LEARNING INDOORS AND OUT IN THE PRIMARY SCHOOL

This fascinating book equips readers with the ability to reconnect children with nature while enhancing their academic achievement. It offers ready-to-use schemes of work with cross-curricular applications and real-world case studies to show how outdoor spaces can be transformed into powerful learning environments that promote connection with nature while delivering curriculum objectives more effectively.

Although outdoor learning has the ability to boost children's motivation, wellbeing, and engagement, many teachers often lack the confidence, time, and structure to implement it effectively. *Learning Indoors and Out in the Primary School* offers a practical solution: a strategic framework that seamlessly integrates outdoor experiences with classroom instruction. This essential resource provides primary educators with a whole-school approach that ensures progression in skills and knowledge across all learning environments – from classrooms to school grounds, local areas, field trips, and residentials. The author provides practical strategies that work in tandem with existing curriculum requirements and clear guidance for teachers and leadership teams on establishing sustainable outdoor learning practices.

This comprehensive guide empowers any teacher or school leader to weave outdoor learning into the very fabric of their school, creating more engaging, immersive experiences for all learners.

Dawn Thomas is the founder and CEO of Nature Days, an outdoor learning, consultancy, and training provider. She is the chair of the Institute for Outdoor Learning (IOL) Curriculum-Based Outdoor Learning (CBOL) Professional Practice Group and a qualified science teacher with over 25 years of teaching experience. She has worked with over 200 different schools supporting the embedding of outdoor learning into the curriculum through staff training, creation of teaching resources, talks, and presentations.

"A breath of fresh air—literally and pedagogically. This book is a powerful reminder that some of the most impactful learning happens beyond the classroom walls. With practical strategies and inspiring case studies, it equips educators to seamlessly embed indoor-outdoor teaching and learning in a cross-curricular way. Thoughtfully written and deeply rooted in both theory and practice, it empowers teachers to reimagine their environments as rich, dynamic spaces for curiosity, resilience, and connection. A must-read for anyone committed to holistic, engaging education."

Cara Evans, Outdoors and Humanities lead, Glyncollen Primary School

"A timely and much-needed, groundbreaking book with the power to transform outdoor learning. Dawn Thomas seamlessly integrates indoor and outdoor environments, creating a new pedagogy that engages everyone—from SLT to students. A future classic, it's set to become the definitive guide for schools looking to embed outdoor learning into their curriculum. I really can't thank you enough for writing it—it is about time that someone took your approach, and I firmly believe that it can, and hopefully will, change the approach to OL in schools."

Zana Wood, Founding Director, Grow to School

"This book is an essential resource for anyone who is keen to use outdoor learning to teach curriculum content but is unsure where to start. Dawn provides useful, practical advice on adapting to an outdoor environment, alongside an abundance of suggested activities, providing inspiration for all areas of curriculum delivery."

Anna Thompson, Education and Learning Manager at Nene Park Trust

"Dawn Thomas delivers a powerful and practical guide for educators seeking to bridge indoor and outdoor learning in primary and special needs settings. Her book is thoughtfully structured and easy to navigate, making it an invaluable companion to curriculum planning. With an emphasis on creativity, engagement, and inclusive education, this resource inspires teachers and school leaders to cultivate enriching, flexible environments where curiosity and holistic development can thrive. A must-read for anyone committed to transforming learning through innovative, integrated approaches."

Claire Williams, Special Educational Needs specialist and former Head Teacher at a school dedicated to supporting students with autism

"*Learning Indoors and Out in the Primary School: An Integrated Approach* provides a series of frameworks for using the outdoors to teach all subjects in the curriculum and embedding outdoor learning strategically across the school. This approach supports schools to use nature as a source of inspiration, and a way to apply the concepts taught in the classroom in real life. The method of weaving indoor and outdoor learning into the planning provides a progressive use of outdoor learning. For many children, being in a classroom is the hardest place to learn, but with an integrated approach to learning indoors and out, the indoor learning is linked to outdoor learning experience and therefore children can see the relevance of what they are taught inside the classroom.

This book will help class teachers and anyone using outdoor learning to teach curriculum content."

Jo Barnett, CEO of Institute for Outdoor Learning (IOL)

"This research-led publication introduces the concept of strategic indoor-outdoor teaching, highlighting its benefits and offering informed solutions to common barriers. It offers clear guidance on leadership roles, staff responsibilities, and effective planning to develop a fully integrated indoor-outdoor learning framework. It also covers lesson structure, progression and assessment, to monitor impact, all brought to life through practical ideas and case studies. With examples across eight curriculum subjects and 20 cross-curricular themes, it provides the tools to embed meaningful outdoor learning throughout your school. This book will empower your team to transform teaching and create an effective, connected learning environment that bridges the indoors and outdoors."

Deborah Lambert, co-author of Bloomsbury's Sustainability and Climate Change Outdoors at KS2 (2024) and the "National Curriculum Outdoors: A Complete Scheme of Work" (2020) series

"We are all surrounded by environments which have some degree of nature to share. This book will help teachers to find that element which can be used in the various subjects of the school curriculum. There is no subject that cannot be improved by being outdoors...School senior staff must give teachers the space and time to explore and provide innovative ways to develop meaningful learning for all youngsters. This book provides a guide for this. Behaviour is also likely to improve with such a teaching strategy. The adults will get a great deal from the experience as well!"

Chas Matthews, Former Head of Geography/Humanities, Walworth School, Southwark. Former Head of Ripple Down House Environmental Centre, Deal. Former Education Officer for East Kent, Kent Wildlife Trust. Former Chairman of the National Association of Field Studies Officers. Honorary Life Member of the Institute for Outdoor Learning

"A companion book that will find welcome space for itself on the shelf of any outdoor leader's classroom, shed, fieldwork kit store, or Celtic roundhouse. Dawn draws from years of experience bringing learners closer to nature, inspiring us with the shared benefits enjoyed by both teachers and students learning together outdoors. *Learning Indoors and Out in the Primary School: An Integrated Approach* anticipates our ambitions for experiential learning outdoors and recognises potential challenges that we may encounter, providing supportive guidance and accessible solutions on our journey together beyond the classroom to somewhere far muddier."

Tom Humphreys, Community Project Manager, North Devon UNESCO Biosphere and Chairman, Network for Environmental Educators in Devon (NEED)

LEARNING INDOORS AND OUT IN THE PRIMARY SCHOOL

An Integrated Approach

Dawn Thomas

LONDON AND NEW YORK

Cover image: Getty Images

First published 2026
by Routledge
4 Park Square, Milton Park, Abingdon, Oxon OX14 4RN

and by Routledge
605 Third Avenue, New York, NY 10158

Routledge is an imprint of the Taylor & Francis Group, an informa business

© 2026 Dawn Thomas

The right of Dawn Thomas to be identified as author of this work has been asserted in accordance with sections 77 and 78 of the Copyright, Designs and Patents Act 1988.

All rights reserved. No part of this book may be reprinted or reproduced or utilised in any form or by any electronic, mechanical, or other means, now known or hereafter invented, including photocopying and recording, or in any information storage or retrieval system, without permission in writing from the publishers.

Trademark notice: Product or corporate names may be trademarks or registered trademarks, and are used only for identification and explanation without intent to infringe.

British Library Cataloguing-in-Publication Data
A catalogue record for this book is available from the British Library

ISBN: 978-1-041-12795-6 (hbk)
ISBN: 978-1-041-12761-1 (pbk)
ISBN: 978-1-003-66671-4 (ebk)

DOI: 10.4324/9781003666714

Typeset in Interstate
by KnowledgeWorks Global Ltd.

DEDICATION

*To everyone inspired by nature to change their teaching
and learning practice.
And the nature of Gower that has changed my life.*

CONTENTS

Preface xiii
Acknowledgements xiv
List of acronyms and abbreviations xv
Introduction xvi
    Aim of this book xvi
    Chapter summaries xvi
    How to use this book xvii

PART I
Introducing indoor-outdoor integrated learning   1
Introduction 1

1 What is it?   3
    What is outdoor learning? 3
    Where can outdoor learning take place? 4
    How is this different from forest school? 5
    What is the aim of indoor-outdoor integrated learning? 5
    How is it different from the outdoor learning I do already? 6
    Why does it have to be strategically embedded? 6
    What do you mean by integrated outdoor learning? 6
    Ideas of how to apply chapter content 7

2 Why do it?   8
    What are the benefits of outdoor learning? 8
    What are the barriers to outdoor learning? 9
    How embedding the indoor-outdoor integrated framework strategically
      overcomes barriers 10
    Why embed a strategic approach to outdoor learning? 12
    How to persuade teachers and SLT 15
    Ideas of how to apply chapter content 16

x Contents

PART II
Strategically embedding the indoor-outdoor integrated curriculum 19
Introduction 19

3 Senior leaders' role 21
Creating an outdoor learning culture 21
How do you create an outdoor learning culture? 21
Strategic leadership in outdoor learning 23
Supporting class teachers 24
A framework for strategically embedding outdoor learning into your school 26
The role of the outdoor learning coordinator 28
Ideas of how to apply chapter content 28

4 Classroom teachers' role 29
How do you undertake effective outdoor learning? 29
Assessment of outdoor learning 31
Assessment for learning outdoors 33
Developing your outdoor learning skills 34
Ideas of how to apply chapter content 34

PART III
Putting indoor-outdoor integrated learning into practice 37
Introduction   37

5 How to start learning outdoors 39
Where do you start? 39
What to do before you go outside? 39
How do you get your class outside? 42
What to do when you get outside 42
Spectrum of outdoor learning delivery 44
Structuring the outdoor learning 45
What to do when you return to the classroom 45
Ideas of how to apply chapter content 46

6 Applying the indoor-outdoor integrated framework 48
What is the indoor-outdoor integrated framework? 48
Inspirational framework 49
Testing theories framework 50
Assessing application of knowledge and skills framework 52
Field work and visits framework 54
Residential framework 56
Combining different frameworks 56
How does a teacher practically undertake indoor-outdoor integrated learning? 56
Using different locations 57
Ideas of how to apply chapter content 58

Contents xi

7 How to ensure progression
59

Progression in outdoor learning 59
How do you know the outdoor experiences are ensuring progression? 59
Measuring the impact of outdoor learning 60
What should you measure? 61
How can you ensure progression in outdoor learning? 62
How do you move the learning along outside? 68
Differentiation outdoors 69
Ideas of how to apply chapter content 70

PART IV
Schemes of work and lesson ideas for using the indoor-outdoor integrated frameworks
71

Introduction 71

8 Subject schemes of work
73

Introduction to the schemes of work 73
How to teach maths with the indoor-outdoor framework 74
How to teach English with the indoor-outdoor framework 86
How to teach science with the indoor-outdoor framework 95
How to teach design technology with the indoor-outdoor framework 98
How to teach information technology with the indoor-outdoor framework 100
How to teach geography skills with the indoor-outdoor framework 101
How to teach history with the indoor-outdoor framework 107
How to teach expressive art with the indoor-outdoor framework 108
Ideas of how to apply chapter content 112

9 Cross curricular application
114

Introduction to cross curricular use of the indoor-outdoor integrated frameworks 114
Science-based topics 115
Geography-based topics 131
Historical-based topics 146
Literacy-based topics 157
Expressive art-based topics 160
Ideas of how to apply chapter content 163

10 Maintaining momentum
164

How to use the indoor-outdoor framework for teaching new topics 164
How to plan with the outdoors in mind 165
How to find inspiration for future outdoor learning 166
How to build on the indoor-outdoor integrated framework 167
Developing long-term outdoor projects 169
How to build on the strategic indoor-outdoor integrated framework 175
Ideas of how to apply chapter content 178

Final thoughts
180

Impacting education 180

Appendix 181
   Whole school outdoor learning audit 181
   Outdoor learning policy outline 183
   Planning ideas 184
   Transition exercises 185
   Extract from Estyn school inspector report for Blaen Y Maes primary school 186
   Extract from Estyn school inspector report for Dan Y Coed specialist school 187
   Glossary 188

Index 191

PREFACE

I have taken thousands of school children on field trips and hopefully inspired them to learn from the outdoors. However, it has always frustrated me when I ask the accompanying staff what their plans are for when they get back to class after the field work, and they seem unsure or mention a recount. I know that nothing would have curbed my enthusiasm more after an exciting day outdoors learning than to have to write it all down. That spark I see enlightened in the pupils who struggle in the classroom when outdoors has the potential to be continued indoors. This book helps teachers to build on the experience and make the best use of what the outdoors can do. Teachers can't do it alone. The structure around them needs to support the integration of outdoor learning in their teaching. That is why a strategic approach to outdoor learning across the school or setting is needed if the most is to be had from outdoor learning. An integrated approach is required at a teaching and strategic level.

ACKNOWLEDGEMENTS

I would like to thank the thousands of children who have come on field trips with me and shown that what I teach them has an impact through the looks on their faces.

Also, the teachers who I have worked with and shown me each of their unique ways to impart knowledge, you are truly amazing.

To Alison Jones for believing in me and dragging this book idea out of me and supporting me to turn a spark into a book.

For outdoor learning providers I have worked with in the IOL who have shared their experiences so generously.

To my local network of Swansea schools for listening to my ideas and providing feedback.

To my family, Stu, Neo, and Gryph, for putting up with not seeing me and going on about outdoor learning all the time.

LIST OF ACRONYMS AND ABBREVIATIONS

CPD	Continual professional development
INSET	In service training. Training undertaken in dedicated non-teaching time within schools for staff.
LOtC	Learning Outside the Classroom. Teaching and learning that takes place outside of the normal school-based teaching and learning. This covers visitors to school, use of school grounds, field trips and visits, and residentials.
NOLA	National Outdoor Learning Awards.
OEAP	The Outdoor Education Adviser's Panel – providers of National Guidance for outdoor learning in the UK.
PPA	Planning, preparation, and assessment times for teachers. Usually covered by another member of staff.
SDP	School Development Plan. A "what we need to do next" plan for a school.
SEND	Special Education Needs and Disabilities. Called many different terms in different countries, ALN – Alternative learning Needs, Special Needs.
SLT	Senior Leadership Team. School staff with management responsibilities.
TA	Teaching assistant.

INTRODUCTION

Aim of this book

So often in schools when outdoor learning is undertaken, it is focused on the early years with indoor-outdoor flow of pupils and continuous provisional experiences. Then, in upper primary, the term outdoor learning is not specified in curricula and therefore seen as a "nice to have" aspect of teaching and learning. An enthusiastic outdoorsy teacher or TA may take out their class or group or a forest school leader may take multiple classes as PPA cover outside. However, there is little coordinated, joined up thinking in this aspect of teaching and learning.

The aim of this book is to provide a framework to:

1. Establish outdoor learning as a respected, appreciated tool for teaching and learning at a strategic level across the school to ensure progression.
2. Help practitioners integrate the outdoor learning into the indoor learning so that there is meaningful progressive use of the outdoor areas.

Chapter summaries

This book is divided into four parts. The first part sets the context of indoor-outdoor integrated teaching and learning.

Chapter 1 defines, describes, and explains what strategic indoor-outdoor embedded learning means and why you should embed it strategically across the school setting.

Chapter 2 describes the benefits of outdoor learning using research and identifies how barriers to outdoor learning can be overcome using indoor-outdoor integrated learning.

The second part provides guidance on the different roles at a strategic and practitioner level.

Chapter 3 looks at senior leaders' roles in providing strategic leadership and embedding outdoor learning into the ethos of the school.

Chapter 4 explains the teacher's and support staff's role in the provision of effective integrated outdoor learning, including assessment and collecting evidence.

Chapter 5 looks at the logistics of structuring outdoor learning sessions and where to start when teaching outside.

The third part provides practical advice on undertaking effective outdoor learning using the indoor-outdoor integrated framework and how to ensure progression.

Chapter 6 describes the indoor-outdoor integrated frameworks and shows how to apply the frameworks to your planning.

Chapter 7 looks at progression in outdoor learning and how to ensure it is happening throughout the year and across the school.

The fourth part provides a practical guide to using the framework to teach different subjects and thematically.

Chapter 8 provides ideas to use the framework for teaching key skills in eight different subjects.

Chapter 9 includes ideas to use the indoor-outdoor framework to teach 20 cross-curricular topics.

Chapter 10 focuses on improving practice by further integration of outdoor learning and broadening learning outside the classroom opportunities in your school through a series of case studies.

How to use this book

This book is designed to be dipped into and revisited. It is aimed at those working in a primary setting teaching nursery to year 6, although it can be used in secondary settings for years 7-9 and in alternative provision such as SEND schools. The principles and aims are applicable to any age group in this range but will be of particular help with years 3-6 when curriculum content needs to be covered in a timely way.

This book will provide school practitioners who lack confidence in teaching outside a framework to help them undertake meaningful outdoor learning. It is also a valuable tool for those more experienced in delivering outdoor learning, as it builds a holistic picture of outdoor learning's role within the curriculum. Following the indoor-outdoor integrated framework provides a progressive structure for planning outdoor learning and making the best use of the experiences.

This book is also for your school's senior leaders to use to embed the outdoor learning at a strategic level. Threading the ethos of meaningful outdoor learning into your school requires support and understanding of all school staff. Integrating outdoor learning into the fabric of your school means that all stakeholders are aware of your commitment and that it is valued as an important part of the life of your school.

The subheadings in the contents and chapters are there to enable you, the reader, to find the aspects of the topics that are of interest to you. Chapters do, however, build on the last, showing a progression in the understanding of outdoor learning.

Each chapter has questions at the end to help you apply the chapter's contents. These can be used by you for your own practice and setting, or used by senior leaders as part of INSET training. The book provides a framework for embedding indoor-outdoor integrated learning strategically across a whole school, but all schools are different, so you will have to apply the framework as fits your setting.

Part I
Introducing indoor-outdoor integrated learning

Introduction

The first part of this book introduces the concept of integrated, strategic indoor-outdoor learning. It defines the many terms included in this idea and how most outdoor learning in schools tends to lack integration with in-school learning. It goes on to explain the value of the full integration of outdoor learning across a school and its benefits to the students. The tool behind this process is the indoor-outdoor integrated framework, which is introduced and its use explained to overcome the barriers teachers find to embedding outdoor learning.

1 What is it?

> **Aims of the chapter**
> - Define and explain strategic, integrated, and embedded, curriculum-based outdoor learning.
> - Identify where outdoor learning can take place.
> - Explain how outdoor learning is different from forest school.
> - Describe the aim of the indoor-outdoor integrated framework.
> - Describe a strategic, integrated teaching approach.

"We already do outdoor learning; we have a forest school leader who takes the class out on a Wednesday". (Many schools feel that they have "ticked the outdoor learning box" when they introduce forest school.)

What is outdoor learning?

The idea of teaching and learning is usually identified as taking place within a classroom. This is not defined as "indoor learning" just as "learning". However, when the term "outdoor learning" is used, it conjures up different ideas to different stakeholders.

Teachers tend to describe it as either taking learning outside or using the outdoors to teach curriculum content.

Governments have defined outdoor learning as "an approach that can be used across all subjects and across a broad range of teaching" [1].

This is different from adventure education, activities such as climbing, caving, and canoeing, also known as adventurous activities which focus on personal and social learning.

Outdoor education has been defined as a pedagogical approach [1].

A way of teaching as opposed to the actual content or skills taught.

Government inspectors focus on the impact of the range of outdoor learning not the actual activity itself.

There is a big problem in the use of language and definitions across different parties.

It is clear that teachers struggle to understand the full concept of outdoor learning [1]. This adds confusion to any research on how much outdoor learning is undertaken by schools.

Although there are lots of definitions of outdoor learning, what is clear is that everyone in your school needs to have the same idea of what it is.

Integrated outdoor learning is undertaken regularly, be that once a year, term, month, or week. It links to the work done in class, so it is part of the formal planning and is built on in future work. It is meaningful as it may contextualise in-school taught concepts or be used to assess understanding or consolidate work.

> **Strategic outdoor learning** is when the whole school embeds outdoor learning into its approach to teaching. It runs as a **thread throughout the school** with all staff being responsible for undertaking it and the leadership supporting a focus on it through long-term goals.

> **Integrated outdoor learning** looks like any other **pedagogy** (a way of teaching), used as a teaching tool by teachers to apply their craft. It is part of the toolbox of approaches used to allow all learners to access the curriculum.

When you visit a school who have strategically embedded integrated outdoor learning, you see that it is part of **how** the whole school functions. It is a fundamental part of the school's identity, and the school would not meet its aims without it.

Where can outdoor learning take place?

Outdoor learning can take place in a range of locations which are not the school building itself.

- School grounds – on the playground, school field, forest school site, vegetable patch.
- Local learning area – the walkable area outside the school gates. For example, local church yard, local park, local farm, local shops, local residential streets, local woods, or other local habitats.
- Field trips – in the local learning area or can involve a bus ride to a suitable location. For example, a river, beach, town centre, mountain, or woodland.
- Residential – when pupils stay overnight, it can be local to the school, a short or long bus journey away, or even abroad.

The choice of the location may be chosen to meet the learning objectives such as collecting data for a river study, or the location may determine to a certain extent the learning outcomes of the outdoor learning, such as going on a residential looking at social skills development.

It is important to understand why the location is the best place for meeting your learning objectives.

In its broadest definition Learning Outside the Classroom (LOtC) is used to encompass learning taking place elsewhere from the school classroom and in other indoor and outdoor locations. For example, museums, mosques, shops, or castles.

How is this different from forest school?

Outdoor learning, in the context of this book, is using the outdoors to teach curriculum content or skills. Sometimes called curriculum-based outdoor learning, it differs from Forest School, which according to the Forest School Association is:

> A child centred, inspirational learning process for holistic growth through regular sessions. A long-term program with a developmental ethos. It develops confidence and self-esteem through learner inspired, hands on experiences in a natural setting [2].

Therefore, undertaking Forest School sessions does not include the coverage of curriculum content but focuses on personal development of students.

What is the aim of indoor-outdoor integrated learning?

The aim of indoor-outdoor integrated learning is to get the most out of outdoor learning opportunities to increase pupil outcomes.

This is done through increasing pupil engagement and sustaining it with the progressive integration of the outdoors in teaching. As a result of this there should be increasing pupil attainment as pupils wish to learn. Outdoor experiences will broaden pupil's horizons motivating them to develop practical and cross curricular skills [3]. The regular engagement with their peers outside will also improve non-cognitive outcomes such as personal qualities and social relationships [4], as well as a greater awareness of nature and the world around us [5].

The indoor-outdoor integrated framework is a teaching tool which builds on indoor teaching through consolidating outdoor activities, which are subsequently strengthened through follow up outdoor learning. This system of progressive indoor and outdoor teaching and learning is a pedagogy, a way of teaching curriculum content using the best location for the pupils to receive the most effective learning experience. The location for teaching and learning changes regularly at the correct point in the teaching to ensure an effective use of outdoor learning to impact pupil's attainment by contextualising the learning.

The indoor-outdoor framework will produce higher attainment in pupils by using the real world outside of the classroom to exemplify concepts taught in class. Teaching in this way also provides much more practical students who can apply concepts taught in school not just pass exams. The use of the outdoors as a thread running through your teaching allows progression in skills such as practical skills, field work skills, application of concepts, and problem-solving. It allows assessment by teachers of the pupil's ability to apply the knowledge and skills taught in a different context and realises the cross-curricular links between subjects.

With regular use of the indoor-outdoor framework, progression is embedded not just in the content, but also in the level of skill, through increasingly challenging locational choices.

The outdoors is used as a resource to exemplify the learning, apply concepts, inspire learning, and increase challenge through immersive experiences in the real world.

How is it different from the outdoor learning I do already?

The biggest difference between the indoor-outdoor integrated framework and outdoor learning, that is taking place in schools already, is that no outdoor learning session happens in isolation. Embedded outdoor learning sessions are linked and connected to in-school teaching, and follow up in-school sessions relate and consolidate the outdoor session, and so on. The outdoor learning is planned alongside the in-school learning simultaneously to build a coherent mapping of the curriculum using the best location for each learning objective. Through this method outdoor learning becomes progressive as it is embedded in curriculum.

Why does it have to be strategically embedded?

For truly embedded, progressive indoor-outdoor learning across a school, it must be adopted by the whole school. Just as outdoor learning sessions cannot be done effectively in isolation, neither can the embedding of the framework be done by one member of staff or one year group or phase.

Integration of indoor-outdoor learning into your school's ethos is paramount to support teaching staff and provide a whole school approach to teaching and learning. For progression across your school then the buy-in and commitment by all staff are required to make the best use of outdoor learning for all learners to meet their needs. This can only be done if senior leaders are on board and support any policy changes, resources, and training requirements.

Oversight by senior leaders of progression across the school through outdoor learning is also required to make the best use of the skills developed through the framework. As well as the creation of a culture of respect for all outdoor learning opportunities.

What do you mean by integrated outdoor learning?

The effective integration of outdoor learning into a school can only be done through its use as a pedagogy. An array of pedagogical approaches is used in schools. The Curriculum for Wales has identified 12 pedagogical approaches [6]. These are all teaching methods and are used to teach all subjects within schools. The embracing of outdoor learning as a pedagogy means that you will integrate its use seamlessly into your teaching when required, when pertinent, and when most effective for the content. This pedagogy of outdoor learning benefits the pupils by enriching the curriculum, adding a depth and breadth of learning experiences which are built on in the classroom. It also provides a resource for teaching and a method to engage learners who learn differently and allow more learners to access the curriculum.

As a pedagogical approach outdoor learning lends itself to cross curricular teaching. The outdoors is not organised into subjects or areas of learning but provides meaningful examples of how subjects are linked and how application of knowledge in one area can be applied in a cross curricular context. When outdoor learning is a thread running through your teaching and learning, it provides opportunities for pupils to experience the curriculum in multiple ways that support topic-based in-school learning.

Ideas of how to apply chapter content

- Undertake an audit of the outdoor learning that takes place now across your school. Use the questions in Appendix.
- Look for evidence of planned outdoor learning. Where is the evidence and is it the same for every teacher?
- Evaluate what is working and what is not. Is there a trend?
- Identify the locations used by different year groups. Is there a trend? What is the reason behind the areas not used?
- Does the outdoor learning build on the indoor learning?

References

1. French, G., Parry, D., Jones, C., McQueen, R., Boulton, P., Horder, S., Rhys-Jones, K., Formby, L., Sheriff, L., & Sheen, L. (2023). Teaching and learning in the outdoors: the current state of outdoor learning in schools in Wales. Published by Welsh Government Education Wales. https://hwb.gov.wales/api/storage/177a33a6-7c70-4843-bb63-903e70a04154/teaching-and-learning-in-the-outdoors-the-current-state-of-outdoor-learning-in-schools-in-wales.pdf
2. Harding, N. (2021). Growing a forest school from the roots up. Published by Forest School Association.
3. Harvey, D. (2025). High quality outdoor learning. A guide for policy and decision makers. Published by Institute for Outdoor Learning.
4. McNatty, S., Nairn, K., Campbell-Price, M., & Boyes, M. (2024). Looking back: the lasting impact of outdoor education for adolescent girls. Journal of Adventure Education and Outdoor Learning, 25(1), 66-83.
5. Sabine, P., Ylenia, P., Panno Angelo, Maurilio, C., Giuseppe, C. (2021). The effects of contact with nature during outdoor environmental education on students' wellbeing, connectedness to nature and pro-sociality. Frontiers in Psychology. *Section Environmental Psychology*, 12, Article 648458. https://pmc.ncbi.nlm.nih.gov/articles/PMC8129515/pdf/fpsyg-12-648458.pdf
6. Curriculum for Wales Guidance. (2020). Published by Welsh Government Education Wales. https://hwb.gov.wales/api/storage/18d0d2f1-0563-4945-a889-d1548ae24c4e/curriculum-for-wales-guidance.pdf?preview=true

2 Why do it?

> **Aims of the chapter**
> - Identify the benefits of outdoor learning.
> - Identify the barriers to outdoor learning.
> - Using indoor-outdoor integrated teaching to overcome these barriers.
> - The advantages of a strategic approach to outdoor learning.
> - How to persuade senior leaders and school staff to strategically embed the indoor-outdoor integrated framework.

"I don't have time to do outdoor learning on top of literacy and numeracy and all the other curriculum content". (Teachers, especially in key stage 2, feel overwhelmed by the volume of teaching they must cover the thought of ADDING outdoor learning as well is seen as a barrier.)

What are the benefits of outdoor learning?

Outdoor learning has been proven through various interventions, projects, and reports to have positive impacts on pupil's wellbeing, motivation, and engagement [1-4].

Research has also shown that not only is attainment improved through increased motivation in pupils [4], but this continues beyond the outdoor learning sessions themselves [5].

Personal development skills improvement through outdoor learning [6] is probably linked to the shared experience as well as increased motivation and engagement from the outdoor learning experience. But I attest that even more benefits could be seen if those experiences are inexplicitly linked to indoor experiences extending it to all teaching and learning taking place.

One of the most important advantages of outdoor learning and the indoor-outdoor integrated framework outlined in this book is the application of the curriculum content.

In an age when you can look up anything on a digital device, be it accurate or not, the problem-solving element of application of skills and knowledge is key in education. Also, with the range of pupils with varying learning styles, differing educational needs, and neurodiversities, the expectation that all pupils can function optimally inside a classroom is unreasonable. The benefits of using the outdoors as a resource as well as a location to teach and learn are that we broaden the scope of the experiences on offer for individual pupils to thrive.

Research by Rickinson et al. [7] reviewing outdoor learning literature identified a range of sources that indicated that the benefits of outdoor learning are not sustained over time if the outdoor learning is not integrated into student's indoor learning and there is a loss of opportunities to "encourage reflection, enhance learning and maintain interest over sustained periods of time". Therefore, the impact of integrated outdoor learning will be more sustained over time when linked to in school teaching.

The Rickinson et al. [7] review also indicated that the value of outdoor learning programs which "incorporated well-designed preparatory and follow-up work" was much more impactful and had greater impact than those that did not include these.

One issue with ensuring outdoor learning realising its full potential in schools is an awareness of the learning objectives of the session. Rickinson et al. [7] outlined that teachers need to be "clear on what they are trying to achieve in outdoor learning sessions" plus "greater attention might be given to exploring ways of building progression within outdoor learning programmes". The indoor-outdoor integrated framework provides clear learning objectives and emphasises the importance of these, as well as building progression in the framework of activities.

What are the barriers to outdoor learning?

Through research I have undertaken teachers report the main barriers to undertaking outdoor learning as:

1. School grounds; concrete playgrounds, no green space or nature.
2. Staff knowledge of what to do outside and how to take learning outside in a purposeful way.
3. Staff confidence in class management outside.
4. Time within the week.
5. Lack of support staff to run authentic outdoor learning or difficulty in safely managing a whole class alone outdoors.
6. Access to the outdoors from the classroom.
7. Staff attitude and willingness to take pupils outside in all weathers.
8. Resources; lack of waterproof clothing or resources for teaching outdoors.

All of these are barriers either real or perceived and vary in their importance from person to person.

Unfortunately, in schools, statutory requirements drive provision. So, the importance of outdoor learning and the ability to overcome barriers to it are influenced by government inspector's view of the value of outdoor learning. When outdoor learning is statutory, such as in early years, then these barriers are overcome, and outdoor learning is respected as an important aspect of teaching and learning. Inspection reports include outdoor learning coverage mainly in early years when it is mandatory; however, in upper primary most mentions are linked to P.E. and no other curriculum areas [8].

How embedding the indoor-outdoor integrated framework strategically overcomes barriers

The indoor-outdoor integrated framework overcomes the barriers above through its whole school approach.

School grounds

Outdoor application of indoor concepts can be undertaken in any outdoor space. The activities planned in the framework will apply to the space available. They also include opportunities to experience a range of other locations which may be more suitable than the school grounds. Integrating outdoor learning includes the consideration of WHERE best to teach, test, discover, explore, inspire, and investigate and the playground will be one of those locations. You do not need amazing grounds to use outdoor learning if it is planned well.

Staff knowledge

As with all teaching an element of knowledge is required, but the integrated framework is based on learning outcomes rooted in the curriculum, of which you as a teacher are knowledgeable. The purposeful use of the outdoors will be created through the planning aspect of the framework which builds on indoor learning and therefore the value is clear through the learning outcome.

Staff confidence

The strategic element of the integrated indoor-outdoor framework requires a whole school approach, and this provides the basis for expectations of behaviour outside. When truly embedded, the outdoor teaching being an extension of the indoor teaching requires the same skills in class management as those utilised in the classroom. Transferable skills need to be identified to staff and routines and rules need to be established across the school. The ethos of the school is vital for instilling in pupils the understanding of outdoor learning as an extension of indoor learning with the same behaviour and learning expectations. Research by O'Donnell et al. [9] identified that teacher's confidence was one of the key factors underpinning the extent of provision and staff belief that they were supported by senior management had a positive influence on the extent of outdoor learning undertaken by teachers. The role of the senior leadership team is therefore to foster this ethos and provide support for staff who still need it. The indoor-outdoor integrated framework also supports teachers to help you make the best use of outdoor learning, increasing your confidence.

Time within the week

The indoor-outdoor integrated curriculum embeds the coverage of the curriculum in the use of outdoors as and when appropriate. So, when outdoors, the curriculum will be covered, skills developed, assessment of learning will be undertaken as you do indoors. If pupils see the outdoors as a location for learning, then effective teaching and learning take place there.

Why do it? 11

This is a mindset shift not an add-on to the busy weeks teaching. The outdoor learning should move the learning on from the indoor learning, consolidate or apply the priory learning, just as would happen indoors. The follow-up work inside after the outdoor session builds on the experience, insuring progression and does not involve repetition of the same content but movement forward.

Lack of support staff

Lack of support and larger class sizes can make staying in the classroom a more manageable solution. If you do not have support staff to either take small groups outside or support the whole class outside, it can be daunting to undertake outdoor learning. Starting the new school year with embedding outdoor learning is a good start to train the pupils to be more independent when getting outside and set the ground rules and expectations outdoors.

The strategic nature of a whole school ethos to outdoor learning also supports this issue as other classes being outside will provide another member of staff to be available if you need to leave your class alone. Planning is key, especially in terms of resources and storage of the resources. If you have outdoor learning boxes at accessible locations outdoors, then there will be no need for the class to be left unsupervised while you locate the resources. Obviously, it depends on the pupils, but with a whole school approach pupils do become better at staying on task outdoors the more outdoor learning they do across the school and the more it is integrated as part of their normal school day.

Most issues with behaviour and class control occur when going outdoors is a novelty and pupils then regard the outdoor space as a play space. As with all outdoor learning, look at strategies you use indoors to overcome large class sizes and lack of support staff, and utilise them outside. For example, carousels of activities, working walls, making supportive resources accessible, and group work can all be employed outdoors if the pupils have a learning mindset there.

Access to the outdoors from the classroom

Obviously, the best setup is one where all classes have direct access to the outdoors. However, with old school buildings this can mean that going outdoors takes more effort and planning. Again, setting up a system that gets the pupils outdoors efficiently is vital; they know what to do and where to go automatically. Trial a system of getting outside that works best and identify muster points outside so your class congregates and is ready to learn outdoors. More details in Chapter 4.

Staff attitude

How to get the staff onboard is dealt with later in this chapter. But the best way to change the attitudes of staff is for them to see the impact that being outdoors is having on the pupils. Making sure staff have appropriate clothing is also important so provision for this helps. Through embracing whole school strategic outdoor learning, it is everyone's responsibility to work outdoors, so staff will have to go out as it is part of your school's ethos.

12 *Learning Indoors and Out in the Primary School*

Resources

If you are utilising the indoor-outdoors integrated framework, then most resources are ones you use in class, so you do not need to go out and buy new and different equipment. Having outdoor learning boxes of resources helps you have the resources you need available outside. These can be stored in outdoor areas or grabbed as you leave the classroom.

Essentials are:

- Clipboards
- Chalk
- Tape measures
- Rulers

Outdoor clothing is also vital. Adding wellies and waterproofs to a uniform policy not only highlights your commitment to outdoor learning but it enforces to parent that these are required for each pupil. To support this, consider looking for funding for class sets of waterproofs or ask for donation from parents of old wellies and waterproofs. Always consider storage of resources and systems to help classes find resources and put them back. A whole school approach on replacing resources and tidying up is important to make sure going outdoors is sustainable for all classes.

Why embed a strategic approach to outdoor learning?

Figure 2.1 shows a progression model for strategically embedding outdoor learning into your school. Chapter 4 on senior leader's role outlines how to use this model to achieve strategic, integrated outdoor learning.

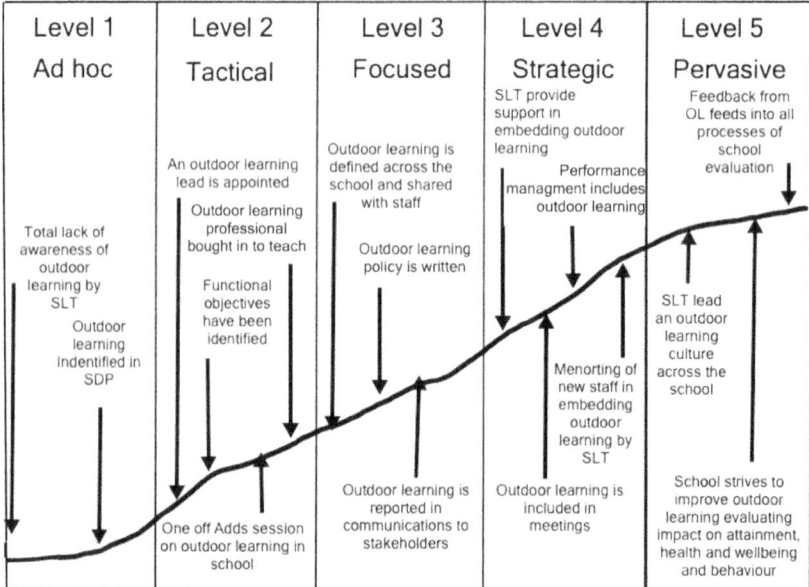

Figure 2.1 Strategic embedded outdoor learning progression model

This model highlights how important it is that the senior leaders are involved and onboard in integrating outdoor learning into your school. Without their support and oversight of the school, outdoor learning cannot be fully integrated, and inconsistencies and barriers will persist. Research by O'Donnell et al. (2006) [9] identified that "the level of school commitment to outdoor learning and headteacher's views of such provision, have a positive influence on the extent of activity undertaken by teachers".

As identified above the strategic approach to outdoor learning overcomes many of the barriers to undertaking outdoor learning. In many schools, when outdoor learning is outsourced to either an external provider or one member of staff then there is a lack of continuity in teaching and learning. Even if there are good lines of communication between staff, the value of knowing the previous experience the pupils have had, and building on that in the future teaching, cannot be overstated. When one member of staff is responsible for teaching all outdoor learning, then the impact of those experiences on the pupils' learning is diminished. Even if they are experts in outdoor learning, they are not experts in what your pupils have learnt so far, or their needs as individuals. Also, what happens if that member of staff leaves and takes all their expertise with them? If longevity and continuity of integrated indoor-outdoor learning is going to take place across the school, then all members of staff need distributed leadership of it.

M. Rickinson et al [7] identified a range of sources that indicated the benefits of outdoor learning are not sustained over time if the outdoor learning is not integrated into student's indoor learning and there is a loss of opportunities to "encourage reflection, enhance learning and maintain interest over sustained periods of time". Therefore, the impact of integrated outdoor learning will be more sustained over time when linked to in school teaching.

The same issues can be applied to limiting the outdoor experiences to one day of the week. Weekly outdoor learning sessions such as Welly Wednesday have been adopted by many schools under one name or another. Although this aims to ensure pupils go outdoor for their learning at least once a week, if it does not happen on that day then, from my experience, it does not happen at all that week. Also, in limiting the outdoors as a place to be experienced at only set times and spaces, you are setting artificial boundaries to learning for teachers and pupils. A whole school approach to embedded indoor-outdoor learning supports learning to take place "when appropriate" and therefore is more meaningful.

Days like outdoor classroom day are a good reminder to get pupils outdoors learning and a starting point for teachers who lack confidence. With a strategic approach supported by senior leaders then a more adaptive approach to integrating outdoor learning will be established in your school.

Pupils with special educational or behavioural needs benefit greatly from being outdoors as and when they need to [10, 11]. The use of outdoor learning as a pedagogy allows inclusivity of all pupils and their learning styles; through a strategic approach staff can use the outdoors to facilitate learning for all. This can only happen if there is a whole school strategic approach with all staff using this and appreciating the importance it has to the school. With everyone on board then any barriers are quickly identified, and senior leaders will see the value of removing these barriers.

Case Study: Dan Y Coed specialist school whole school approach to strategic outdoor learning

Dan y Coed is a specialist school and home for children with autism and learning disabilities based in Swansea, South Wales. They approached me as they felt that more curriculum content could be drawn from the visits the pupils were having in the local area. As a specialist school, they had access to cars and many pupils needed to go out for their personal development of key life skills as well as for emotional regulation.

I started by taking the whole school teaching staff to a number of the local areas which they regularly visited and went through all the curriculum-based activities they could undertake there and on route to the locations. This was followed up with staff discussions of what would work for each of their pupils.

While the staff trialled the activities and were building confidence with the integration of outdoor learning into their teaching, I met with the outdoor learning coordinator. Together we discussed the vision for outdoor learning at Dan Y Coed school and with the coordinator's understanding of the school and mine of outdoor learning we wrote an outdoor learning policy. The contents of this policy were fed back to the teaching staff and the outdoor learning coordinator supported the staff to follow the policy and implement the plan for more meaningful outdoor learning.

I met with the outdoor learning coordinator at the start of each term, and we went through the topics for each class and identified potential outdoor learning opportunities. These were then fed back to the staff and evaluations of the outdoor learning were included in feedback Fridays and pupil and teacher reviews.

On top of the support for the teachers the outdoor learning coordinator also collated the many links to external providers the school has worked with and fostered networks to develop an ongoing relationship that has grown over the years. Now pupils at Dan Y Coed have access to strategic progressive outdoor learning activities which have been mapped to key skills and qualifications which the pupils undertake such as ASDAN life skills.

The impact of this strategic approach was recognised in a school inspection.

"Leaders at the school have developed valuable opportunities for pupils to learn in a range of exciting activities outside the classroom. As a result, pupils develop a range of important skills such as independence, confidence, and resilience. These skills prepare pupils well for experiences beyond the school".

"As a result of pupils' engagement in work-related opportunities, many pupils' attendance has improved, and a very few pupils have transferred to a local mainstream college because of skills acquired on work experience placement. In addition, the school has recently been presented with a recognised quality award for its outdoor and work-related curriculum offer" [12].

More details of the Estyn school inspection report in the Appendix.

An embedded approach also means that any requirements for staff training or support will be identified, and any needs met through systems of staff development and monitoring. The inclusion of outdoor learning in staff meetings, pupil progress meetings, and tracking will ensure progression across the school in the skills and knowledge learnt outdoors. Also, miscommunication in policies and practice can be identified such as having wet break when pupils are undertaking outdoor learning and out-of-bounds areas being used for outdoor learning. With the whole school staff being involved in the inclusion of outdoor learning, better joined up thinking about school grounds use and trips and visits can be achieved.

"Deeply embedding outdoor learning into the school like this will make it much more likely to survive the shifting sands of education where headteachers and teachers move on, political boundaries shift, budgets change, management systems, and organisational structures morph" [13].

How to persuade teachers and SLT

Hopefully, the above has convinced you of the importance of strategically embedding an integrated indoor-outdoor framework, but how do you get the rest of the staff on board?

Depending on who they are or where they are in terms of the outdoors, there are several arguments you can use.

Application of the curriculum

The fact that embedded outdoor learning provides opportunities to practically apply the curriculum will provide the pupils with real-life skills. Linking these to the consolidation of in-school work will engage pupils as they will see the relevance of what they have learnt.

Motivating

Using the outdoor space, which is a free resource, to broaden and enrich the learning experience in your school will improve motivation and encourage a better connection to nature.

Pedagogy

Outdoor learning is a pedagogy not another subject so will not add to the volume of work required to be taught.

Access for all pupils

Covering the curriculum in a variety of ways allows access for all pupils.

Behavioural improvements

Scheduled, regular outdoor learning reduces behaviour issues and fosters independence [7].

Added value

Every teacher wants all pupils to have the opportunity to achieve their best. With outdoor learning you can add value to your curriculum offer and expand horizons.

Ideas of how to apply chapter content

- Building on the audit of outdoor learning undertaken in Chapter 1, identify the barriers in your school to undertaking integrated outdoor learning.
- Investigate if outdoor learning is occurring consistently across the school and if not why not?
- Identify outdoor learning that is working well and analyse why it works and how you know it is impactful.
- Is there progression across the year groups in outdoor learning? Map the time spent outside the classroom for each year group, what activities are undertaken, the learning objectives, and the level of challenge.

References

1. Sheldrake, R., Amos, R. & Reiss, M. (2019). Children and nature: A research evaluation for the Wildlife Trusts. Published by UCL Institute of Education. https://www.wildlifetrusts.org/sites/default/files/2019-11/Children%20and%20Nature%20-%20UCL%20and%20The%20Wildlife%20Trusts%20Full%20Report.pdf
2. Estyn. (2023) The use of the outdoor learning environment to support pupils learning and well-being. Effective Practice. Published by Estyn. https://estyn.gov.wales/improvement-resources/the-use-of-the-outdoor-learning-environment-to-support-pupils-learning-and-well-being/
3. Twohig-Bennett, C. & Jones, A. (2018). The health benefits of the great outdoors: A systematic review and meta-analysis of greenspace exposure and health outcomes. Journal Environmental Research, 166, 628–637. https://pmc.ncbi.nlm.nih.gov/articles/PMC6562165/pdf/main.pdf
4. Canal and Rivers Trust (2024). Waterways, wildlife and wellbeing, School Impact Report. Published by CLOtC. https://canalrivertrust.org.uk/media/document/XnTH9n9zLyp3LAedMWR9Zw/GrODXxYIws_jZoPF7_L1OpNafQvb_1Qda2SgiJ4SnNg/aHR0cHM6Ly9jcnRwcm9kYy21zdWtzMDEuYmxvYi5jb3JlLnd-pbmRvd3Mubm V0L2RvY3VtZW50Lw/01903b40-5747-7618-a0fe-31b7235941c8.pdf
5. Harvey, M., Rankine, K., & Jensen, R. (2017). Outdoor learning hubs. A Scottish Attainment Challenge Innovation Fund Project. Published by Education Scotland. https://www.sapoe.org.uk/wp-content/uploads/2018/01/Outdoor-Hub-Learning-Report-Dec-2017-V1.pdf
6. Kendall, S., & Rodger, J. (2015). Evaluating learning away final report. Learning Away. Published by Paul Hamlyn Foundation. https://learningaway-org-uk.stackstaging.com/wp-content/uploads/LA-Final-Report-May-2015-1-1.pdf
7. Rickinson, M., Dillon, J., Teamey, K., Morris, M., Choi, M, Y, Sanders, D., & Benefield, P. (2004). A review of research on outdoor learning. Published by National Foundation for Educational research and King's College London. https://informalscience.org/wp-content/uploads/2019/02/Review-of-research-on-outdoor-learning.pdf
8. Prince, H. E., and Diggory O. (2023). Recognition and reporting of outdoor learning in primary schools in England. *Journal of Adventure Education and Outdoor Leering*, 24(4), 553–565. https://www.tandfonline.com/doi/full/10.1080/14729679.2023.2166544
9. O'Donnell, L., Morris, M., & Wilson, R. (2006). Education outside the classroom: An assessment of activity and practice in schools and local authorities. Published by National Foundation for Educational Research. https://dera.ioe.ac.uk/id/eprint/6550/1/RR803.pdf
10. Heath, J. F. (2020). What is the impact of outdoor education on pupils with complex needs? Published by Educational Institute of Scotland. https://www.eis.org.uk/Content/images/cpd/Action%20Research%20Grants/OutdoorLearningHealth(1).pdf

11 Glanville, K. (2023). Exploring outdoor learning in primary education for children with special educational needs and disabilities. Doctoral thesis. Birmingham City University. https://www.open-access.bcu.ac.uk/id/eprint/14183
12 Estyn (2023). Dan Y Coed inspection report. Published by Estyn, His Majesty's Inspectorate for Education and Training in Wales. https://estyn.gov.wales/system/files/2023-11/Annual%20monitoring%20inspection%20Dan%20y%20Coed%202023.pdf
13 The Eden Project. (2019). Embedding outdoor learning in a primary school. *Alverton Community Primary School*. Published by The Eden Project. https://www.edenproject.com/learn/schools/teacher-training/embedding-outdoor-learning-in-a-primary-school

Part II
Strategically embedding the indoor-outdoor integrated curriculum

Introduction

Building on the ideas introduced in Part I, Part II clearly defines the roles of the senior leadership team in supporting classroom teachers to strategically embed indoor-outdoor learning. A whole school approach to outdoor learning is necessary for all students to receive the greatest impact. With this in mind, senior leaders have to be on board and also provide support and guidance for all other staff so that their use of outdoor learning is appreciated and respected. Part II provides a teacher's guide to providing effective outdoor learning and ways to record the impact.

3 Senior leaders' role

Aims of the chapter

- To identify what the senior leadership team needs to do to embed outdoor learning into the ethos of the school.
- How to provide strategic leadership.
- How to support teaching staff in embedding indoor-outdoor teaching.
- The role of senior leaders in the strategic leadership of outdoor learning.

"It's on the School Development Plan so now teachers have to teach outside, but they still aren't". (Following inspections senior leaders often put "develop outdoor learning" on their school development plan with no real understanding of what that looks like.)

Creating an outdoor learning culture

Every school is individual, and this is the essence of the culture and ethos of your school. The way your school strategically embeds indoor-outdoor learning is through its values and beliefs. If your senior leadership team has passion and belief in the purpose of outdoor learning, then this will trickle down through the school into the practice of all your staff.

Schools have approached this in different ways and the wording varies, but the reasoning is that if you value outdoor learning then the benefits of outdoor learning align to your school's values. The application of those values is what has the impact on the pupils and so instilling those values is vital for a whole school approach to outdoor learning.

How do you create an outdoor learning culture?

The setting of an outdoor learning culture starts with an understanding of the benefits to the pupils and staff of outdoor learning. The communal acceptance that undertaking outdoor learning is positive will remove the fear by staff of it being viewed as "not real teaching and learning". This will lead to the upward spiral of increasing confidence and more effective use of outdoor learning to meet pupils' needs as seen in Figure 3.1.

DOI: 10.4324/9781003666714-5

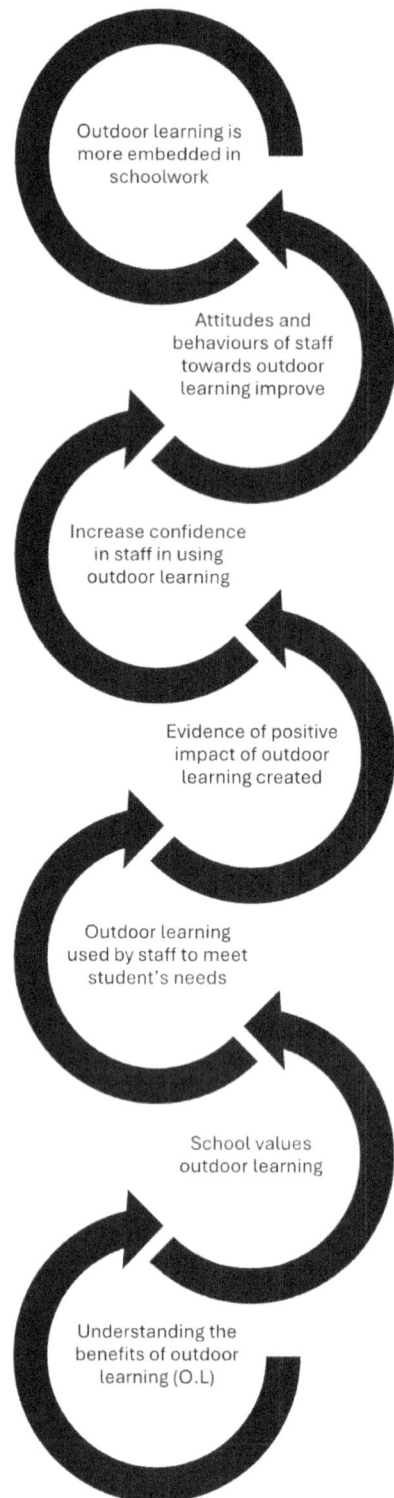

Figure 3.1 Creating an outdoor learning culture

Your senior leaders need to highlight the fact that embedding outdoor learning should not add more workload through the collection of additional evidence. When indoor and outdoor learning is fully integrated, the outdoor learning part is evidenced in the work created by the pupils and does not need additional evidence through photos, QR codes, or recounts for it to be valued in the learning.

Evidence of the impact of the outdoor learning will be explicit in the follow-up work which is linked and builds on the outdoor experience.

If your senior leaders want evidence of the outdoor aspect of the learning, then you can implement a simple marking process, e.g. a green dot showing the work was linked to an outdoor session. More importantly, the outdoor learning is monitored as part of the pupil performance monitoring and performance management observations as a key part of the role of teachers and support staff. Building the understanding that the outdoors is used to add value to the pupil's experience, and this should be evident in the pupil's responses to questions and understanding of concepts and skills.

Setting a culture of celebrating and respecting outdoor learning as a pedagogy requires the inclusion of it in all monitoring of teaching and learning as is done with other pedagogies such as group work or problem solving. So, there should be no requirement for it to be evidenced in addition to the work generated and moderated to look for pupil progress.

Strategic leadership in outdoor learning

On a practical level, the strategic embedding of outdoor learning requires its understanding and inclusion in all the procedures and policies used within your school.

The main policies which affect the daily application of the curriculum and running of the school should include using the outdoors as an explicit part of school life.

Policies

Depending on the names of the policies within your school, understanding of the role of outdoor learning should be included in:

- Any curriculum or teaching policies as a pedagogy to implement the curriculum.
- Health and safety, and safeguarding policies so the values of being outdoors align with the requirements of the school's health and safety.
- Uniform policy so that the requirements for outdoor learning, such as wellies and waterproofs are a clear requirement to parents, removing barriers to getting outside.

Procedures

Outdoor learning also needs to be included in all procedures within your school and so a consistent message is sent across the school. The best example of this is wet play. If pupils are undertaking outdoor learning in the rain in their waterproofs and then must get changed to come in for wet play, then this does not send a consistent message to the pupils. The same goes for boundaries at break time. When areas are out of bounds to pupils at breaktime and then used for outdoor learning, there is a lack of congruence.

24 *Learning Indoors and Out in the Primary School*

Senior leaders need to look at attitudes that are embedded in policies and procedures and consider if these align with valuing outdoor learning. What reason is there for these decisions on wet play and limiting space at break time? Is it due to the attitudes of staff or an outdated belief? As your school embeds outdoor learning these clashes may come to light and lead to changes in procedures to further indicate the school values the outdoors and encourages it.

Risk management

The attitude to risk management may also differ through your school staff. Consistent outdoor rules and understanding of risk should be a topic for whole school training.

Senior leaders can provide support for outdoor learning through provision of risk assessments for your school's site, local learning area, and off-site visits, plus activity risk assessments. However, all staff need to be confident in these risk assessments and understand their role in putting in place the control measures they identify for **their** pupils.

Whole school awareness

To highlight the value attached to outdoor learning senior leaders can also include it in the ongoing communications with school staff and governors. For example, inclusion in your staff meetings, staff observations, governor's meetings, and any meeting which the value feeds into.

See the strategic outdoor learning graphic (Figure 3.2) for how these elements all work together.

Supporting class teachers

Training

To enable your teachers to embed effective outdoor learning, training may be required. Surveying your staff and identifying training needs will allow your senior leaders to bring in experts who can share best practice and improve confidence in the staff.

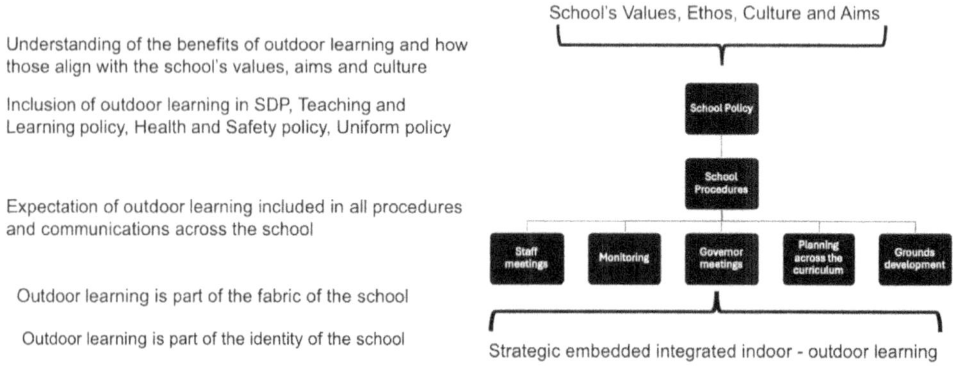

Understanding of the benefits of outdoor learning and how those align with the school's values, aims and culture

Inclusion of outdoor learning in SDP, Teaching and Learning policy, Health and Safety policy, Uniform policy

Expectation of outdoor learning included in all procedures and communications across the school

Outdoor learning is part of the fabric of the school

Outdoor learning is part of the identity of the school

School's Values, Ethos, Culture and Aims

School Policy

School Procedures

Staff meetings | Monitoring | Governor meetings | Planning across the curriculum | Grounds development

Strategic embedded integrated indoor - outdoor learning

Figure 3.2 Strategic outdoor learning system

Resources

Your teachers may also identify other needs such as resources. This does not necessarily mean having to purchase a lot of new equipment. It is much better to audit the resources your school already has and see what can be used for outdoor learning and then create resource boxes which are accessible for use during outdoor learning sessions.

These could be in each classroom or in outdoor storage containers. Probably the most useful outdoor resource is waterproofs and wellies. If you can purchase a set for a class/es it helps remove the barrier of the weather from undertaking outdoor learning. Asking for donations from your parents can also provide a school set of waterproofs over time. Consider the storage of these also and the logistics of getting your pupils ready to go out and learn in wet weather.

Other resources which your senior leaders can provide are those to support the actual learning undertaken outside. For example, outdoor learning ideas and lesson plans to help with the development of progress in outdoor learning across the school.

Mentoring

To support new staff or staff who lack confidence in outdoor learning, a team teaching, buddying, or mentoring system can be established to allow your staff to observe best practice and feel supported in their use of outdoor learning.

Case study of mentoring of new staff at King Edward VI King's Norton School for Boys

King Edward VI King's Norton School for Boys is part of the King Edward VI multi-academy trust in Birmingham, England. KNBS is a secondary boys' school with a long history of using outdoor education to enrich students' lives and inspire young people to achieve at the highest level.

The school has a dedicated outdoor education lead who supports all staff to plan and run outdoor learning, including off-site visits. The outdoor education lead has weekly meetings with new staff and supports them to complete the appropriate paperwork ahead of any trips, such as risk assessments and trip forms. The outdoor education lead also accompanies the new staff members on their first outdoor learning session to provide support and constructive feedback. This mentoring continues for a long as the staff require it, until they feel confident to carry on alone.

The distributed responsibility of planning and leading outdoor learning is key to embedding outdoor learning, but senior leaders have key roles as supportive mentors to empower new staff to feel confident with this role.

26 *Learning Indoors and Out in the Primary School*

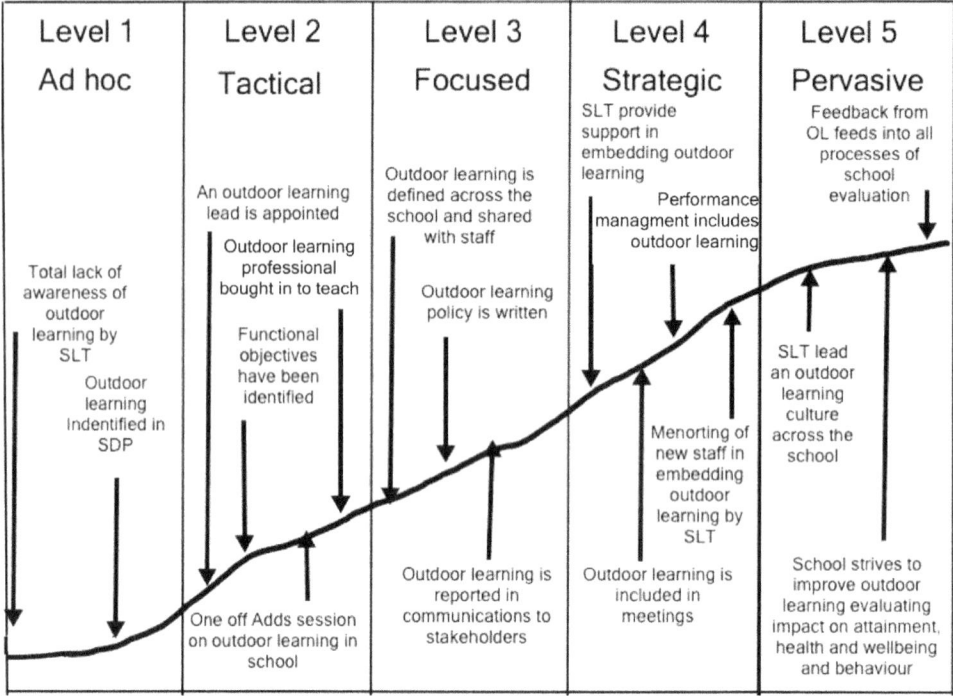

Figure 3.3 Strategic embedded outdoor learning progression model

Monitoring

To ensure that outdoor learning is happening across your school and is embedded and impactful, monitoring needs to take place. This process needs to be integrated into the ongoing monitoring of teaching and learning already in place in your school. The aim is to ensure outdoor learning is progressive and impactful across the school and that feedback from past outdoor learning feeds into future outdoor learning.

Auditing of how strategically embedded outdoor learning is within the school can be undertaken using the framework in Figure 3.3.

A framework for strategically embedding outdoor learning into your school

Figure 3.3 outlines a progression model for use by your school to determine where you are in your journey to embedding outdoor learning and identify the next steps to move towards more strategically embedded outdoor learning.

Start with an audit of where the school is now strategically and then use the framework to identify the next steps to progress in a whole school approach to outdoor learning.

Use the progression model and descriptions below to support the strategic embedding of outdoor learning through your school.

A description of the levels in the strategic progression model.

Level 1 Ad hoc

- Outdoor learning is poorly defined and understood within the school.
- Its use is not understood or appreciated by senior leaders as a pedagogy and there are no processes in place to support teachers to embed effective outdoor learning.
- Therefore, any outdoor learning is unpredictable, reactive to inspections or incoming initiatives, and short-lived.
- No measure is made of the effectiveness or impact of any outdoor learning.

Level 2 Tactical

- Outdoor learning has been identified as an area for development in the school.
- One member of staff is responsible for coordinating outdoor learning.
- Basic management practices have been initiated such as a training session for staff on outdoor learning or membership to an outdoor learning organisation.
- The school has identified functional objectives such as increasing outdoor learning but a route to this is unclear.
- An outdoor learning provider may be drafted in to run outdoor learning sessions.

Level 3 Focused

- Outdoor Learning is defined across the school and this is shared with the staff.
- An outdoor learning policy is written and shared with the staff.
- Processes for undertaking outdoor learning are documented and standardised throughout the school to ensure consistency.
- A route plan to improving outdoor learning across the school is created and shared with all stakeholders.

Level 4 Strategic

- Support is provided by senior leaders in embedding outdoor learning.
- Best practice of outdoor learning is shared in meetings and there is a sharing of outdoor learning resources.
- Performance management includes outdoor learning for all staff.
- Outdoor learning is respected as part of every member of staff's role and there is mentoring of new staff.
- Outdoor leaning is included in communications with stakeholders such as in staff and governor meetings.
- School emphasises outdoor learning in all they do such as through policies and procedures.

Level 5 Pervasive

- Embedded, integrated outdoor learning is part of the fabric of the school.
- The school strives for improvement through embedding outdoor learning in processes, evaluating attainment, policies, and procedures.

- Feedback from current and past outdoor learning is utilised to enhance and refine school's standards and procedures continuously.
- Outdoor learning is an integral part of the school's self-evaluation process and school improvement.

This progression model can be used as a road map for your school so that systems are in place to support all staff, so they feel confident in undertaking effective, impactful outdoor learning.

The role of the outdoor learning coordinator

On a leadership level the strategic embedding of outdoor learning requires someone to oversee it throughout the school. This coordinator will ensure there is progression in outdoor learning across the school and there are a range of opportunities for all students to undertake regular, frequent, meaningful outdoor learning.

This role will be supportive but should ensure that procedures are in place to monitor outdoor learning across the school and feed the findings back into future outdoor learning. Having systems in place that encourage all staff to participate in evaluating and monitoring outdoor learning is vital, but the collation of this data and looking for impact is key to ensuring continual improvement in the outdoor learning provision.

The creation of an outdoor learning policy may be a useful way of consolidating all aspects of outdoor learning and expectations of leaders, staff, and pupils in one document. An outline is available in the Appendix.

Ideas of how to apply chapter content

- Use the strategic framework progression model to identify where your school is on embedding outdoor learning, and identify the next steps required.
- Identify how outdoor learning can be used to support the ethos and values of your school.
- Create an outdoor learning policy for your school – outline in the Appendix.
- Survey your staff to find out their requirements in terms of training and resources.
- Embed outdoor learning into relevant policies and procedures, such as outdoor clothes in uniform policy, tour of school grounds in induction for new staff.
- Audit the outdoor learning resources you have.
- Create a bank of resources – generic risk assessment, outdoor learning boxes, plant identification guides, etc.
- Embed outdoor learning into procedures of your school – staff meetings, staff observations, governors' meetings.

4 Classroom teachers' role

> **Aims of the chapter**
> - To provide a teacher's guide to undertaking effective outdoor learning.
> - Ideas for collecting evidence of outdoor learning.

"I know it is good for the children to be outside, but then we just have to write it all up in their books or print off photos or QR codes to show they've done it. It just takes up too much time". (Many teachers feel that unless there is evidence in the children's books, it doesn't count.)

How do you undertake effective outdoor learning?

All the skills to undertaking an effective outdoor learning session are the same as those in the teaching standards. Most teaching skills you use in the classroom are transferable to teaching outside the classroom. Some adaptation may be required to the techniques used, and like all teaching, it takes practice to see what works for you and your pupils.

Planning

The key to an effective outdoor learning session is planning. When planning an outdoor learning session, the focus, as with indoor teaching, is the learning objective. Ensuring you know why you are outside and whether it is in fact the best place to reach that objective will put you in good stead for having an effective session.

When undertaking long-term planning consider topics that fit with the seasons and stimulate ideas for going outdoors. For example, looking at nature's calendar provides a good grounding for topic choice: Harvest in autumn, mini beasts in spring, flowers and growing in summer. Also, the weather at different times of the year can feed into science topics or geographical topics which can link to the conditions. For example, insulation experiments in winter, Africa or deserts in summer, monsoons in spring, hurricanes in autumn.

Books can also provide an opportunity for embedding outdoor learning sessions when they are set in an environment you can visit or replicate outside, for example, The Explorer by Katherine Rundell [1], Kensuke's Kingdom by Micheal Morpurgo [2], and Stick man by Julia Donaldson [3], see Chapters 8 and 9 for more ideas.

Routine outdoor learning is also a way to embed going outdoors into the routine of your class. One school I worked with had introduced the taking of temperature readings outdoors and indoors and comparing the two numbers as part of their daily weather observation. (Incidentally, the teacher has recently told me that she no longer teaches the skill of reading thermometers in class time, as this skill is learnt independently through this activity, saving her teaching time.)

This can be further extended to create a primary source of data for your school. See the weather and climate framework in Chapter 9 for more details.

Medium-term planning

Unlike indoor planning, you may want to look at the forecast when planning the weekly indoor-outdoor sessions. Flexibility in timings across the week may be necessary if the weather will impact your ability to achieve the learning outcomes. If your long-term planning has considered the seasonal weather, then it may be that challenging weather is what you need. For example, if you want the pupils to experience the cold of the Arctic, or the driving rain in a hurricane, or the blistering heat of the desert. However, if the outdoor learning session requires worksheets and writing, then this can be challenging in high winds and rain.

> **Top tip**
>
> **You can matt laminate worksheets to make them waterproof, but you can still write on them in pencil and rub out with an eraser.**

Schools use different methods and tools for planning. Whatever system you use for your planning to embed outdoor learning the structure needs to prompt you to ask.

"Where is the best place to teach this?"

If you are to truly embed the indoor-outdoor framework of learning, then think what the best prompt will be to ask this question "where is the best place to teach this", as you plan. You could add an outdoor learning symbol to your planning to indicate where you will teach or highlight outdoor learning opportunities in a certain colour.

It is vital that you do not complete your planning and then look at what you have planned and put in the outdoor learning retrospectively. This is what happens in most schools and leads to the "add on" nature of outdoor learning. Following the indoor-outdoor framework will guide you to integrating outdoor learning (see Chapters 8 and 9 for examples). This should mean that the planned outdoor and indoor sessions are linked and make the best use of the experiences.

Short-term planning

Day-to-day planning may focus in the first term on establishing routines for outdoor sessions and training your pupils in the expectations for those outdoor sessions. It is important that your expectations for your pupils outside are the same as inside.

Congruence is essential as this will impact pupils' attitude to learning outside. If you have set rules inside that don't fit outside, such as pupils being able to get their drinks without asking, then create appropriate outdoor rules together. If these are agreed across the school, then this helps when pupils change classes, but involve the pupils in understanding why the rules are necessary. Once these rules and routines are ingrained in the pupil's understanding, then going outside will be much more effective. See Chapter 5 for more practical tips.

You will also find that you have to adapt to the circumstances outside as distractions arrive. For example, the field is being mown, you find a dead vole, the children spot an animal track or poo, and an ambulance rushes past. There is no point in trying to ignore what the pupils are distracted by. Embrace it and find the teaching opportunity within the discovery. If you can be flexible with your learning outcomes, then student voice and interests can feed into an engaging session.

Assessment of outdoor learning

Assessment is a key part of teaching and learning and therefore to outdoor learning. The purpose of assessment is to support pupil progress. Like your teaching skills, most assessments you use indoors can be transferred outdoors. Teachers worry that if there is nothing in the books then there is no evidence of outdoor learning. However, when outdoor learning is integrated with the indoor learning then the evidence of learning is found in the evidence of indoor learning. For example, follow up work done in class books and learners' understanding and skills. Do not invent a new method for evidencing and assessing outdoor learning in isolation.

An example of how assessment of outdoor learning is evidenced in books.

Case study of assessment of outdoor learning session – Science investigation in year 4

The outdoor learning session involved a mini beast hunt and a science investigation into the speed of the caught mini beasts. The class drew the animals they found and then collected data in a results table on the speed of the different mini beasts. The animals raced across a tray and the students timed how long each different mini beast took.

Back indoors they coloured and labelled their pictures using the correct terms. They then created a bar chart of the speed of the different animals. Figure 4.1 shows the book work created as a result of this indoor-outdoor learning.

32 *Learning Indoors and Out in the Primary School*

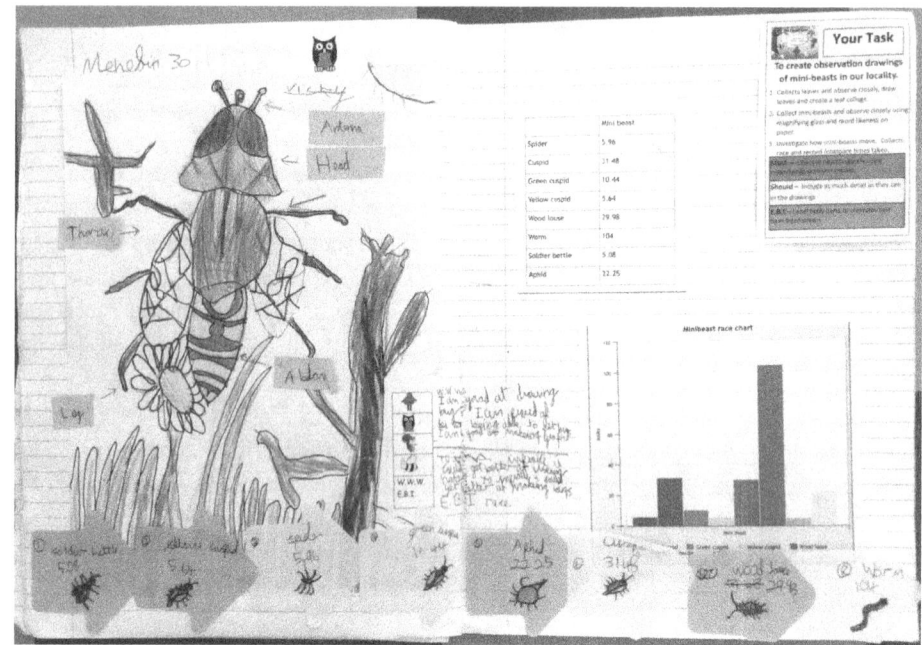

Figure 4.1 Assessment of outdoor learning in books

Self-assessment, peer assessment, and teacher assessment were then undertaken of their outdoor learning through the work in their books, which was all part of the total teaching and learning experience.

If your school is looking for evidence in books, then this example shows how the indoor-outdoor framework will facilitate that.

Table 4.1 outlines an example of how the indoor-outdoor framework can be used to generate content for assessment in books for a literacy session.

Learning objective: To set the scene for an original traditional tale, myth, or legend.

Table 4.1 Example for using indoor–outdoor framework in a literacy lesson

Location	Activity
Indoors:	Introduction to traditional tales, myths, or legends with research done in class on the text type.
Outdoors:	Read some tales that link to the environment you have in your school grounds.
Indoors:	Reflect on the use of the environment to set the scene or tone of the tale.
Outdoors:	Choose a location for the setting of their tale. Collect descriptive words for that location or take photos.
Indoors:	Use the descriptive words or photos to inspire a description, setting the scene for the tale.
Outdoors:	Read the description outside in the location and evaluate the impact of the description.
Indoors:	Redraft the description using the evaluation to improve the impact.

The assessment of the learning will be undertaken in the written work, which is the outcome, but the outdoor learning is also assessed as the evidence will be in the quality of the written work. The outdoor learning is integral to the quality of the book work.

If you do want to assess the impact of outdoor learning itself, for example, if you are using it as an intervention or want to collect empirical data on outdoor learning specifically, then you need to compare this piece of work with a group of students who undertook the same task with no outdoor learning. See Chapter 7 for more ideas on collecting data on the impact of outdoor learning. It is important to know what the assessment is for and select the right type and time to assess to make it meaningful and helpful to move pupil's learning forward.

Why provide evidence of outdoor learning?

If you are taking photos of outdoor learning and printing them off and placing them in student's books with assessment comments, consider who this is for. Does it help with pupil progress? If your school insists on evidence from outdoor learning sessions, then consider the use of digital outdoor learning folders to upload photos or tools such as Seesaw or Squid. If the collection of evidence of outdoor learning does not help to move pupils' learning along, then share chapter three of this book with senior leaders so they can instil a supportive strategic culture of embedded outdoor learning.

Assessment for learning outdoors

Assessment for learning strategies can also be transferred from inside the classroom.

What pupil assessment tools do you use?

Figure 4.2 identifies a range of assessment tools used by teaching staff. Which of these do you use indoors and which ones could you use to assess outdoor learning?

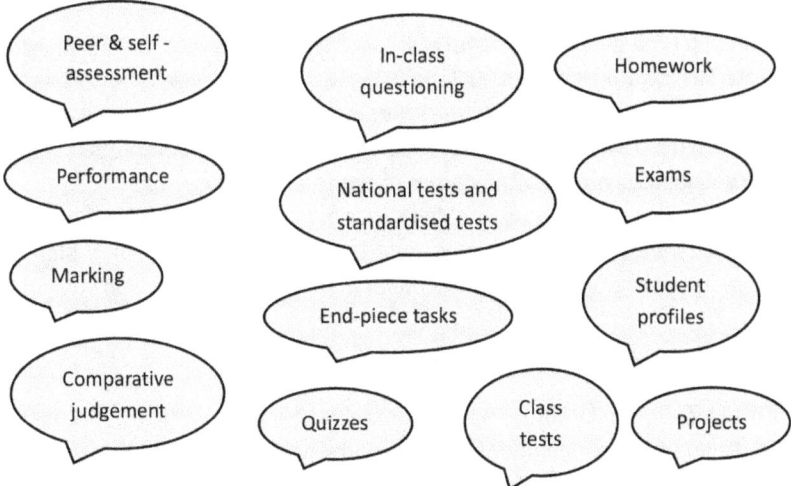

Figure 4.2 Assessment tools

The best time for assessment for learning is **at the moment of learning**, so it needs to be undertaken outside as well as inside.

Observation is best done outside. The indoor-outdoor framework can provide a **reflective cycle for assessment** for learning as you reflect on what the pupils learnt when returning inside. Then ask them to consider how they can progress their learning when they carry on inside or return outside. Embedding assessment into the teaching and learning both indoors and out will provide the most effective teaching strategy for assessment.

Monitoring

Pupil progress monitoring is part of assessment and again you can use the monitoring cycles and systems set up in your school for indoor teaching and learning. Consider including the use of the observations undertaken outside when feeding back on pupil progress. As you embed these experiences you will see that pupils who struggle to make progress inside may show much more progress in skills and attainment outdoors. This is especially true of pupils with additional learning needs, so consider how the monitoring of their progress can reflect the outdoor experiences they are having.

Developing your outdoor learning skills

Training and CPD

If you want more expertise in the skill of using the outdoors to teach, then you will find experts in your Early Years staff. The embedding of outdoor learning is integral to Early Years provision, so get advice from the experts and adapt the strategies they use to your class.

Teacher's prior knowledge

If you feel you lack subject knowledge in the outdoors because you can't name trees this should not be a barrier to taking pupils outside. You do not have to be an expert in nature to use it to teach. The key is to be aware of your learning objectives. It is unlikely that the objective is for the pupils to be able to identify all the trees. If it is, then what you are probably developing are observational skills or skills in using Identification keys. If you do not know the tree's names, then you can use the same strategies as the pupils to find out, with the class. This will provide a much more informative experience for everyone and a much better teaching tool than you just telling them the names of the trees.

Using the outdoors to teach transferable skills is much better than just gaining knowledge such as names of things. There are many apps that you can use to identify plants now, but focus on the skills you are developing in the pupils and therefore the reason you are outdoors.

Ideas of how to apply chapter content

- Explore a system for integrating outdoor learning into your long-term, medium-term term and short-term planning – Ideas in the Appendix.
- Identify methods you can employ for assessment or adapt your assessment methods for use outdoors.

- Integrate monitoring the impact of outdoor learning into your ongoing monitoring of teaching and learning.
- Identify any training needs you have linked to your role as an outdoor learning provider.

References

1. Rundell, K. (2017). The explorer. Bloomsbury.
2. Morpurgo, M. (1999). Kensuke's kingdom. Harper Collins.
3. Donaldson, J. (2008). Stick man. Scholastic.

Part III
Putting indoor-outdoor integrated learning into practice

Introduction

Now that you understand the theory and structure required to integrate indoor-outdoor learning, Part III goes into the practicalities of actually doing it. It provides guidance for class teachers on how to get outdoors for the first time and what to do when you get there. It also introduces the indoor-outdoor integrated frameworks. Five frameworks for teachers to use to support their teaching so they know how to weave the indoor and outdoor teaching and learning. It then goes on to provide further guidance in ensuring there is progression in the outdoor learning you are undertaking, and how to know if there is progression in the student's knowledge or skills.

5 How to start learning outdoors

> **Aims of the chapter**
> - How to start teaching outside.
>   - Resourcing; dealing with the weather, staffing, and safety.
>   - Logistics; getting outside, muster points, establishing routines.
>   - Teaching outside; managing behaviour, structuring outdoor learning sessions, transition, teaching styles.

"I know I should be taking my class outdoors, I just don't know how to start". (Teachers who have had "improve outdoor learning" added to their School Development Plan do not necessarily have the follow-up support to implement this).

Where do you start?

In an ideal world strategic outdoor learning throughout the school, implemented by the senior leadership team, as described in Chapter 3, should lay the groundwork so that any teaching staff starting out using the indoor-outdoor curriculum are supported and mentored. This provides the culture of outdoor learning as a respected and key tool for teaching.

What to do before you go outside?

Being prepared is key to a successful outdoor session. Chapter 4 covered planning and you should know the learning objectives of the outdoor session and following indoor sessions.

Resources

With your learning objectives clear, resources need to be accessible for any outdoor learning session.

You could create outdoor learning boxes which can be stored in class and grabbed when going outside. Or you can use outdoor storage, like sheds, so that they are accessible when

Table 5.1 Outdoor learning boxes contents

Maths	Literacy	Science	Humanities	Art	PE
Tape measures Rulers Clinometers Number stones	Lined paper Letter stones Reading books	Magnifying glasses Pots Sweep nets Stop watches Trowels	Maps Compasses Rulers Tape measures	Paint brushes Pots Crayons Paper	Balls Hoops Bean bags Stop watches

you are outside. Nothing breaks the flow of an outdoor session more than having to go back indoors to find the necessary equipment.

Items which are useful in a generic outdoor learning box are:

- Clipboards
- Pencils
- Waterproof paper (matt laminated)
- Chalk
- Sit mats

You may also want to create subject-specific outdoor learning boxes or class outdoor learning boxes such as those in Table 5.1.

The most useful resource is waterproofs. If you can't go outside to teach because your students are not dressed appropriately, then it is very difficult to plan an effective indoor-outdoor curriculum. See Chapter 3 for ideas to help ensure your class is fully kitted out for the weather and make sure all staff have sufficient clothing too.

Ratios and staffing

Your staffing levels and permissions will vary depending on where you are undertaking your outdoor learning. Within your school grounds, if you have a member of support staff, then you should be able to go out to the school grounds easily.

Make sure that you have considered the roles of the adults, especially with logistics such as toileting and head counting.

If you are going further afield than your school grounds, then approval may have to be sort from the local authority. There are no specified ratios from the Outdoor Education Advisers Panel (OEAP), the provider of guidance for all outdoor educational activities, apart from in Early Years. But your employer, which may be the head teacher or local authority, may have some set ratios for specific locations such as beside water.

Ratios will vary and are a risk management issue for each school depending on:

- Group requirements
- Any special needs of the group
- Location

- Remoteness
- Age of students
- Weather

Aim for the more the merrier in the case of adults and undertake a risk assessment for the conditions and group to determine what is an acceptable minimal level.

Permissions

Establishing pre-approval for visits to your local learning area in the school operational procedures makes going out of the school gates much easier. Check that your school has all new students' parents or guardians complete a permission form for use through the year for visits to the local learning area.

Always have at least two members of staff when off site and a mobile phone in case one adult needs to return. Inviting parents or governors will increase your staffing numbers and provide opportunities for sharing what the students are doing. Give these volunteers clear roles and guidance of your expectation. Parents are usually very keen to take over the activity and "help" the children. Brief them on how to be observers and supporters and not hands on. I have seen a lot of dens being built by parents while their children watch, clearly not meeting any useful learning objective.

Having systems and procedures in place for local visits will streamline your job in planning visits. Refer to your school's outdoor learning policy and health and safety, and risk management procedures before you set off.

School visits will require authorisation by the local authority and head teacher, so you should consider trips as soon as possible when planning so that there is time to achieve the prior learning before the visit is undertaken.

External providers

If the visit is being led by an external provider, then make sure your learning objectives are clear, and you know how they will adapt to meet your class's needs.

Communication is key to a successful visit and the provider should be told:

- Learning objectives
- Prior knowledge and work undertaken
- Post visit work planned
- Behavioural needs of your students
- Learning needs and range of your students
- Disabilities or other needs of all participants
- What strategies you use for class control
- Any routines in place which they can adopt such as freeze words

If providers do not ask for this information, then inform them so they can be effective in their instructing.

A site rec or visit with the provider is a perfect opportunity to pass on this information. If you look for the Learning Outside the Classroom Quality badge, then you know their safety and teaching have been assessed and are of a high quality.

If you are undertaking your own offsite visit, then a site reconnoitre is vital so that a thorough risk assessment can be made.

Safety

When using the school grounds, you need to consider what would happen in the case of an accident or a fire alarm. Always take the fire register with you outside and a first aid kit to avoid children and a member of staff having to return to the school for any small accidents.

Strategic outdoor learning should mean that risk assessments are shared by senior leaders but do not just adopt them. Risk varies with the students and the weather, and you should look at the risk assessment and then address any risks with control measures necessary for your class on that day. If you find there are additional risks missing from the risk assessment, then add these as they should be dynamic documents.

How do you get your class outside?

Training students to get outside efficiently should happen in the first term alongside the establishing of other school routines. Identify where students will store their waterproofs and put them on. Teach the class what the procedure is when you say you are all going outside. This should lead to a sequence of actions which happens quickly to allow the transition from indoors to outdoors to happen as efficiently as possible.

For example, when you say, "get ready for going outdoors," the students go to the toilet, get waterproofs and wellies on, pick up a clipboard, and line up by the fire door.

This will be different for each year group and so needs to be established at the start of the new academic year.

Knowing the routine to get outside should be established through regular use of the same system and procedure. Eventually, students will be so efficient that a five-minute outdoor session will not be preceded by 20 minutes of faffing time.

Unless it is very hot outside, taking water bottles is usually unnecessary. Consider what your class usually needs inside for the time you are planning to be outside and prepare accordingly.

What to do when you get outside

Once outside the building you need to identify a place for your class to congregate. This could be a seating area or in a circle on the playground. Experiment with different muster locations as the weather changes. Make sure there are no distractions like windows into classrooms. Can the students hear you or are you close to the road or nursery playground? Can your whole class sit or stand in the area?

The location may vary depending on the weather. If it is raining, you may want to use a covered area or if it is windy, stand on the side of the building which blocks the wind. In summer you don't want the sun in your classes' eyes or yours. If it is very cold, then consider introducing the activity inside and just do a quick reminder outside to keep your class moving.

When first starting outdoor learning with a class, you need to set the ground rules. Make it clear that your expectations for behaviour and level of working are the same as inside the classroom. Transfer the same rules you have for behaviour and class working to the outdoors. The more the students learn outside, the better they will be at concentrating and staying on task outdoors. If they only use the outdoors for playtime, then they will immediately expect to run and play once outside.

If your class is not focused when you get outdoors or you need to lower the level of excitement, then consider using a transition exercise, see the appendix for some examples. With regular indoor-outdoor learning, students will become more focused outdoors and the need for transition exercises will reduce.

Class control

Once the rules of indoor teaching and learning have been established outside then the skills for managing behaviour can also be transferred. For rules that are specific to being outdoors discuss and come up with a class set of rules in collaboration with the students. This way they understand these new rules or restrictions.

Consider:

- Boundaries
- Using sticks
- Picking plants
- Picking up animals
- Moving around the space

It is useful to have consistent rules across the school for the above so that when students move classes, they follow the same rules.

Teaching

When teaching outside remember that all your teaching skills are transferable to the outdoors. You may want to experiment with different teaching styles to those you use in the classroom as the outdoors can provide much more scope for facilitation and kinaesthetic styles than the indoors does. Let the students experiment with problem solving and just observe. You can learn a lot from listening to their conversations and asking key questions at the right time will move the learning along without you interfering with the flow of the activity. Use questioning to challenge, motivate, and inspire them to push themselves.

Observation of the student's activities will provide opportunities for assessment and also identification of their interests. A great way to embed outdoor learning is to follow the interests of the students and build the planning around these.

Start small

If you are new to outdoor learning, or your class is, then start small.

- Use the space closest to your classroom or just outside the door you exit the school building from.
- Aim for part of lessons to be outside and not the whole morning.
- Use the outdoors as a resource by going out and collecting items to use inside.
- Have small groups go outside with a teaching assistant and use worksheets for observing the seasons, colours, numbers, or angles.
- Build up the time and distance from the school as you gain confidence, and the class gets better focused outdoors.

Spectrum of outdoor learning delivery

Below is a spectrum for outdoor learning delivery.

These different levels of outdoor learning each have their place, and it is not that level six is better than level three, although level one is really an entry point for less confident teachers and does not really provide all the outdoor learning benefits.

Embedded integrated outdoor learning should include different levels to allow students who respond to outdoor learning in different ways, positive or negative, to succeed and develop better outdoor learning skills and resilience.

It is important that staff are aware of where they are comfortable on the spectrum of delivery and aim to start at that level.

Level 1 - Space
Take work to do outdoors.
Example: It's a sunny day so you do your literacy carousel, worksheet, reading outside.
Level 2 - Store
Collect items outdoors to use indoors.
Example: Teacher or pupils bring in leaves to draw inside.
Level 3 - Run
Undertake activities that work better outdoors.
Example: Daily mile, P.E. outside. Messy activities such as painting and planting.
Level 4 - Explore
Explore the outdoors to inspire work.
Example: Scavenger hunt to write a poem. Seasons spotter sheet to look at signs of spring. Magic spot to focus or calm students.
Level 5 - Apply
Reinforce learning by seeing the concepts in the real world.
Example: Grow plants in different conditions. Measure on a different scale to reinforce understanding of area and perimeter. Map skills. Designing a den.

Level 6 – Inspire
Using the outdoors to teach concepts. Immersive experiences.
Example: Survival day – discovering what it would be like to survive outdoors. Adventurous activities – teamwork through climbing. Residential – living away from home.

As your confidence increases aim to move up a level in your delivery of outdoor learning.

Structuring the outdoor learning

The way you structure your outdoor learning session can mirror the way you do indoor learning.

- Prepare the class for the activity; this can happen indoors or out.
- Transition to the outdoors if they are not there already.
- Undertake the main activity with you facilitating and undertaking assessment for learning through observation.
- Review the activity and link to prior learning and skills.
- Transition back into the classroom and build on the experience with the follow-up activity.

Example outdoor learning session:
Den building.
Learning objective: To create a how-to guide for den building.

1. Prior learning. Understand the design process.
2. Looking at the design process and creating model dens following a design brief.
3. Transition to outside.
4. Preparation outside by identifying suitable locations for building and collecting resources.
5. Main activity den building.
6. Each group feeds back to the class how their den meets the design brief and reflects on the process and how it could have been improved. Take photos or sketch their dens.
7. Transition inside.
8. Use photos of dens or drawings and label them to identify how the den meets the design brief.
9. Write a "how to" guide on building a den using the ideas that came up in the reflection process when outside.
10. Give the how-to guide to another year group for them to use to build a den outdoors.

Making it clear to the class that they will be creating a "how to" guide and following a design brief, identifies the learning objectives and the mode of assessment of the outdoor learning.

What to do when you return to the classroom

Reflection

When your class and you are starting to integrate outdoor learning, it is important to take time to reflect on how the session went. Try to be objective and get feedback from the children and other support staff. Were there issues you had not planned for? How could you better tackle these next time? Were there any surprises in the student's attitude and behaviour?

Do not expect every outdoor session to be perfect. With so many confounding factors it is hard to tell why a session does not work sometimes. The change may be out of your control or just needed a slight tweak to adjust to the mood of the class. Experiment with different styles of teaching, locations, groupings, and types of activities. You and your students are learning a new way to teach and learn so experiment and embrace the change.

Routines

To improve outdoor learning and indoor learning then sessions need to be frequent and regular. Students need to go out regularly to start to associate the outdoor locations with learning. Infrequent sessions are usually much harder to manage as the excitement of the children is too great and the attitudes and rules have not been embedded. If you and your class are struggling to teach and learn outside, you probably need to go outside **MORE.**

Every year group can integrate a short outdoor session into their daily routine. It could be tagged onto break time or after lunch time to avoid having to get dressed again. Or story time could be in an outdoor space or group work. Look for opportunities to undertake meaningful outdoor learning daily which builds skills in your students of being outdoors.

Be flexible

Even though planning indoor-outdoor learning requires clear learning objectives, don't forget to embrace opportunities to adapt those objectives if things happen outside.

The weather may not be right for the activity you had planned one day, for example, you were planning to use bits of paper outside, and it is windy. If you can be flexible and shift around your weekly activities to consider the changing weather, then you can make the best use of what you have.

The weather can also be a great learning device so embrace the opportunities it can provide.

Table 5.2 contains a number of ideas to work with the weather.

Ideas of how to apply chapter content

- Identify several muster points for your class outdoors and experiment with them in different weathers.
- Explore transition activities and monitor the impact on your pupils.
- Establish routines which encourage independent efficient preparation for outdoor learning.
- Discuss the rules and expectations for outdoor learning with your class.
- Reflect on an outdoor session you have undertaken and look for areas that went well and areas for improvement.

Table 5.2 Working with the weather ideas

Rain	Wind	Sun	Frost and ice	Snow
Collect water and measure volume in different shaped containers	Measure wind speed with windsocks	Investigate shadows	Look for frost shadows	Track animal footprints
Investigate waterproof materials	Look at where the wind blows the litter or leaves	Investigate what colour is the hottest	Investigate the structure and properties of ice	Build an igloo
Follow the water around the school building	Seed dispersal investigation	Make a UV shield and test with UV beads	Investigate the temperature of different parts of the grounds	Insulation experiment
Make a model water slide for a ball	Find a wind shadow	Build a solar oven	Look for frost crystals	Investigate friction
Measure the volume of a puddle	Design and test a windmill model	Investigate evaporation	Explore melting ice with salt	Go looking for objects hidden in the snow

6 Applying the indoor-outdoor integrated framework

> **Aims of the chapter**
> - To describe the indoor-outdoor integrated frameworks.
>   - inspirational framework
>   - testing theories framework
>   - assessing application of knowledge and skills framework
>   - field work and visits framework
>   - residential framework.
> - How to combine different frameworks.
> - Implementing the indoor-outdoor framework into your planning.
> - How to use different locations with the indoor-outdoor integrated framework.

"That all sounds great but how do I do it"? (Once I introduce the idea of the indoor-outdoor framework to teachers they recognise the value in the integration but are not sure how to implement it).

What is the indoor-outdoor integrated framework?

The aim of the indoor-outdoor integrated framework is to help teachers use outdoor experiences to consolidate, progress, and enhance learning inside the classroom.

To make the most of the multi-sensory experience of outdoor learning the activities need to build on the skills and knowledge acquired in the classroom. Likewise, the follow-up indoor activities need to draw out the learning from the outdoor experience and apply it to the following progression of knowledge and skills being taught.

This interweaving of indoor and outdoor sessions can provide a framework for learning and application that enriches the teaching and learning experience.

The indoor-outdoor integrated framework can be summarised by asking two questions.

1. How can we build on that outdoor experience?
2. Where is the best place for that to take place?

Applying the indoor-outdoor integrated framework 49

If the location for the teaching is considered when undertaking planning, then the best use will be made of outdoor experiences. Then recognising the shift in experience and skills in the students after being outdoors, teachers develop ongoing indoor or outdoor teaching that ensures progression. In this way, the best use will be made of any outdoor experience and the potential for applying the curriculum in the real world will be clear, increasing interest and attitudes in pupils.

There are five indoor-outdoor integrated frameworks.

Three based on different focuses of teaching and learning, Tables 6.1-6.3, and two based around outdoor experiences beyond the school grounds, Tables 6.4 and 6.5. Each framework is described below with an example of an activity to help explain its application. More examples can be found in Chapters 8 and 9.

Inspirational framework

The inspirational framework, outlined in Figure 6.1 and Table 6.1, uses an outdoor experience to drive the planning, motivation, and excitement of the topic. The initial activity is the hook, and the outdoors is used to inspire questions which are followed up in the most appropriate location.

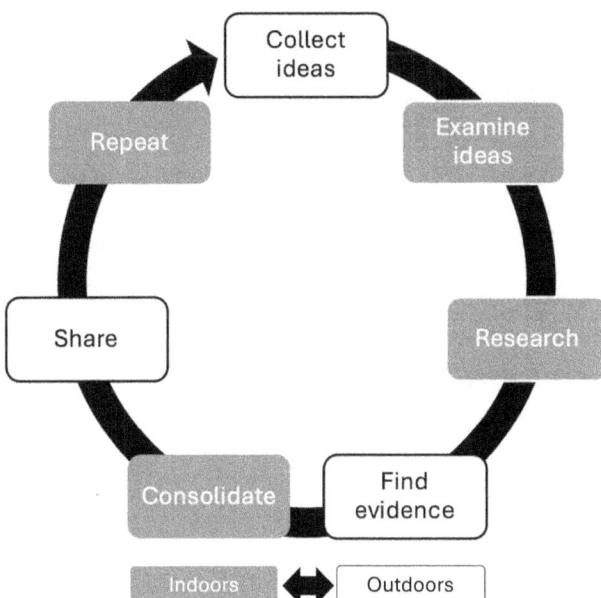

Figure 6.1 Inspirational framework. A system of teaching that uses inspiration from an outdoor experience to generate ideas to explore in class. These ideas are then researched indoors, followed by identifying supporting evidence outdoors. The evidence gathered in both settings is consolidated and shared with others, using the outdoors as a space to present and explain discoveries. The process is then repeated, with learning moving fluidly between outdoor and indoor environments as the framework progresses.

Table 6.1 Inspirational framework

Location	Learning objective	Example
Outdoor	Inspire students, using an outdoor experience, to be curious and **collect ideas.**	Walk around the school grounds or local learning area and come up with questions to explore on the topic of "My place".
Indoor	**Examine the ideas** collected and sort them.	Sort the questions generated from the experience outdoors into categories. Combine all the questions on plants, or animals, or landforms, or people, or history.
Indoor	Select one idea to focus on and **research** further.	Explore the natural history of the local area through research.
Outdoor	**Find evidence** of the research you have undertaken indoors, outdoors.	Visit places you have researched and explore them, talk to local historians, ecologists, or residents.
Indoor	**Consolidate** the research and practical visits together in an end product.	Create a natural history walking guide to your local learning area.
Outdoor	**Share** with the wider community.	Take local people on the walking tour using the guide.
Indoor	Choose a different idea and **repeat** the process.	Choose a different category and repeat. e.g. historic buildings.

Testing theories framework

This framework, outlined in Figure 6.2 and Table 6.2, works well with scientific investigations. Bringing taught concepts to life and allowing students to explore how science relates to the real world.

It is important to focus on the skill of the scientific process, not on discovering groundbreaking new science. Also, the application of skills in data collection and problem solving as well as data presentation and evaluation.

The scientific experimental process

1. Generating questions
2. Understanding variables
3. Predicting results
4. Writing a method
5. Collecting data
6. Presenting data
7. Drawing conclusions
8. Evaluating methods

The results will not necessarily prove the taught theory, but a deeper understanding of the concept will be acquired through the experimental process. The learning objective is to investigate and apply the taught concept in the real world and the skills associated with the scientific process.

Applying the indoor-outdoor integrated framework 51

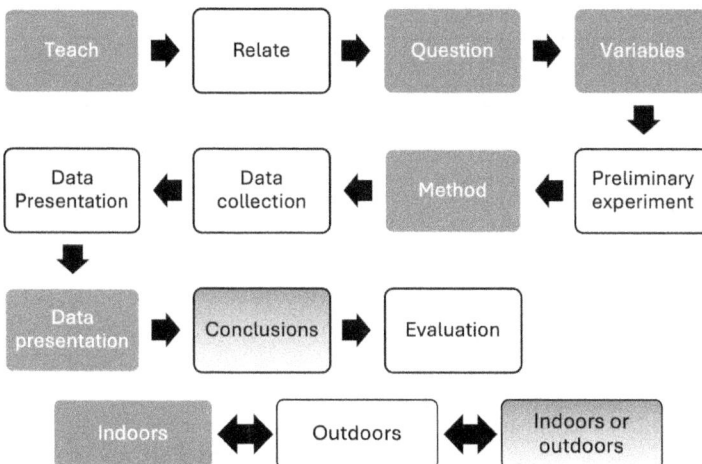

Figure 6.2 Testing theories framework. A teaching system that uses the outdoors to exemplify concepts first introduced indoors. Students then investigate these concepts using the scientific method, beginning with a preliminary outdoor experiment to test methods and practice data collection skills. Data is gathered outdoors to address the investigation question and later presented in both indoor and outdoor settings to draw conclusions. Finally, students evaluate the data collection method outdoors, reflecting on possible improvements. As learners move through the framework, the balance of activities gradually shifts from indoor to outdoor environments, though some tasks may take place in either setting.

Table 6.2 Testing theories framework

Location	Learning objective	Example
Indoor	**Teach** the concept.	Teach the concept of insulation and heat transfer.
Outdoor	**Relate** the concept to the real world.	Explore the temperature in different parts of the school grounds.
Indoor	Using experience and knowledge on the concept, come up with **investigation questions.**	Generate an investigation question. e.g. Why is it warmer on the playground?
Indoor	Discuss and explore **variables** you could measure and test.	Discuss all the factors that affect the temperature outside and how they could be measured.
Outdoor	Undertake a **preliminary experiment** to test ideas for a method and skills in data collection.	Explore possible locations for undertaking an investigation into temperature. Trial using the equipment to measure the variables. Use this information to choose the appropriate location.
Indoor	Write a **method** for the investigation.	Use the outdoor experience to write a method to follow. Include instruction for location and how to use the equipment.

(Continued)

52 Learning Indoors and Out in the Primary School

Table 6.2 (Continued)

Location	Learning objective	Example
Outdoor	Undertake the **data collection** for the investigation.	Follow the method to measure the variables in the different locations and to collect the data in a results table.
Outdoor	**Present** the results.	Use chalk or loose materials to create a rough graph of the results outside on the playground.
Indoor	**Present** the results.	Use the most appropriate method to present the results. It could be a graph in books or using a computer program, or as a presentation.
Indoor/Outdoor	Draw **conclusions.**	Present your conclusions to the experiment either in books or as a presentation.
Outdoor	**Evaluate** investigation.	Use the space outside to describe what you did and how it generated reliable data, and how your method could be improved.

This framework, outlined in Table 6.2, can also be used for undertaking geographical enquiries into more broader areas such as on place, see Chapter 8 for more examples.

Assessing application of knowledge and skills framework

All topics that include the teaching of concepts which have a practical application can be taught using the assessing application of knowledge and skills framework outlined in Figure 6.3 and Table 6.3.

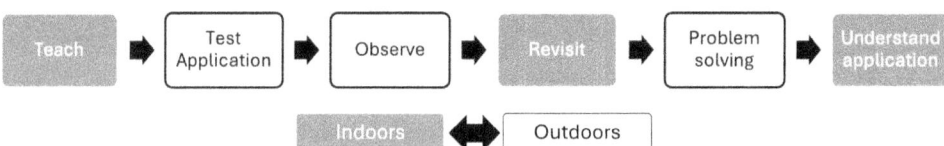

Figure 6.3 Assessing application of knowledge and skills framework. A teaching system that uses the outdoors to test students' understanding, skills, and application of concepts in a new environment. Concepts are first introduced indoors, then applied outdoors through tasks that reveal how well students have understood them. Teachers can observe any misconceptions during these activities and address them back in the classroom. A deeper grasp of the concept is then assessed through outdoor problem-solving, followed by reflection on how the concept applies to students' everyday lives. The outdoors serves both as a setting for assessing understanding and as a way to encourage cross-curricular application of learning.

Table 6.3 Assessing application of knowledge and skills framework

Location	Learning objective	Example
Indoor	**Teach** the concept, knowledge, or skill.	Teach measuring perimeter and area using a ruler.
Outdoor	Test the **application** of the knowledge and skills in a different environment and on a different scale.	Outdoors ask students to measure items such as the perimeter of the playground, the area of the field using tape measures, trundle wheels, or meter sticks.

(Continued)

Table 6.3 (Continued)

Location	Learning objective	Example
Outdoor	Observe any **misunderstanding** of concepts and gaps in practical skills.	Listen and watch the students applying the processes taught in class. Observe how different equipment is being used effectively.
Indoor	**Revisit** any concepts, knowledge, and skill requirements.	Clarify or revisit any misconceptions identified through the application of the measuring task. Look at the suitability of equipment for measuring different scales.
Outdoor	Assess deeper understanding and application of the concept through **problem solving**.	Present a problem to the class which requires the application of the mathematical concept to answer. e.g. Can we fit a full-size football pitch on the field?
Indoor	Identify the **value** of the concept in real-life application.	Highlight why this mathematical concept is important by asking the class to come up with different ways this may be of use in their lives. e.g. Measuring for a carpet, AstroTurf, solar panels for a roof.

The progression to outdoors allows the assessment of pupils' understanding of the concept in a different environment, but also how they apply the knowledge they have gained practically. This framework provides the opportunity to discover misconceptions in the learning and identify any skills gaps.

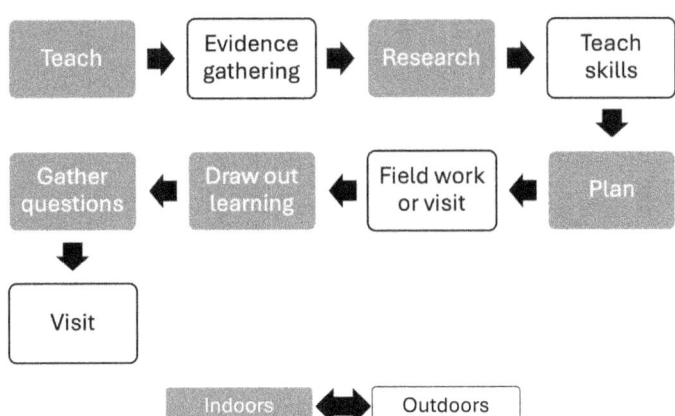

Figure 6.4 Fieldwork and visits framework. A system that uses field work to build on prior teaching undertaken in school. Students compare the field visit site with their school through research. Before the trip, the necessary fieldwork skills are introduced and practiced outdoors in the school grounds. The field visit is planned to develop skills in navigation and timetabling. After the field visit, learning is consolidated by reflecting on the experience and exploring any new questions it raises. Further visits are then used to investigate these questions in greater depth. The outdoors is used as a tool to develop skills and enhance the fieldwork experience.

Table 6.4 Fieldwork and visits framework

Location	Learning objective	Example
Indoor	**Teach** the prior knowledge for the subject of the field trip or visit.	Teach the process of adaptation.
Outdoor	Look for **evidence** of the subject in your school grounds.	Look at plants or mini beasts and identify adaptation features. e.g. Streamlined worms for burrowing, or camouflage.
Indoor	Discuss and **research** the place or location you are going to visit to compare to your school grounds. Use maps to identify the location for the field trip or visit.	Use Google Earth to take a virtual journey from your school to the field trip location. Look for similarities to your school grounds.
Outdoor	**Teach skills** you will be using on the field trip or visit.	Explore the best place to find mini beasts, use keys to identify them, discuss best practice to keep your students and animals safe.
Indoor	**Plan** the route to the location and use timings to create a timetable for the day.	Use maps to find the most direct route to the visit location. Calculate the time to drive there. Work out a timetable for the day to fit in with the school day.
Outdoor	Go on **field trip or visit.**	Go to the field location to explore adaptation such as a rocky shore, pond, or river. Take photos and collect data on the number of different types of animals.
Indoor	**Draw out learning** from the experience.	Draw pictures of the animals found on the field trip. Draw graphs of data collected on the numbers of each animal.
Indoor	**Gather questions** generated by the field trip or visit.	Discuss what questions your class has about the field trip or visit. e.g. Do we have similar animals to the rocky shore in your school pond?
Outdoor	Identify where these questions could be answered and **visit** these locations.	Visit the school grounds or another location to answer the questions generated. e.g. Explore animals in a wetland habitat such as a pond and see how their adaptations compare to those in the sea.

Field work and visits framework

Going on a field trip or visit provides a unique opportunity to explore places beyond those found in your school grounds and local learning area. Linking the right visit or field trip to the topic or learning objective is key, as well as choosing the right time in the learning of the topic. Many life skills can be hung on a field trip or visit which teach cross-curricular skills such as route planning, timetabling, and budgeting. Also consider other opportunities available during a field trip or visit such as road crossing, risk management, water safety, and perception studies.

Figure 6.4 and Table 6.4 outline how the fieldwork and visits framework can be used to make the best of any school visit including an example of a field trip. This framework can also be used for trips to museums, art galleries or the theatre to ensure best use is made of these experiences.

Applying the indoor-outdoor integrated framework 55

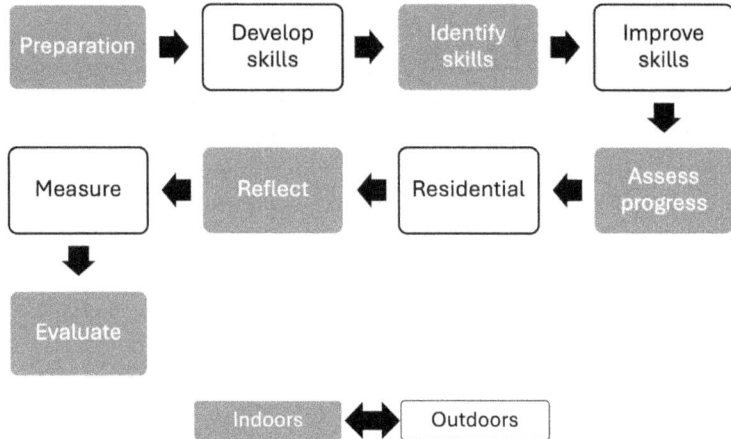

Figure 6.5 Residential framework. A system that uses the residential experience as a way to build key skills needed during such activities. Before the residential, students identify the skills they need to develop. Their current skill levels are measured through outdoor activities, which provide a baseline. Activities are undertaken outdoors to improve these skills and any progress is reflected on. After the residential, their skills are reassessed to evaluate the improvements made through the experience.

Table 6.5 Residential framework

Location	Learning objective	Example
Indoor	**Preparation.**	Look at the plan for the residential and identify what your class are excited or worried about. Discuss skills which would make the experience even better, e.g. confidence, team building, communication, trust, problem solving, resilience.
Outdoor	**Develop skills** required during a residential.	Undertake activities which will develop the skills identified, e.g. team building and communication through problem solving games and activities like walk the plank, toxic waste, den building, and team games.
Indoor	**Identify** the skills level.	Evaluate what went well and what skills they need to develop.
Outdoor	**Improve** the skills.	Design their own game or activity to help develop the skills that need improving, e.g. games that help with communication such as line up games.
Indoor	**Assess** progress.	Discuss how their skills have improved, how they can tell they have improved, and what the results were.
Outdoor	**Residential.**	Go on a residential.
Indoor	**Reflect.**	Discuss what skills they developed while on residential and choose an activity to repeat outside to see how much they have improved.
Outdoor	**Measure** progress.	Choose an activity that was used before the residential for which the classes' skills have improved. Repeat the activity again using the skills they have learnt from the residential.
Indoor	**Evaluate** improvement.	Discuss how their approaches to the activity differ from before the residential and how they can apply these new skills in their lives.

Residential framework

Like the fieldwork and visits framework a range of life skills can be developed through residential experiences as outlined in Figure 6.5 and Table 6.5. Think about the potential learning outcomes which are difficult to cover within the school day. It is more difficult to embed a residential framework into planning if not all the classes are attending the residential. Hopefully, this framework in Table 6.5 can still develop their life skills even if some students do not take part in the residential. Be mindful when undertaking follow-up sessions in the lack of a residential experience by some pupils.

Residentials also provide other opportunities for teaching knowledge and skills. During the residential consider how you could explore these experiences:

- Being self-reliant, e.g. keeping track of their belongings
- Time keeping
- Listening skills
- Exploring the night sky and nocturnal animals
- Map reading and route planning in an unknown location
- Domestic skills like clearing away, setting the table, hanging up wet clothes
- Responsibility for their own and others safety and enjoyment
- Reflection on their emotions
- Appreciation of awe and wonder of nature
- Self-improvement

Combining different frameworks

The different frameworks outlined above can be combined over the school year to create structured progression in indoor and outdoor experiences. The field work and visits framework can be used to test theories when the field work is a scientific or geographical enquiry.

The outdoor experience at the start of the Inspirational framework may be a visit or field trip or a visitor coming into the class or a residential.

The important idea is that the outdoor teaching and learning and the indoor teaching and learning are not **undertaken in isolation** but are inextricably linked.

How does a teacher practically undertake indoor-outdoor integrated learning?

You can implement the integration of the indoor-outdoor frameworks at the different stages of your planning, long-term, medium-term, and short-term.

The essence of the indoor-outdoor integrated framework can be applied thematically to long-term planning when topics are chosen that link to outdoor learning opportunities. Consider the topic associated with the residential or visit when planning that term's topic. How can you make the best use of the outdoor experience in choosing the topic?

For example, if you are undertaking a residential where the class will be undertaking team building activities or adventurous activities, the topic could be Belonging or Community.

You could also apply key skill development planning through the outdoor learning experience. For example, if you are planning a visit to the theatre, then the skill could be around creativity or communication such as oracy and presentation skills.

Other skill development may be planned before the residential or field trip to provide better use of the time you are offsite. For example, learning compass and map work skills so that orienteering activities can include a higher level of progression and challenge. Learning skills in data collection, sampling, or using identification keys so that fieldwork can be done more efficiently and gather robust data. You are then revisiting the skills and knowledge which reinforces the learning, especially when applied in a different situation.

Incidental outdoor learning and routine outdoor learning can be embedded into daily activities using the frameworks too. Consider which daily tasks will be more impactful outdoors and how you can build that experience into your class teaching. For example, reading, numeracy, or literacy carousel. Or introduce daily or termly outdoor activities that build skills such as data collection, perception studies, or nature connectiveness. For example, monitoring the weather, measuring plant growth, surveying traffic levels, measuring noise levels, mindful walks, observing nature, and the seasons.

Explore ways of generating long-term data sets through **continuous monitoring** throughout the year. For example, temperature readings in the school grounds over the year can be used to draw climate charts for your school. Over the years you can use this data to see the impact of global climate change on your local area.

Using different locations

When using the indoor-outdoor integrated framework try to make the best use of all the locations available to you. When you plan, aim to integrate all the areas in your school grounds and link the activity to the area best suited to it.

Different locations can be used to provide variety when revisiting concepts or assessing understanding in the framework. For example, when your class gets confident in applying skills in one area of the school grounds move to a different area to see how they apply their thinking there.

For example, take your class on a walk to be inspired to find adjectives for a story, visit a range of locations, and give them the opportunity to contrast how the different locations make them feel and how they could use this to impact the narrative of a story. When the students have finished their stories, they can choose a location for it to be read in and see how that immersive experience effects the reader.

For more details on using different locations for progression, see Chapter 7.

As your students progress in outdoor learning, a great learning opportunity is to involve the class in deciding where the best place will be to learn the skills or explore concepts. This will build a better understanding of place and purpose of any visit. For example, after using the inspirational framework the questions can be used to prompt students to think of locations in the school grounds or further afield which will provide

Figure 6.6 An example of how to identify potential use of the various locations in your school grounds

Source: Screenshot courtesy of © Google Earth.

the answers to the questions. Providing pictures of local areas and sites to visit will help pupils see the potential for learning in all environments. It is therefore important that teachers have a good awareness of the school grounds and local learning area so they can choose the best place for the learning. If you are not local, then consider asking a local member of staff or governor to take you on a tour of the local sites and share their experience of the place.

Figure 6.6 provides an example of how different locations within your school grounds could be used for a variety of activities. Using a map of your school's site can help you identify any areas underutilised for teaching and learning.

Ideas of how to apply chapter content

- Use a map to identify the different locations in and around your school where you could undertake outdoor learning. See Figure 6.6.
- Use the above to feed into your outdoor learning planning.
- Look at your planning and see how you could embed one of the frameworks into your future topics.
- Explore the topics on your long-term plan and establish how you could embed outdoor learning into them. Start with an easy topic.
- Consider a range of long-term data your class could routinely collect.
- Look at the planning tools or sheets you use. How can you adapt them to facilitate the embedding of the indoor-outdoor framework?

7 How to ensure progression

Aims of the chapter

- How to ensure progression in outdoor learning.
- Monitoring progression.
- Differentiation outdoors.

"All the year groups go into the woods; they love making dens even the year 6s". (In schools every aspect of learning is about progression, but schools rarely map progression in their outdoor learning provision.)

Progression in outdoor learning

The role of schools is to facilitate pupil's progress in all that is taught. Teachers spend hours completing spreadsheets and pupil progress reports focusing on progress in one aspect or another. Although outdoor learning is neither a subject nor a skill if we are using it as a pedagogy and to improve the experience of the students, then you would expect progression in outdoor learning experiences across the school and an improvement in the skills associated with being outdoors. Unfortunately, most schools find that the volume of outdoor sessions decreases dramatically as you go up the age groups as shown in Figure 7.1.

This is usually due to teachers citing the volume of content that older year groups must be taught. However, if outdoor learning is used to teach content or assess understanding using the integrated indoor-outdoor framework, then the level of outdoor learning need not decrease so dramatically as the students go through the years. I don't expect year 6 classes to be outside as much as nursery, but how would your pupils respond to more regular outdoor learning experiences in the higher age groups?

How do you know the outdoor experiences are ensuring progression?

Like all aspects of teaching and learning outdoor learning must be progressive.

DOI: 10.4324/9781003666714-10

60 Learning Indoors and Out in the Primary School

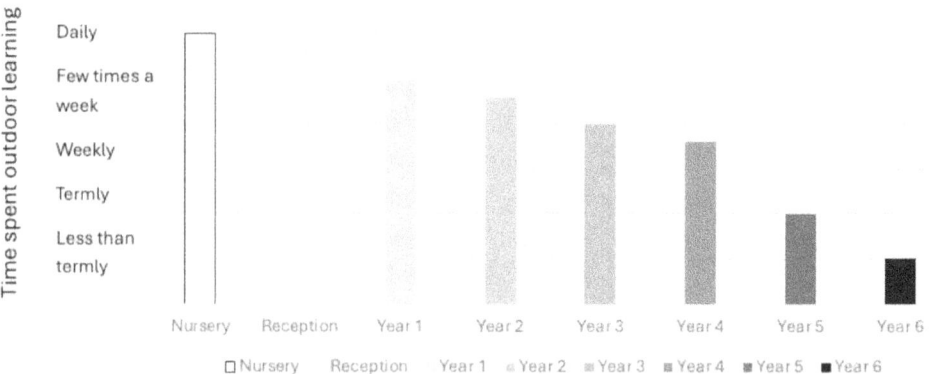

Figure 7.1 A graph showing the trend in the amount of outdoor learning taking place across the primary setting

If you are undertaking an outdoor activity in year six which is also undertaken in reception you need to justify that it is an appropriate activity to challenge the pupils.

It is possible that the same activity may be suitable for different age groups and the progression occurs in what happens next, inside the classroom. For example, a mini beast hunt with nursery may be repeated in year six, but the aim of the hunt in year six is to gather data to present on graphs or as part of a science investigation into habitats and the conditions found there. The outdoor session may look similar with just the addition of a results table for year six, but the learning objectives are very different. This is why embedding the outdoor learning into the indoor learning is so important and being aware of prior learning and post activities is vital. In nursery any follow-up or prior learning may be limited to identifying the names of mini beasts or playing with models of them, the learning outcomes being "recognition of living things and being kind to animals".

Awareness of what outdoor learning pupils have experienced in the previous school years will ensure outdoor learning builds on prior knowledge and skills. This can be the role of senior leaders such as an outdoor learning coordinator, who can monitor outdoor learning experiences across the school to see that progression in the outdoor experiences takes place. You and your support staff can also benefit from speaking to lower age group class teachers to understand what outdoor learning has taken place.

Measuring the impact of outdoor learning

Measuring the impact of the outdoor learning experiences will also be key to ensuring progression. If you want to collect empirical data on the impact of outdoor learning to generate evidence of impact, it would be useful to use a baseline assessment by measuring pupil's abilities or level of understanding at the start of the academic year to make sure progress and challenge follow. To ensure strategic integrated outdoor learning these strategies should not be done in isolation but as an integral part of the other baseline assessment or data collection undertaken by your school in their evidence collection as part of your self-evaluation process.

Looking at the impact of outdoor learning can be undertaken through a number of routes:

- Evaluating outdoor learning skills – for example, the practical application of concepts like map reading, identifying landforms, measuring, or problem solving.
- Intervention impact – for example, a small group undertakes outdoor learning to improve their ability to concentrate or self-esteem.

To measure the impact of outdoor learning you need to consider the type of data you want to collect. Quantitative data provides numbers to be graphed and used in reports to prove impact but, what should you measure?

What should you measure?

Academic attainment

The answer to this question should stem from the reasoning behind the use of outdoor learning in your school and your main objectives for the use of outdoor learning. If you are looking at improving academic attainment through outdoor learning, then you can use the outcomes and markers you use to measure pupil attainment and compare to a control group who have not undertaken outdoor learning or the group's progress before outdoor learning was instigated.

Health and wellbeing

If the focus of the integration of outdoor learning is to improve health and wellbeing, then quantitative data can be gathered through questionnaires which rate how students are feeling and coping with school. These can provide ratings of levels of happiness and confidence before outdoor learning starts and then compared to after outdoor learning has been undertaken. The time scale can be short, before and after one session, or long, at the start and end of the year.

Attendance

Other quantitative data that is collected in your school which can be used as evidence of improving pupil's health and wellbeing is attendance. Analysing increases in attendance and equating them to outdoor learning may not be possible, but this data may add to the overall picture of the impact when combined with other data that is collected.

Pupil voice

Talking to students and observations of pupils while outdoors and in class can also provide qualitative data on the impact of outdoor learning on health and wellbeing.

This data usually provides much more detail and nuance behind any numbers generated by a questionnaire. For example, if a student has said that they feel they are calmer, you may observe that they deal better with conflict in the classroom or are more likely to be on task after an outdoor learning session.

More targeted impacts of outdoor learning may be linked to specific interventional uses of outdoor learning or school improvement targets. This data generation needs to be planned into the teaching and assessment processes so that data can be collected at the right time.

Some examples of methods for collecting data on impact on attainment:

- Book looks of work to assess understanding of concepts.
- Talking to students before and after outdoor learning session to assess understanding.
- Assessments of skills specifically fostered outdoors through pupil observation, such as map reading skills, mobility and motor skills, resilience, adaptability, attention, independence.
- Tests to measure application of knowledge through problem solving.

You may want to consider identifying the key skills developed through outdoor learning experiences so that these can be mapped and evaluated when outdoor sessions take place. This should not be in addition to other tracking but should be integrated into the school's pupil progress tracking and school evaluation processes already in place.

How can you ensure progression in outdoor learning?

Progression through location

Different locations can be used to increase challenge in an outdoor learning activity.

A variety of surfaces can increase difficulty physically by making movement more challenging. For example, if you have a slope in your school grounds or uneven surfaces with obstacles such as forest, then undertaking a walk will be more challenging in these locations compared to on the playground or field.

Location can also be used to differentiate an activity by giving different ability groups different locations to work in. For example, building shelters is easier in a woodland where there are trees to use as supports compared to the same activity in a field or playground. Embedding progression in shelter building skills across the year groups can be achieved by moving from the woodland to the fence line, to the field, and finally to the playground. This revisiting of activities in different locations will test their problem-solving skills and ability to reframe the challenge. It is important to review the level of challenge as the activity is taking place and then relocate groups to provide more or less support. Follow-up activities could involve assessing their ability to adapt or problem solve as well as teamwork and dealing with conflict.

Case study: Nature Days den building on a beach field trip

I regularly undertake field trips on a beach which involves shelter building. Pupils are presented with a range or resources, broom handles, string, tarpaulins, and spades. They then must build a shelter from the weather.

Without fail most of the class will attempt to build their shelters in the middle of the beach as a free-standing structure dug into the sand with spades. This is extremely challenging especially on a windy day.

After letting them try for some time I usually intervene by questioning them as to why they are struggling. They recognise that the poles are not supporting the tarp and keep falling, but it takes a lot of questioning before they admit that the location is the wrong choice, and they should move to a more sheltered spot which has trees to support the shelter.

Using the same location in your school grounds, especially if you lack habitat variety, can require creative planning. As your students get more efficient outdoors then look for opportunities to go further afield to find habitats that are not available on site.

Think about progression in location through the year moving from school grounds, areas close to the school, further from the school building to local learning area, field visit on a bus to a longer bus journey as shown in the progression model in Figure 7.2.

Throughout the school, progression in location can be linked to an increase in competence outdoors by the pupils and confidence in the staff. Moving from an easy location such as the school grounds to a more challenging terrain such as river side, hill or mountain, or a busy city centre. Depending on the rurality of your school taking pupils to a busy city may be much more challenging than visiting a local wood. Try to embed contrasting locational opportunities throughout the student's school life.

Progression over time

As the student's progress through the year then the amount of time you spend outside can increase. This progression fits in well when the summer term comes at the end of the academic year. However, I would always advocate for higher levels of outdoor learning in the first term to train your pupils in the skills of getting outdoors efficiently. These do not have to be long sessions, however, and can be just a 5 – 10-minute part of your lesson, whereas by the summer term you could be spending the whole afternoon outdoors. The weather and the busyness of Christmas will influence the amount of time you can spend outdoors.

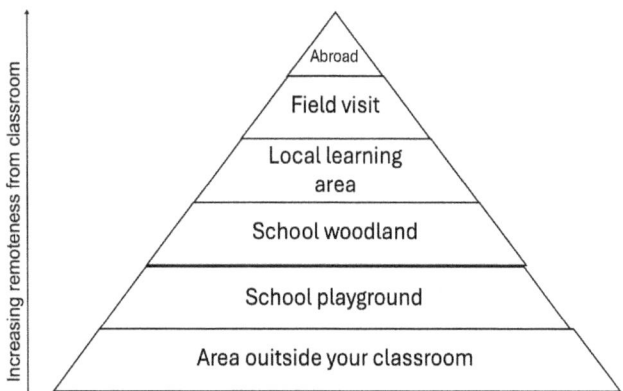

Figure 7.2 Model of progression by location

Model of progression in time spent outdoors

5-minute sessions ⟶ A weeks residential
Once a year ⟶ Daily sessions

In colder months activities that require being still outside and using fine motor skills such as writing can be very challenging and are not advised if there are required to meet your learning objectives.

Adjust the time outside compared to the time inside appropriately to make sure pupils can undertake the activity. Consider more active activities in the colder months and more transitions inside so they can warm up. It is important to maintain a level of outdoor learning even in the winter months as the weather always looks worse when you are inside, and students will lose those skills of being outdoors if you stop outdoor learning completely in the winter.

Figure 7.3 shows a suggested model of progression in the time spent outdoor learning across the school year, with an explanation of why the length of time should vary.

Progression in outdoor skills

A good way of monitoring and ensuring progression in outdoor learning is to map the skills that outdoor learning can be used to teach or assess and then create a skills progression model for your school that relates to outdoor learning.

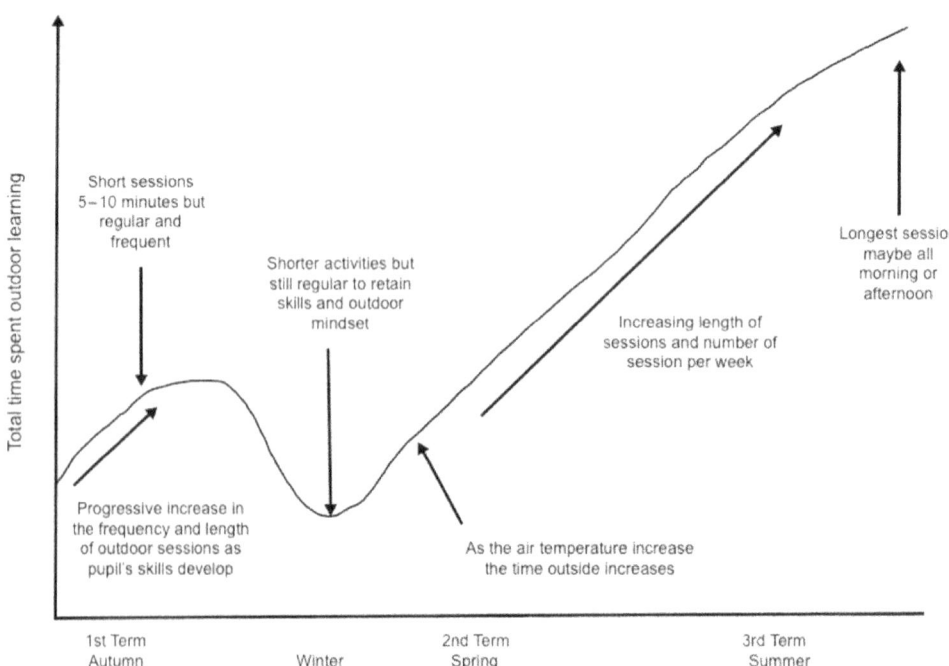

Figure 7.3 Model of progressive outdoor learning in terms of time spent outdoors

How to ensure progression 65

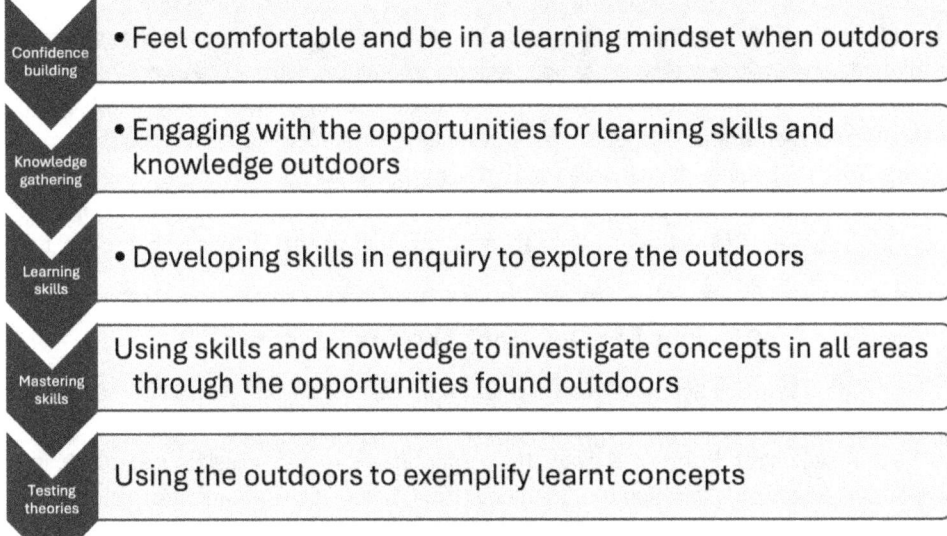

Figure 7.4 A general progression model for outdoor learning skills

This progression model can relate to outdoor learning skills, as in Figure 7.4, and can be referred to when planning outdoor learning sessions across the school.

Outdoor skills can also relate to other aspects of school life such as sustainability goals, nature connectiveness, or health and wellbeing goals. Developing a holistic view of the outdoor environment and how pupils interact with it is a key skill to developing students who respect and care for the environment.

Figure 7.4 general progression model for outdoor skills is also underpinned by progression in building connections to the outdoors. As well as developing knowledge and skills we need to use outdoor learning to allow students to foster a connection to nature so that they value it and appreciate and protect the environment in the future.

Building connections progression model.

- Using knowledge of the natural world, learners begin to understand the impacts of their actions on the environment
- Feel empowered by their skills and knowledge to make a positive impact on the environment
- Learners develop their own values about the natural world and develop greater empathy for it
- Learners take ownership over the state of the natural world
- Learners build positive impacts on the environment into their lives
- Learners link outdoor experiences to life choices and the impacts of their behaviour

More practical outdoor skills can also be mapped across the school as a benchmark for progress. For example, woodcraft skills, knots, den building and design skills, fire lighting skills, plant and animal identification skills. Awards can be designed around these skills, or you can use frameworks from ready-made outdoor skills awards such as the National Outdoor Learning Award (NOLA) which are free and capture personal development outcomes of your students on an outdoor learning experience, as opposed to academic outcomes. The award can be used with any age group, any outdoor activity in any outdoor environment over any length of time.

I have also seen primary schools create bespoke awards for their students based on the National Trusts' 50 things to do before you're 11 ¾ and a passport of outdoor activities that students aim to complete before they leave the school. These should be developed to challenge pupils but also planned into the school calendar so that they are achievable within school time.

Case study: Blaenymaes Outdoor Learning Passport

Blaenymaes Primary School is in an area of Swansea, South Wales, UK, which has high levels of poverty.

At Blaenymaes Primary School, their school vision and mission statement is 'Planting Seeds of Inspiration to Bloom and Grow'. It shows their commitment to offer authentic learning opportunities and experiences which maximise every child's potential, whatever their potential may be.

The Pupils have created the 50 Things of Blaenymaes and topics are planned with these at the heart of the learning. The pupils have a 50 things learning journal where they document their achievements throughout their Blaenymaes school journey.

This was recognized as a strength of the school in the latest school inspection report.

"They help manage the school finances effectively and work hard to mitigate the impact of poverty on families. For example, through grant funding and links to other organisations, leaders provide valuable activities, on and off site. These help to broaden pupils' experiences".

"The curriculum is based on the fifty experiences Blaenymaes primary pupils should access and this helps ensure that there is a breadth of knowledge and learning experiences for all" [1].

Blaenymaes Primary School inspection report 2024 (More details in the Appendix.)

Curriculum-linked skills can also be mapped and progression measured through the pupil assessment processes. Skills in fieldwork, navigation, as well as skills taught through using the outdoors such as independence, spatial awareness, risk management, mobility, and movement.

Progression across the school

To monitor progression across the school in outdoor learning, a central repository of the outdoor activities, especially field trips and visits, should be developed and shared with teaching staff. The role of an outdoor learning coordinator would be to monitor external visits across the curriculum, and within the school grounds, and look for a range in the breadth and depth of the experiences provided. Collecting feedback from teaching staff and pupils on any

How to ensure progression 67

outdoor learning can be used to feedback on the outdoor learning offered and identify how it can be improved and built on.

Progression in field trips

If you are revisiting sites multiple times for visits across the school, then make sure that you are clear that the activities are progressive. Use of external providers of outdoor experiences should also be aware of your objectives so that you don't repeat the same activities. If an outdoor location or experience is revisited this should not be a problem if there are different aims for the session.

For example, a field trip to a beach could be undertaken by all year groups.

- Nursery/Reception: Explore the beach and build sandcastles.
- Year 1: Collect items from the strand line and sort the items into human-made and natural or plants and animals. Rock pooling to look for sea animals.
- Year 2: Collect items to create artwork on the beach. Look for animals in the sandy shore, dig for lugworm. Rock pooling collect and identify animals.
- Year 3: Investigate floating and sinking of found materials. Make boats out of natural materials to sail on the sea or in a rock pool.
- Year 4: Collect items when beach combing. Identify shells or materials using a key and create a story to explain their journey.
- Year 5: Go rock pooling and draw the animals and identify their adaptations to the environment. Undertake a microplastics investigation on the beach.
- Year 6: Undertake a science investigation into the location of animals with distance from the sea. Explore the coastline looking at coastal landforms and create models in the sand of them.

Progression in residential

You can also provide progression in your residential offer as shown in Table 7.1.

Table 7.1 Progression in residential

Year	Residential experiences
Year 1	Extended day with evening session in the school grounds after school finishes. Family camp in the school grounds.
Year 2	Extended day in a residential centre close by or one-night residential sleeping in the school hall or camping in the school grounds.
Year 3	One to two nights residential in a close by residential centre. Centre staff or teachers design the program of activities.
Year 4	Two to three nights residential in a residential centre close by. Activities chosen by the pupils but run by the teachers or centre staff.
Year 5	Three to four nights residential further away from the school. Co-design of the activity program with the pupils.
Year 6	Four to five nights residential an hour or more drive from the school. Children plan their own program.

Including progression in residential experiences helps pupils develop the skills required to be independent away from home over their school life and if they miss the residential in year 6, they still have other opportunities. It is unrealistic for us to expect all pupils to be able to undertake a week's residential in year 6 if they have never had any experience of being away from home before that. Introducing this progression model should increase the uptake of year 6 residentials as pupils become more confident in being away from home.

By giving students more responsibility and input into designing their outdoor learning experiences, they will develop other transferable skills.

How do you move the learning along outside?

Within an outdoor learning session strategies used to ensure pupils are progressing can be undertaken using the same practices used indoors.

Questioning

Questioning is key to facilitating progression in outdoor learning sessions. If you have staff that tend to step in too soon than consider supplying a set of question starters for them to refer to when approaching pupils who are struggling. Using Bloom's taxonomy [2] is a good starting point to support progression and the tell, show, do, apply model of instructing in Figure 7.5, but ask them first.

Extension tasks

As with indoor teaching having extensions for pupils to undertake when they have completed their activity is important. Look at the methods you use indoors and identify which can be transferred outdoors.

An extension could involve the students **reviewing** their progress and then improving on it. Some of the most valuable skills are not developed during the activity but in the reviewing afterwards. To allow for more independence in this reviewing, a standard set of review questions could be used so students know what is expected. Again, if you have a reviewing system you use indoors transfer it outdoors, one star and a wish, what worked well, even better if, what a good one looks like (WAGOLL), but think of a way of recording it which works outdoors.

One source of extension tasks you can introduce is **independent outdoor challenges**. These can be created to build on the outdoor learning activity or be stand-alone activities for pupils to go on to when they have completed their work. Missions or challenges can be provided in the form of laminated cards that pupils can undertake independently or with others

Figure 7.5 Tell, show do model

Table 7.2 Outdoor learning extension challenges

Subject	Challenge
Literacy	Write a survival guide to your school grounds.
Numeracy	What volume of water is in the puddles outside?
Science	Which colour flower do pollinators prefer?
Design Technology	Design a way of protecting your school from flooding.
Geography	Create a map of your school grounds.
History	What was your school ground like in the past?
Expressive Arts	Create your own sculpture using natural materials.
Religious education	Create a positive message using the outdoors for inspiration.
Physical Education	Design an obstacle course.

using the outdoors to complete them. Table 7.2 contains examples of independent outdoor challenges for each subject.

Differentiation outdoors

The same factors used to increase challenge outdoors can be used to support pupils outdoors. For example, when den building in your school grounds:

- Location – Placing lower ability groups where there are trees or a fence to support the shelter.
- Resources – Providing enough resources or removing resources from more able groups such as limiting the amount of string.
- Providing help and support.
- Adding guidance – Providing guidance by demonstrating ways to build a den or providing a selection of pictures of design ideas to choose from.
- Adding rules – Adding more rules for the more able such as the shelter needs to be 1m high or big enough for the whole group to sit in.
- Removing choice – Sometimes the biggest obstacle to success is the ability to choose. Allowing free reign can be very challenging and so giving exact instructions on where to go and what to do will help support their decision making.

Just remember that the learning objectives of a den-building activity are not building a den. It is the cooperation, communication and teamwork skills, design and planning skills, associated with building a den that are important. Therefore, it is vital that you leave time to review those skills at the end so the pupils can see what they have achieved and not focus on the actual den itself.

Review questions:

- What did you do well?
- What did you struggle with?

- How could you have improved your attitude/teamwork/communication?
- What skills have you developed?
- What have you learnt?
- What advice would you give to another group doing the same activity?

Ideas of how to apply chapter content

- Look at the learning objectives of your outdoor learning sessions in your planning. How have you ensured there is progression?
- Identify skills which can be taught and tested progressively through outdoor learning. Create a skills progression framework.
- Look at your school cohort and create a progression of outdoor experiences which meet their needs and provide them with new transformative experiences.
- Choose one location that you revisit multiple times; it can be within one year with one year group or across the school. Identify a progressive set of learning outcomes to build on each visit.
- Create a bank of independent outdoor challenges for your next topic to build on the indoor teaching.
- Look at the school grounds and consider ways to differentiate an outdoor activity such as den building.

References

1. Estyn, His Majesty's Inspectorate for Education and Training in Wales. (2024). A report on Blaenymaes Primary School. https://primarysite-prod-sorted.s3.amazonaws.com/blaenymaes-primary-school/UploadedDocument/4e05efa2-861a-4352-b83b-91b97b5189aa/inspection-report-blaenymaes-primary-school-2025.pdf
2. Bloom, B. S., Engelhart, M. D., Furst, E. J., Hill, W. H., & Krathwohl, D. R. (1956). Taxonomy of educational objectives: The classification of educational goals. Handbook I: Cognitive domain. Longman.

Part IV
Schemes of work and lesson ideas for using the indoor-outdoor integrated frameworks

Introduction

Part IV provides a series of schemes of work which show you how you can teach subjects, skills, and topics using the indoor-outdoor frameworks. For each subject, ideas of activities which build on in-class teaching are outlined, and then follow-up activities to undertake indoors are described. A continuous series of sessions, undertaken in the appropriate location, following one of the indoor-outdoor frameworks, supplies inspiration for your planning of the curriculum. Once you have utilised or adapted the ideas described, you can then see how to build on this work by using the indoor-outdoor frameworks for future planning of more adventurous and progressive teaching and learning.

8 Subject schemes of work

> **Aims of the chapter**
> - To provide a range of activities to use to integrate the indoor-outdoor frameworks into the teaching of subject-related skills.
> - Using the indoor-outdoor frameworks to teach skills in:
>   - Maths
>   - English writing
>   - Science investigations
>   - Design technology
>   - Information technology
>   - Geography skills
>   - History
>   - Expressive arts

"I just need some ideas to help me take the learning outside" (Most teachers want inspiration to take their learning outdoors and ideas to make it impactful and worthwhile.)

Introduction to the schemes of work

The following teaching ideas, based on the indoor-outdoor integrated frameworks, address skills required in the main curriculum subjects. Each subject has several key concepts which can be taught directly through the indoor-outdoor integrated framework using these ideas.

This is not a rigid scheme of work, more a framework to guide you to integrate outdoor learning into your indoor teaching. To this end the indoor teaching is not explained in detail just outlined and the outdoor activities are more descriptive with questions to ask and focus on. Take what is useful and integrate them into your planning with the indoor-outdoor system in mind.

The year group each scheme is aimed at is identified but can be differentiated up or down depending on your classes' needs.

74 Learning Indoors and Out in the Primary School

More ways to teach some of these concepts are included in Chapter 9, where they are embedded in topic work. This can help with the understanding of the relevance or application of the key concepts. All the ideas include application of the concepts in the real world outside, and their use in problem-solving to challenge students and allow for potential independent work.

The following series of ideas will probably be undertaken over a series of days or weeks and not completed in one day. Find the essence of the framework and adapt it for your school and students, don't expect to follow every activity rigidly.

How to teach maths with the indoor-outdoor framework

Maths and numeracy are probably the easiest subjects to teach outside. I have included two different frameworks: the assessment and application of knowledge and skills framework in Table 8.1 for teaching number in years 1-3, and the inspirational framework for measuring length in years 2 and 3 in Table 8.2.

Number: Years 1-3

Table 8.1 Scheme of work for using the assessment of application of knowledge and skills framework to teach number

Assessing Application of Knowledge and Skills Framework – Number		
Location	Learning objective	Activity
Indoor	Be able to count to 10, 20, or 100	Teach the concept of counting to 10, 20, or 100
Outdoor	Test the ability to count to the number in a different environment with different objects.	Ask your students to collect the number (10, 20, 100) of loose parts, e.g. sticks, stones, leaves, grass.
Outdoor	Count backwards and forwards. Identify and represent numbers using objects.	Ask your students to line the objects up and count them, write the numbers underneath in chalk, count backwards and forwards.
Indoor	Revisit counting to 10, 20, 100 Count in twos, fives, and tens.	Bring natural objects used outdoors indoors and group into twos, fives, and tens to count in multiples.
Outdoor	Test the ability to count in multiples of 2, 5, and 10.	Collect plants that are in multiples, e.g. in twos – sycamore keys, pine needles, in fives – horse chestnut leaves, sycamore leaf points, buttercup flowers – five petals, in tens – leaves, grass, stones.
Indoor	Use the language of equal to, more than, less than, most, least.	Fill plates with different numbers of Lego bricks/multilink blocks. Ask your class which has the least, count them. Hold another plate and ask if there is more, less, or an equal number to the other plate.

(Continued)

Subject schemes of work

Table 8.1 (Continued)

Assessing Application of Knowledge and Skills Framework – Number		
Location	Learning objective	Activity
Outdoor	Test the ability to understand the concept of equal to, more than, less than, most least.	Ask your class to collect objects and sort them into piles of the same type, e.g. stones, leaves, sticks, flowers. Ask them to arrange the piles by number starting with the least and ending with the most.
Outdoor	Estimate numbers.	Ask students to estimate how many objects are in each pile and write the number under the piles. Then count the number of objects to check their estimate.
Indoor	Understand strategies for estimating numbers.	Give examples of benchmarking, using number lines to estimate larger numbers, and rounding. Fill cups with balls or Lego and put cups in number order estimating the number.
Outdoor	Use strategies for estimating numbers in context of problem solving.	Find natural groups of items outside, e.g. daisies in the grass, leaves on a plant, windows on the school, bricks in a wall, tiles on the roof. Ask your class to use strategies to estimate the number. Discuss the strategies they used. Which is the most accurate strategy? Then together count the number to check your estimate.

Measuring length: Years 2–3

Table 8.2 Scheme of work for using the inspirational framework for teaching measuring of length

Inspirational Framework – Measuring Length		
Location	Learning objective	Activity
Outdoor	Compare and order lengths.	Ask your students to collect a stick that is the same size as their hand. Help them arrange your whole class's sticks in size order to see whose are longer or shorter.
Indoor	Measure and record lengths and heights.	Ask your class to use rulers to measure the length of objects in the classroom and record using the correct units. Ask your class to estimate the lengths of objects outside.
Outdoor	Use rulers to measure using appropriate standard units.	Lay out equipment on the ground, rulers, meter rulers, tape measures, trundle wheels, weighing scales, measuring jugs. Provide a results table with objects listed, such as playground length, door height, tree height, bench length. Ask your class to measure objects listed on the results table using the equipment they think is best.

(Continued)

Table 8.2 (Continued)

Inspirational Framework – Measuring Length		
Location	Learning objective	Activity
Outdoor	Understand different scales of measuring.	Go through the equipment and units they used to measure and ask them to justify their choice. Discuss the strategies they used to measure larger lengths or heights. Evaluate the methods and units used.
Indoor	Calculate different measurements.	Help your class use the answers from the results table to calculate the total length of all the objects and total height. Ask your class to estimate if the total height is taller than the school and the total length is longer than the field.
Outdoor	Solve problems involving measuring.	Ask your class to prove their answer.
Indoor/outdoor	Apply measuring skills to problem-solving.	Set a series of measuring problems for your class to answer using the correct equipment and units, e.g. who has the longest legs, who is the tallest, which classroom is the longest?

There are more measuring ideas for years 4–6 in information technology ideas.

The inspirational framework can be used to teach measuring of perimeter in years 4–6 as shown in Table 8.3 and again for measuring area in years 5 and 6 shown in Table 8.4.

Measuring perimeter: Years 4–6

Table 8.3 Scheme of work for using the inspirational framework for teaching measuring perimeter

Inspirational Framework – Measuring Perimeter		
Location	Learning objective	Activity
Outdoor	Inspire interest in measuring perimeter.	Ask you class some perimeter questions, e.g. How long is that tree trunk? Not tall but the length around it? Is it longer than I am tall? Ask students to come up with methods to find out. For example, putting arms around the tree. What units would the length be in?
Indoor	Measure and calculate the perimeter of rectilinear shapes.	Teach the concept of perimeter and that it is a measure of length. Ask your class to measure the perimeter of items in the classroom. Discuss how to calculate the perimeter of rectilinear shapes, e.g. square and rectangle.

(Continued)

Subject schemes of work 77

Table 8.3 (Continued)

\multicolumn{3}{l}{Inspirational Framework – Measuring Perimeter}		
Location	Learning objective	Activity
Outdoor	Measure and calculate the perimeter in a different environment using a different scale.	Ask your students to measure the perimeter of objects and parts of the school grounds, for example, the playground, the field, the car park.
Indoor	Measure and calculate the perimeter of composite rectilinear shapes in cm.	Discuss in groups strategies for measuring perimeter for composite rectilinear shapes. Ask your class to complete some examples on paper.
Outdoor	Measure and calculate the perimeter of composite rectilinear shapes in metres on a different scale.	Give out an aerial photo of the school and its grounds. Ask your class to calculate the perimeter of the school building (if all sides are accessible outside) or school field and playground.
Outdoor	Identify strategies for calculating perimeter of composite rectilinear shapes. Use appropriate scale and units for measuring. Convert between standard units.	Discuss the strategies used to calculate the perimeter with your class and compare answers. Evaluate the accuracy of the answers and suitability of the units used. Ask your class to convert the units used into cm.
Indoor/Outdoor	Apply measuring skills to problem-solving.	Set a series of measuring problems for your class to answer using the correct methods, equipment, and units, e.g. How much fencing would we need to fence in the whole school field? Which tree has the greatest perimeter? Is the tree with the greatest perimeter the tallest?

Measuring area: Years 5 and 6

Table 8.4 Scheme of work for using the inspirational framework for teaching measuring and calculating area

\multicolumn{3}{l}{Inspirational Framework – Measuring and Calculating Area}		
Location	Learning objective	Activity
Outdoor	Inspire interest in measuring area.	Ask your class questions on area, e.g. Is the playground bigger than our classroom? How can we find out? Discuss different ways your class could measure it. Identify all the spaces in the middle they aren't measuring when they measure length.

(Continued)

Table 8.4 (Continued)

Inspirational Framework – Measuring and Calculating Area		
Location	Learning objective	Activity
Indoor	Measure and calculate the area of squares and rectangles.	Teach the concept of area and how to calculate it. Discuss how to calculate the area of rectilinear shapes, e.g. square and rectangle. Measure and calculate the area of items in the classroom, e.g. table, book.
Outdoor	Measure and calculate the area of squares and rectangles in metres.	Give out an aerial photo of the school and its grounds. Ask your class to calculate the area of the playground or school field.
Outdoor	Identify strategies for calculating area of rectangles. Use appropriate scale and units for measuring. Convert between standard units.	Discuss the strategies used to calculate the area with your class and compare answers. Evaluate the accuracy of the answers and suitability of the units used. Convert the units used into cm.
Indoor	Estimate the area of compound and irregular shapes.	Use paper of irregular shapes on squared paper to investigate strategies for calculating the area of irregular shapes.
Outdoors	Apply strategies for estimating and calculating the area of compound and irregular shapes.	Using the aerial photo of the school grounds identify irregular composite shapes. Discuss how you could calculate the area of these. Have equipment available such as meter rulers, tape measures, trundle wheels, and rulers. Choose one location to measure and calculate the area of, e.g. the school building, the field and playground, the pathway.
Outdoor	Identify strategies for calculating area of compound and irregular shapes. Use appropriate scale and units for measuring. Convert between standard units.	Discuss the strategies used to calculate the areas and compare answers. Evaluate the accuracy of the answers and suitability of the units used. Ask your class to convert the units used into cm.
Indoor/ Outdoor	Apply measuring skills to problem-solving.	Set a series of measuring area problems for your class to answer using the correct methods, equipment, and units, e.g. Can we fit a full-size football pitch in our field? Is our classroom bigger than the playground? Who has the biggest classroom? How many solar panels $2m^2$ can we fit on our school roof?

Subject schemes of work 79

Geometry

The testing theories framework can be used to teach geometry including shape for years 1–6 as shown in Table 8.5, and angles for years 3–6 as in Table 8.6.

Shape: Years 1–6

Table 8.5 Scheme of work for using the testing theories framework for teaching shape

Testing Theories Framework – Shape		
Location	Learning objective	Activity
Indoor	Identify and describe 2D shapes.	Teach the names and properties of 2D shapes.
Outdoor	Identify and describe 2D shapes in a different environment. Collect data in a tally chart.	Take your class on a shape hunt identifying the different 2D shapes they can find, e.g. square windows, triangular roof, rectangular playground. You can collect the data in a tally chart.
Indoor	Analyse data. Draw a bar chart from data.	Look at the data and discuss which shape there is the most and least of. You could make a bar graph of the data.
Outdoor	Identify and describe 2D shapes in a different environment.	In groups, get your class to use rope tied in a circle to make 2D shapes on the ground. Ask them to prove that it is the right shape by identifying the properties. Start with a rectangle, square, triangle, circle.
Indoor	Identify and describe 3D shapes.	Teach the names and properties of 3D shapes.
Outdoor	Identify and describe 3D shapes in a different environment.	Take your class on a shape hunt identifying the different 3D shapes they can find, e.g. cuboid-shaped buildings, sphere-shaped balls.
Outdoor	Make simple 3D shapes. Identify and describe 3D shapes in a different environment.	In groups, ask your students to use sticks cut to size or broom handles to make 3D shapes. Ask them to prove that it is the right shape by identifying its properties.
Indoor	Build simple 3D shapes.	Ask the class to follow a design template to make a 3D shape from its net, e.g. a cube.
Outdoor	Build a 3D shape. Draw a net. Measure the dimensions of the shape.	Ask the class to build a regular-shaped 3D den. Then they have to draw the net of the 3D shape. Ask your class to measure the dimensions of the den.
Indoor	Draw 2D shapes using given dimensions and angles. Convert units.	Using the drawing and the measurements of the net of your class's den, ask your class to redraw an accurate scale net for your den. Students then build the net into a 3D model to see how accurate their measurements were.

(Continued)

Table 8.5 (Continued)

Testing Theories Framework – Shape		
Location	Learning objective	Activity
Outdoor	Evaluate the net.	Ask the students to compare their model 3D den to the actual den and evaluate the model.
Outdoor	Apply understanding of nets. Convert units.	Ask the students to swap model nets around the group. Each group then tries to identify the den their net is for by measuring the den and the model and comparing the two.

Angles: Years 3–6

Table 8.6 Scheme of work for using the testing theories framework for teaching angles

Testing Theories Framework – Angles		
Location	Learning objective	Activity
Indoor	Recognise angles as a property of shape.	Teach what angles are, e.g. right angles, and half turns.
Outdoor	Identify right angles.	Take your class on a right-angle hunt. Using the right angle between outstretched thumb and first finger to compare to objects outside.
Outdoor	Collect data. Identify right angles.	Ask students to collect data, identifying the number of right angles in nature or built environment such as the building. They could complete a tally chart of the data.
Indoor	Find trends in data. Draw a bar graph.	Analyse the data and look for patterns. Are there more right angles in nature or the built environment? Students could draw a bar graph of the data.
Indoor	Identify acute and obtuse angles. Measure the size of angles.	Teach the names and properties of acute and obtuse angles. Ask students to use a protractor to measure different types of angles.
Outdoor	Measure the size of angles.	Ask your students to measure the angles of different objects outside and put the angles in order in a table.
Indoor	Find trends in data. Analyse data. Draw a bar graph.	Ask the class to analyse the data collected. Is there a pattern in the number of obtuse and acute angles in the built and natural environment? Which is there more of? They could add the data for obtuse and acute angles to their bar graph.
Indoor	Complete a simple symmetrical figure.	Get your students in pairs. Then one of the students has to construct half of a symmetrical picture using loose parts, for example, they could make an insect or a house. Ask their partner to complete the picture using symmetry.

(Continued)

Table 8.6 (Continued)

Testing Theories Framework - Angles		
Location	Learning objective	Activity
Indoor	Recognise angles as a description of a turn.	Introduce the idea of angles as a description of a turn.
Outdoor	Demonstrate understanding of angles as a description of a turn.	Return to the symmetrical picture. Ask your students to rotate the picture by 90°, and 180°.
Indoor	Identify angles at a point on a straight line.	Task your students to create a trail around the playground lines using angles to explain the route, half turn and 180° and other multiples of 90°.
Outdoor	Follow instructions in degrees.	Ask the students to test their route out on their partner. Then as a pair they can evaluate their instructions.
Indoor/ Outdoor	Apply measuring skills to problem-solving.	Set a series of measuring angle problems for the class to answer using the correct methods, e.g. Does the angle of the branch to the trunk increase as you go up the tree? Which angle is the strongest?

Data collection

The testing theories framework can be used to teach data collection and presentation in year 2 and 3 as shown in Table 8.7 and years 4-6 as in Table 8.9.

Data collection and presentation: Years 2 and 3

Table 8.7 Scheme of work for using the testing theories framework for teaching data collection and presentation for years 2 and 3

Testing Theories Framework - Data Collection and Presentation		
Location	Learning objective	Activity
Indoor	Interpret and construct simple pictograms and tally charts.	Teach the concept of pictograms and tally charts and ask students to undertake data collection with objects inside.
Outdoor	Sort objects. Construct a tally chart. Construct a pictogram. Interpret simple pictogram.	Ask the class to collect loose parts, e.g. leaves, flowers, stones, pinecones. Then sort the objects into piles of the same type. They could make a tally chart of the results. Ask your students to make a line on the ground or use a line on the playground and place one of each object along the line. Students then place the objects above the line to make a pictogram.

(Continued)

Table 8.7 (Continued)

Testing Theories Framework – Data Collection and Presentation		
Location	Learning objective	Activity
		Stand your class so they can see the whole class pictogram of objects. Discuss the data with your class. Which object is there the most of? Which is the longest line? Which object is there the least of? Which is the shortest line?
Indoor	Construct block diagrams. Interpret block diagrams. Ask simple questions.	Teach your class how to construct block diagrams with objects and interpret block diagrams. Discuss as a class what else you could count and sort outside, e.g. mini beasts, plants, children, materials, furniture.
Indoor	Construct a simple table. Ask simple questions. Make a prediction.	Ask your class to draw a simple results table for collecting data for your chosen items (see Table 8.8). How can they make sure the data is accurate? Ask them to come up with a plan for counting and categorising. They can make a prediction of what they think will be the results.
Outdoor	Collect data. Count and categorise objects. Present data using a table.	Ask the class to follow the plan to count the number of objects. They can record the data on the tally chart.
Outdoor	Construct a block diagram. Interpret data using a block diagram. Answer questions about totalling and comparing categorical data. Solve one-step and two-step questions using information presented in bar charts and tables.	In small groups, get your class to use chalk or loose materials (cones, sticks, hoops, beanbags, multilink blocks) to create a block graph of the results outside on the playground (see Figure 8.1). Ask them to interpret the data by answering questions on the group data as above. Ask interpretive challenging questions, e.g. How many more …? How many fewer …? Discuss if their predictions were correct.
Indoor	Construct a bar graph.	Support the class to use the most appropriate method to present their results. It could be a graph in their books or using a computer program. Remind them of the graph they built outside.
Indoor/Outdoor	Use data to draw conclusions.	Ask your class to present their conclusions to the data collection either in books or as a presentation.

(Continued)

Table 8.7 (Continued)

Testing Theories Framework – Data Collection and Presentation		
Location	Learning objective	Activity
Outdoor	Evaluate results.	Get the class to use the space outside to describe what they did and how it generated reliable data and how their method could be improved. Discuss if all the groups collect the same data and got the same results?

Table 8.8 Discrete data results table

Different Types of Objects				
Tables	Benches	Signs	Bins	Goal posts
⊮Ⅲ Ⅲ	Ⅲ	Ⅰ	ⅠⅠⅠⅠ	ⅠⅠ

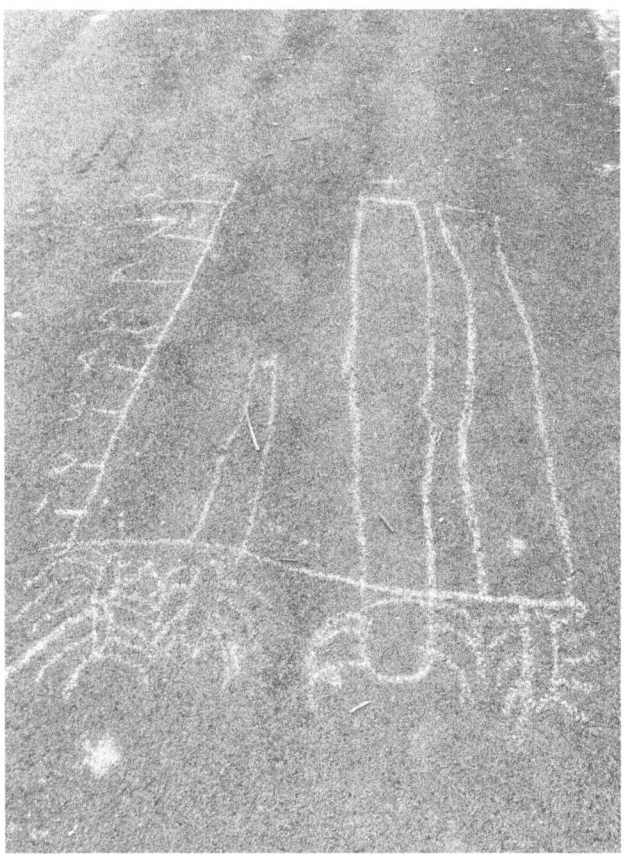

Figure 8.1 Block graph on the playground
Source: Photograph by the author.

Data collection and statistics: Years 4-6

Data collection and graphs can be applied to real-life context through the scientific investigation and geography enquiry process. See science investigation table and geography enquiry table for more examples.

Table 8.9 Scheme of work for using the testing theories framework for teaching data collection and statistics

Testing Theories Framework - Data Collection and Statistics		
Location	Learning objective	Activity
Indoor	Understand discrete and continuous data.	Teach the concept of different types of data, how discrete can be sorted and displayed in a bar graph, and continuous is on a spectrum and can be presented on a line graph.
Outdoor	Identify discrete and continuous data.	As a class survey the school grounds and identify sources of different data types. What can we count? E.g. number of trees, number of mini beasts, species of plants. What can we measure? E.g. temperature, wind speed, time to walk the path, heart rate, height of trees or children.
Indoor	Interpret line graphs. Make a prediction using data.	Decide on one of those pieces of data to investigate and measure. If you have past data from the school grounds such as temperature data over time, use this to interpret information and make a prediction. Use this data to get your class to generate an investigation question, e.g. is it warmer on the playground closer to the school? Does the hedge stop the wind? Can the tallest person walk fastest?
Indoor	Create a results table. Write a method to collect data to answer a question. Demonstrate an understanding of collecting relevant data.	Based on the question chosen, ask your class to create a suitable results table (see Tables 8.8 and 8.10). Ask your students to decide how they will collect the data and to come up with a method.
Outdoor	Test method of data collection. Test skills in data collection.	Get your students to explore possible locations for undertaking their data collection for their question. Students then trial using the equipment to measure the variables. They can then use this information to choose the appropriate location.

(Continued)

Subject schemes of work

Table 8.9 (Continued)

Testing Theories Framework – Data Collection and Statistics		
Location	Learning objective	Activity
Indoor	Redraft the method. Write a method for the data collection.	Ask your class to use the outdoor experience to write a method to follow. Include instruction for location and how to use the equipment.
Outdoor	Collect data to answer a question. Complete a table.	Students can then follow their method to collect data for the variables in the different locations and fill in their results table.
Outdoor	Represent information in an appropriate chart. Interpret a range of graphs.	Ask your students to use chalk or loose materials to create a rough graph of their results outside on the playground. See Figures 8.1 and 8.2. Ask your students to explain to the class why they used their chosen graph and how the graph helps to show trends.
Indoor	Construct a line graph. Interpret a line graph.	Ask your class to use the most appropriate method to present the results. It could be a graph in their books or using a computer program. Then they must describe the trend shown in the line graph.
Indoor/ Outdoor	Use the data to draw conclusions.	Get your students to present their answer to the question either in their books or as a presentation.
Outdoor	Evaluate data collection method.	Allow students to use the space outside to describe what they did and how it generated reliable data and how their method could be improved.

Table 8.10 Continuous data results table

Independent variable – Data you choose to count or measure	Dependent variable – Data you are measuring
E.g. Distance from the building	Temperature of the ground
E.g. Height of person	Time to run around the path
E.g. Number of star jumps	Heart rate
E.g. Distance from the hedge	Wind speed
E.g. Distance from the road	Noise level
E.g. Age of tree	Tree height
E.g. Time of day	Length of shadow

Figure 8.2 Line graph in the sand
Source: Photograph by the author.

How to teach English with the indoor-outdoor framework

The outdoors can provide a place of inspiration for fiction writing as well as a subject for functional non-fiction writing. The ideas in Tables 8.11-8.17 below use the inspirational framework to outline how different text types can be taught using the indoor-outdoor integrated framework.

Tables 8.11, 8.12, outline how the inspirational framework can be used to teach fiction writing text types such as narrative writing for different age groups.

Narrative writing - Fiction years 1-2

Table 8.11 Scheme of work for using the inspirational framework for teaching narrative writing for years 1-2

Inspirational Framework - Narrative Writing		
Location	Learning objective	Activity
Outdoor	Becoming familiar with stories.	Take a suitable book outside. Read it to your class in the environment it is based in. For example, Stickman beside a tree, Bog baby beside a pond, we're going on a bear hunt on the field.
Indoor/ Outdoor	Describe the character in detail.	Ask your students to describe their own experience of the environments in the book. Have they visited them and what did they do there?

(Continued)

Table 8.11 (Continued)

Inspirational Framework – Narrative Writing		
Location	Learning objective	Activity
		Ask your class to create the main character of the story, e.g. find a stick man, use clay to make a bog baby.
Outdoor	Orally retell the story using the school grounds as inspiration. Using story language and structure to create your school's version of a classic story.	Using your class's made characters, students take one part of the story at a time and find the right location for each scene in the school grounds. When they get to the right location, ask them to take it in turn to retell the scene of the story using the natural environment as a backdrop. Then move to the next location for the next scene. If there is no appropriate location, then your class must rewrite the scene with the location and resources they have. For example, there is no river for stick man to float down in your school grounds, so a child takes the stick to the forest to build a den. In We're going on a bear hunt there is no cave, so they crawl into a bush and find a badgers sett.
Indoor	Retell the story. Collect ideas into chronological order.	Ask your students to use pictures to make a book of your school's version of the retelling of the story. They can add simple sentences to describe the scene. Each student can do one scene and then combine them to make the book.
Outdoor	Share your story. Speak audibly and fluently. Read simple sentences.	Take the new book outside and ask your class to retell the story in the right locations for each scene, for another class such as Reception.
Indoor	Retell a story.	Choose a different story book and repeat the process.

Narrative writing – Fiction years 3–6

Table 8.12 Scheme of work for using the inspirational framework for teaching narrative writing for years 3–6

Inspirational Framework – Narrative Writing		
Location	Learning objective	Activity
Outdoor	Understand the language conventions and grammatical features in adventure story sentences and narrative texts.	Take a suitable book outside to the environment it is based in to read a chapter to the class. For example, The Explorer [1] chapter "At the top of the cliff", Kensuke's Kingdom [2] chapter Gibbons and ghosts. Discuss with your class how the author has captured the essence of the location. How have they developed atmosphere?

(Continued)

Table 8.12 (Continued)

Inspirational Framework – Narrative Writing		
Location	Learning objective	Activity
Indoor	Plan a story of a certain genre, using the correct language conventions and grammatical features.	Ask your class to write a plan for an adventure, mystery, legend, or fantasy story based in your school grounds.
Outdoor	Create the setting for your story.	Allow your students to visit the locations where scenes from their story are set. Get them to sit in those places and gather adjectives to capture the atmosphere of the location.
Indoor	Use experiences to create atmosphere in descriptive text.	Students write a description for each location for the story. They can look for places in the story which could be improved with metaphors or similes.
Outdoor	Use metaphors and similes to improve narrative text.	Get your students to sit outside and observe. They can look for potential metaphors or similes in the environment. For example, "his heart soared like the buzzard as it circled upward", "the stillness was a leaf waiting to fall"
Indoor	Use metaphors and similes to improve narrative text.	Students redraft their story to include their metaphors and similes.
Outdoor	Read aloud their own writing with fluency. Use appropriate intonation and tone to make meaning clear. Assess the effectiveness of their own and others writing and suggest improvements.	Allow your students to share their story with others in the best location to provide context and atmosphere to their story. The rest of the class listen to other's stories and provide feedback on their stories. Did the description of the location set the scene? Did the metaphors work? Was the story engaging and easy to follow? Were the characters realistic? They could provide suggestions for improvement for others.
Indoor	Redraft narrative text. Proofread for spelling and grammatical errors.	Get your students to redraft the narrative to include the suggested improvements. Then proofread for spelling and grammar.

Poetry - Fiction years 1 and 2

Tables 8.13 and 8.14 outline how the inspirational framework can be used to teach fiction writing text types such as poetry for different age groups.

Table 8.13 Scheme of work for using the inspirational framework for teaching poetry writing for years 1 and 2

Inspirational Framework - Poetry Writing		
Location	Learning objective	Activity
Outdoor	Becoming familiar with poetry structure.	Read a poem outside at a season and in a place that relates to the poem, for example, from the Lost Words Bluebell or Acorn [3]. Ask your students to identify the natural objects in the poem.
Outdoor	Observe natural objects.	Ask your students to collect any objects from the poem they can find. You could provide pictures of the objects for them to match, consider the time of year for flowers in spring and summer, nuts in autumn, leaves in summer. Take the objects inside.
Indoor/Outdoor	Collect ideas into chronological order. Create an observational poem.	Ask the students to place the objects in a row in chronological order of the poem. They can describe each object and collect the adjectives in a word bank. Then use each object in turn to create an observational poem using a simple structure, e.g. name the object, describe the object, ask a question of the object. I am a conker. Shiny, brown, smooth ball. I wonder what's inside?
Outdoor	Create an observational poem.	Ask your class to collect new objects outside. Together, create a new observational poem using the same structure and the new objects.
Indoor	Speak audibly and fluently. Read simple sentences Write a poem.	Help students write their poems down or draw pictures and record the poem.
Outdoor	Create a poem. Perform a poem.	Take your class for a walk around the school grounds collecting observations for a travelling observational poem. In small groups they can create the poem as you travel. For example, I am a seagull, flying round and round in the sky, where have I come from and why am I here? Take turns for groups to share their poems and perform it to bring the poem to life.

Poetry – Fiction years 3-6

Table 8.14 Scheme of work for using the inspirational framework for teaching poetry writing for years 3-6

Inspirational Framework – Poetry Writing		
Location	Learning objective	Activity
Outdoor	Understand the language conventions and grammatical features in poetry structure.	Choose an appropriate location outside to listen to a poem which is connected to the environment found there. For example, poems from the *Lost Words* book [3], *Tiger Tiger Burning Bright* [4], and *I Am the Seed That Grew the Tree* [5]. Read the poem to your class. Discuss what inspiration the author has taken from nature. Take a walk around the school grounds to look for inspiration for a poem. Ask the class to note down things that inspire them, for example, objects, landscapes, and feelings.
Indoor	Plan a nature-inspired poem.	Ask the students to choose a topic for their poem inspired by their time in nature.
Outdoor	Plan a nature poem.	Visit the locations where each pupil's poem best fits. Allow them to sit in those places and gather details to capture the atmosphere of the location.
Outdoor	Find inspiration in nature for poetry writing.	Students can gather adjectives and objects which could be included in their poem.
Indoor	Use experiences to create an impactful poem. Write a poem.	Ask your students to draft a poem using the adjectives they have collected outside.
Outdoor	Read your poem outside. Reflect on the content of the poem.	Ask your students to read the poem in the location and see if it fits with the location. Students can experiment by moving to another location and reading their poem. How do different locations make the poem sound?
Indoor	Redraft to improve the emotion of the poem.	Students read the poem indoors. Ask your class if the poem has more impact in one location? Get your students to look for parts in their poem where the emotion or atmosphere could be improved. Add atmosphere or emotion.
Outdoor	Use metaphors and similes to improve poetry text.	Take students to the location where their poem most fits. Get them to sit outside and observe. They can look for potential metaphors or similes in the environment. For example, from the Lost Words [3], "A hank of rope for a snake, bramble is on the march again, sun of the grass – dandelion".

(Continued)

Table 8.14 (Continued)

Inspirational Framework - Poetry Writing		
Location	Learning objective	Activity
Indoor	Use metaphors and similes to improve poetry text.	Students can redraft their poem to include their metaphors and similes.
Outdoor	Read aloud their own writing with fluency. Use appropriate intonation and tone to make meaning clear. Assess the effectiveness of their own and others' writing and suggest improvements.	Students share their poem with others in the best location to provide context and atmosphere to their poem. The rest of the class listen to other's poems and provide feedback on them. What words provided atmosphere for the poem? Did the structure bring the meaning to life? The class can provide suggestions for improvement for others.
Indoor	Redraft the poem. Proofread for spelling and grammatical errors.	The class redraft the poem to include the suggested improvements. Proofread for spelling and grammar.

Table 8.15 outlines how the inspirational framework can be used to teach non-fiction writing text types such as instructional writing for different age groups.

Instructional/Procedural text writing - Non-fiction years 3-6

Table 8.15 Scheme of work for using the inspirational framework for teaching instructional writing

Inspirational Framework - Instructional Writing		
Location	Learning objective	Activity
Outdoor	Create a den to inspire instructional writing. Communicate instructions.	Task your students to build a den. You can provide resources such as sticks, tarpaulins, string, clothes pegs, tent pegs. They can work in groups, and you can include parameters or let them decide. Discuss what worked well in building their dens.
Indoor	Understand the language conventions and grammatical features of instructional text writing.	Teach the features of instructional text writing.
Indoor	Use research and experience to write instructions to build a den.	Ask the class to use the text type features to write instructions for building a den.
Outdoor	Give clear instructions. Follow a set of instructions. Test out a set of instructions.	Ask the class to swap instructions with another group. Then they can follow the instructions to build a new den.

(Continued)

Table 8.15 (Continued)

Inspirational Framework – Instructional Writing		
Location	Learning objective	Activity
Indoor/Outdoor	Assess the effectiveness of their and others' writing.	Ask each group to explain how clear the instructions were.
Indoor	Revise instructions. Propose changes in vocabulary, grammar, and punctuation to enhance effects and clarify meaning.	Using the feedback from the other group ask your students to improve their instructions.
Outdoor	Give clear instructions. Follow a set of instructions. Test out a set of instructions.	Using their revised instructions, ask each group to give clear oral instructions to a different group to build a den.
Indoor/Outdoor	Assess the effectiveness of their and others' writing.	Ask each group to explain how clear the instructions were and give feedback to the group giving the instructions.

Table 8.16 outlines how the inspirational framework can be used to teach non-fiction writing text types such as explanatory texts for different age groups.

Explanatory/Informational texts – Non-fiction years 5 and 6

Table 8.16 Scheme of work for using the inspirational framework for teaching explanatory/Informational writing

Inspirational Framework – Explanatory/Informational writing		
Location	Learning objective	Activity
Outdoor	Observe nature. Collect information for an informative text.	Take your class to explore your school grounds and identify the variety of nature living there. Ask the class to choose a topic to learn more about. For example, each group could be given a different tree, plant, or animal such as a mini beast to focus on. Ask students to take photos, make observational drawings, and descriptions of the organism creating a fact file of what they see.
Indoor	Understand the language conventions and grammatical features of explanatory text writing.	Teach the features of explanatory text writing.

(Continued)

Table 8.16 (Continued)

Inspirational Framework – Explanatory/Informational writing		
Location	Learning objective	Activity
Indoor	Research further about the organism. Use subheading to organise the text.	Task your students with researching the organism they have observed. They could choose what aspects to include in their explanatory text and use subheadings.
Outdoor	Find evidence of the research you have undertaken indoors, outdoors.	Students then find the organism they are studying outside and see if the research they have found relates to it. For example, the research said that oak trees sometimes has wasp galls growing on them. Students could look for any wasp galls on your oak tree. The research said that the plant Alexandar has hollow stems.
Indoor	Consolidate the research and practical visits together to produce an informative information guide.	Students then create an informative fact file with an introduction and a conclusion and all the points they have gathered about the organism.
Outdoor	Share the informative text with the class. Read aloud their own writing with fluency. Use appropriate intonation and tone to make meaning clear. Assess the effectiveness of their own and others' writing and suggest improvements.	Students can share the informative text with the rest of the class at the place the organism lives. They then listen to others' informative text and provide feedback on them.
Indoor	Redraft the informative text. Proofread for spelling and grammatical errors.	Students redraft the informative text to include the suggested improvements. Proofread for spelling and grammar.
Outdoor	Share with the wider community.	Your class can then take local people or another class on a walking tour of your school grounds using the information on each organism to teach them about the biodiversity of your school grounds.

Table 8.17 outlines how the inspirational framework can be used to teach non-fiction writing text types such as persuasive writing for different age groups.

Persuasive text writing – Non-fiction years 5 and 6

Table 8.17 Scheme of work for using the inspirational framework for teaching persuasive writing

Inspirational Framework – Persuasive Writing		
Location	Learning objective	Activity
Outdoor	Identify a cause for your persuasive writing.	Take your students on a walk around your school grounds and find something that needs improving or changing. For example, no seating, no play equipment, grass is too muddy, no access to the field at lunch time, poor maintenance, rubbish being dropped, not enough flowers or trees. It could relate to a local issue in the school grounds or local learning area such as graffiti, parking, speeding. Or a broader topic that impacts the area such as global climate change, air pollution, ash die back tree clearing.
Indoor	Write a survey. Undertake a survey and analyse the results to come to a conclusion.	Ask students to look at all the potential issues they have discussed. They then undertake a survey of the classes' opinions on the issues. For example, which one of these issues do they think is the most important? Students then find the most interesting and emotive issue to write about.
Indoor	Learn the features of persuasive text writing.	Teach the features of persuasive text writing.
Outdoor	Find evidence of the need for the persuasive writing.	Take your class to visit the places outside which relate to the issue they have identified. Students list the main problems and why they are problems.
Indoor	Undertake research on an issue. Consolidate the research and practical visit together to create a persuasive letter.	Students undertake research into their issue to find facts and figures to support their argument. They need to choose a suitable form for the persuasive text, e.g. a poster, letter, blog post, email. Then draft the persuasive text using the identified features.

(Continued)

Table 8.17 (Continued)

Inspirational Framework - Persuasive Writing		
Location	Learning objective	Activity
Outdoor	Share persuasive writing with the class. Read aloud their own writing with fluency. Use appropriate intonation and tone to make meaning clear. Assess the effectiveness of their own and others' writing and suggest improvements.	Students read their persuasive text to the class in the location it relates to. The rest of the class listen to other's persuasive writing and provide feedback on them.
Indoor	Redraft persuasive text. Proofread for spelling and grammatical errors.	Students redraft the persuasive text to include the suggested improvements. Proofread for spelling and grammar.
Indoor/Outdoor	Share with the wider community.	Your class can send the persuasive text to the appropriate person, e.g. governing body, head teacher. Or read their persuasive text out in assembly.
Indoor	Choose a different idea and repeat the process	Choose a different issue and repeat.

How to teach science with the indoor-outdoor framework

Scientific method years 5-6

The ability to follow the scientific method is a key skill in science. Using the indoor-outdoor testing theories framework shown in Table 8.18 below, your students can be inspired to ask scientific questions to investigate outside. The link this provides between the in-class concept teaching and the real-world testing can bring meaning to the topic they are studying. This framework can be used for any topic which links to the outdoor environment you have locally. It is important to understand that the **results are not what is important** here and the **process** is what we are teaching. If the results do not back up the theory, then this is an opportunity to evaluate the method and data.

Table 8.18 Scheme of work for using testing theories framework teaching the scientific method

Testing Theories Framework - Scientific Method		
Location	Learning objective	Activity
Indoor	Understand what adaptation is.	Teach the concept of adaptation.

(Continued)

Table 8.18 (Continued)

Testing Theories Framework – Scientific Method		
Location	Learning objective	Activity
Outdoor	Investigate adaptation in nature. Identify adaptative features in plants and animals.	Take your class outside and look at mini beasts and plants. Observe and describe their features, e.g. mini beast's numbers of legs, plants' variety in shape, size, and colour. Ask your class to list all the ways they differ from each other. Ask your students to come up with questions to investigate about adaptation, e.g. do plants with bigger leaves live in sunnier places? Do animal with more legs run faster?
Indoor	Using experience and knowledge on adaptation to come up with an **investigation question.**	In groups get your class to discuss all the questions they could investigate on adaptation. Together discuss one question which it would be possible to collect the data for. Structure the question so that the two variables relate to each other. For example, do plants have larger leaves in sunnier places? Do mini beasts with more legs run faster? Do plants grow taller in more light?
Indoor	Recognise the independent and dependent **variables.**	Teach or revisit variables. Get the class to discuss all the factors that affect adaptation and how they could be measured, e.g. in plants – sunlight, water, space, and animals – where they live, predator prey, habitat, and size. Help your class identify the independent and dependent variable for their chosen question.
Outdoor	**Trail a method** for the experiment. Identify the control variables for the experiment.	Allow students to explore possible methods for undertaking the investigation into adaptation, e.g. find a place with lots of sunlight and a place with not a lot of sunlight and measure the size of the same plant's leaves. Collect mini beasts with different numbers of legs and time them running a set distance. Get students to use this information to choose their control variables, e.g. the species of plant, the distance the minibeasts run.
Indoor	Identify the control variables for the experiment. Plan a **fair test**. Write a **method** for the investigation. Write a **prediction**. Draw a **results table.**	Discuss with your class what control variables are needed and why. Which variables are hard to control? Can you control if the mini beast runs in a straight line? Can you control the amount of rain a plant gets? Discuss fair testing with your class. Allow the students to use their outdoor experience to adapt or change the investigation method. Students write a method to follow. They can include instruction for how to use any equipment and make it a fair test. Students can come up with a prediction based on their preliminary experiment. Students then use the independent variable and dependent variable to draw a results table (see Table 8.19).

(Continued)

Table 8.18 (Continued)

Testing Theories Framework – Scientific Method		
Location	Learning objective	Activity
Outdoor	Undertake **data collection** for the investigation.	Ask students to follow their method to measure the variables and collect the data in a results table, keeping the control variables the same.
Outdoor	**Present** the results.	Ask students to use chalk or loose materials to create a rough graph of their results outside on the playground. For example, put the independent variable on the horizontal axis and the dependent variable on the vertical axis (see Figure 8.3). They could use a bar graph for categorical data, e.g. snail, ant, woodlice, and a scatter or line graph for continuous data, e.g. numbers of legs.
Indoor	**Present** the results.	Ask students to repeat the graph they made outside using the most appropriate method to present their results. It could be a graph in books or using a computer program.
Indoor/ Outdoor	Draw **conclusions.**	Students then present their conclusions to their experiment either in books or as a presentation. They need to answer the investigation question using proof from their results.
Outdoor	**Evaluate** the investigation.	Students can use the space outside to describe what they did and how it generated reliable data and how their method could be improved.
Outdoor	**Apply** the conclusions. Come up with **questions** to investigate.	Allow students to look around the school grounds for more evidence that their results on adaptation are correct. Then students can predict what adaptations animals would have in a pond or the beach, plants in a sand dune system or woodland. You can then take your class to visit a pond or beach and look for animals adapted to the water. Discuss if the student's predictions were correct? For example, visit a woodland or sand dune system and look at how plants are adapted to less light and water. Students then use their knowledge of adaptation to explain how these adaptations help the plants and animals survive. As a class come up with further questions on adaptation that this experiment has brought up.

Table 8.19 Results table for scientific method

Independent variable	Dependent variable	Control variables
E.g. Amount of light (Location; long grass or short grass)	Width of the leaf	Species of plant, how you measure, number of plants measured, amount of rain (pick locations close together)
E.g. Number of legs	Speed of running	Distance, how you measure speed, number of animals you measure.

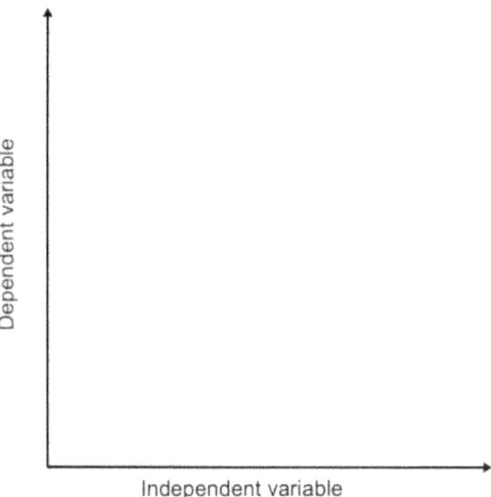

Figure 8.3 Scientific results graph axis

How to teach design technology with the indoor-outdoor framework

The design process – Years 5–6

Through use of the design process, your students learn to follow a design brief and meet the needs of a project which has purpose. The end product does not have to be a full-size version of the object; it could be a model, but the creative process is the aim of the task as well as the test and review aspect of the design process. The learning outcome is that your students understand and can follow the design process, not create an amazing piece of design technology.

Table 8.20 shows how the inspirational framework can be used to teach the design process.

Table 8.20 Scheme of work for using the inspirational framework for teaching the design process

Inspirational Framework – The Design Process		
Location	Learning objective	Activity
Outdoor	**Collect ideas** to identify a need.	Take your students on a walk around your school grounds or local learning area and come up with ideas of something that is missing that they could design and build. For example, an obstacle course, an outdoor game, an animal home.
Indoor	**Examine the ideas.** Collect and sort them.	In groups you class can sort the ideas generated from the experience outdoors into categories. They could combine all the ideas for games, wildlife, furniture, etc. Then the class votes or has a debate on the need for the object.

(Continued)

Table 8.20 (Continued)

Inspirational Framework – The Design Process		
Location	Learning objective	Activity
Indoor	**Research** the design of the chosen item. Create a design brief.	Once the item has been decided on, the students research what a good one needs to have. What is its function? Students need to identify the key features required of the item, e.g. What does it need to do? What material should it be made out of? How do they make it? Using all the answers the students create a design brief for the item. For example, the animal home must attract mini beasts, be made from natural materials, have lots of holes, have space for animals to hide, be free standing.
Outdoor	**Find evidence** of the research they have undertaken indoors, outdoors. Make a sketch of a similar item and annotate features.	Students need to find an example of the item they plan to make and examine it. This may be in your local learning area or on a school visit. What design has been used? Does it meet their design brief? Could they copy the design or improve it?
Indoor	**Consolidate** the research and practical visits together to create a design for the prototype for their design.	Students create a design plan from the information they have gathered. They could describe the material and design they will use and how it will meet the design brief.
Outdoor	**Build** a prototype of the item.	Allow students to experiment with different materials to build the prototype.
Outdoor	**Test** the design.	Students then use the design brief to evaluate if their design meets the brief. If not, they need to change the design or material and rebuild. They continue testing and adjusting the design until it meets all parts of the brief.
Indoor	**Present** their idea and communicate their results.	Groups present their idea to the class explaining how it meets the design brief and describe how they made it.
Outdoor	**Implement** their design idea.	Students can then place their design in its location in your school grounds. They can monitor its use or development to see if the design was fit for purpose. For example, survey the mini beasts that enter their animal home to see how it is being used, ask children what they think of the obstacle course.

How to teach information technology with the indoor-outdoor framework

The use of technology outdoors can be a practical way of teaching the use of computers in data collection. There are apps that can be used as sensors for taking measurements such as decibel meters and can be used in undertaking geographical enquiries such as those described in Table 8.25. However, digital technology can also be used to collect, collate and process data for a scientific investigation or geographical enquiry. Using the app Survey123 by Esri, a survey can be created to collect quantitative and qualitative data which can be downloaded as a spreadsheet, or used to generate graphs directly through the app. It can also be used to geolink data to specific locations using GPS and can map the collected data.

Table 8.21 provides an example of how Survey 123 and other geographical information systems such as Google Earth can be used with the testing theories framework to develop skills in information technology and digital data collection and processing.

Digital data collection – Years 5–6

Table 8.21 Scheme of work for using the testing theories framework for teaching digital data collection

Testing Theories Framework – Digital Data Collection		
Location	Learning objective	Activity
Indoor	Introduce digital data collection.	Introduce your class to geographical information systems such as Google Earth and Google Maps. Look at your school on Google Earth to see what they can identify.
Outdoor	Identify sources of data.	Take your class for a walk around the school grounds and identify what they could plot on a map of your school grounds by geolinking. For example, they could plot the location of the trees, or the plant species, height, age, circumference. They could plot the location of microclimate such as temperature, wind speed, sunlight, or shadow length. They could geolink litter or mini beasts.
Indoor	Using experience outside to come up with a focus for the data collection.	As a class discuss what to measure and decide on several factors.
Indoor	Design a digital survey.	Using the app Survey123 get your students to write a survey to collect data in your school grounds on the factors they have chosen. Insure they make the first question what is your location? See Figure 8.4.
Outdoor	Trail the survey.	Students take a digital device with the survey open outside. They then go to several locations in your school grounds and complete the survey at each location. They then send the data to Survey123.

(Continued)

Table 8.21 (Continued)

Testing Theories Framework - Digital Data Collection		
Location	Learning objective	Activity
Indoor	Upload digital data to a mapping system. Display digital data.	Get the class to open the results on Survey123 on a computer and display on a base map of their school grounds. They can look at the graphs created by the app, or download the excel document of the class data and create bar charts to analyse.
Outdoor	Test the digital data presentation method.	Students can then take the digital device with the screenshot of the map out to the school grounds. Use the map to locate a place on the ground where they have collected some data. They can then check the data by measuring it again. For example, walk to the tree on the map and remeasure the circumference and check the data.
Indoor	Evaluate the presentation tool.	Discuss with your class if the GIS map was accurate. Get your class to discuss how this data collection method could be used. For example, showing where rubbish is so they can decide where to place bins. They might think of a way to use this digital device on a field trip. Then allow your students to plan to use Survey123 to collect their data when they go.

School grounds tree survey

1. Where is the tree?

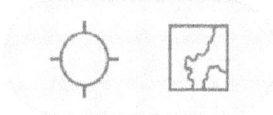

2. What species is the tree?

3. What is the circumference of the tree at 1 m height?

4. Estimate the height of the lowest branch.

5. Claclulate the age of the tree.
   To calculate the age of a living tree, divide the circumference in cm by 2.5

Figure 8.4 An example of a questionnaire for Survey123

How to teach geography skills with the indoor-outdoor framework

Mapping is an excellent progression model for indoor-outdoor learning. It can be taught at each age group with increasing complexity and independence, and progression in the skills required. In Table 8.22 the testing theories framework can be used to teach map making to

102 Learning Indoors and Out in the Primary School

years 1-3, the focus is on understanding how objects and landforms are spatially perceived. In Table 8.23 the map making framework for years 4 - 6, moves to a more accurate representation of objects as seen from above. The use of 2D shapes to identify what structures look like from above broadens skills in maths also.

As the maps get more complex, they should also get more accurate. This will result in a very useful resource for your school. This scaled map can be used in maths to calculate distances and directions and be used for other activities when a scale map is required such as trails and orienteering courses.

Map making years 1-3

Table 8.22 Scheme of work for using the testing theories framework for teaching map skills for years 1-3

Testing Theories Framework - Map Making		
Location	Learning objective	Activity
Outdoor	Identify landscape features on the ground.	Take your class on a walk around your school grounds and ask them to identify the landforms that you pass, e.g. the field, the school, the playground, forest, flower beds, paths, roads.
Outdoor	Create a map. Understand relative position.	Ask your students to collect loose parts to make a model of their school grounds, e.g. sticks, small stones, larger stones, shells, pinecones, conkers, cut grass. Ask them to think about what loose part can represent what feature, e.g. sticks to make the path outline, gravel to show the buildings. Ask them to think about what landforms are next to which other ones; is the field next to the school? Get them to consider the relative size of the landforms; is the playground bigger than the field?
Outdoor	Describe their map. Listen to feedback.	Get groups to share their map with the rest of the class and explain what each feature represents. Allow other groups to ask questions about the map and give feedback. Take a photo of the maps or older students can draw a picture of their map.
Indoor	Label a map. Create a key for a map.	Print off the photo of your student's loose parts map and get your students to label the landforms. They can use different colours and create a key or use labels.
Indoor	Design a route on a map. Use directional language.	Ask your students to draw a route on their map to a specific location. Depending on their ability, they can write instructions to follow with the map, e.g. start by the door. Walk to the goal post. Go uphill to the playground. Or they can use symbols, see Figure 8.5, using your own symbols.

(Continued)

Subject schemes of work 103

Table 8.22 (Continued)

Testing Theories Framework – Map Making		
Location	Learning objective	Activity
Outdoor	Use directional language accurately. Design a route on a map. Communicate instructions orally.	Take your class back outside to the loose parts map with their paper map. Get them to put an X on the papermap at the same specific location their instructions go to. Then they have to give directions for their route to another group and give them the map so they can walk to the right spot on their loose parts map. The groups compare the route they took to see how accurate the directional instructions were.
Outdoor	Follow a map. Follow directions. Assess the effectiveness of their own and others writing and suggest improvements.	Repeat with another group who follow the instructions and the map to see if they can get to the real location in the school grounds. Other groups provide feedback to the group on their route, map, and directional language.
Indoor	Refine your map.	Students listen to the feedback on their map and instructions and change their map as necessary.
Outdoor	Complete the map of the school grounds.	Students walk around the school grounds and add details to their paper map to improve accuracy.
Indoor	Use the map.	Students share their maps with another class. They could set up a treasure hunt for another class using their map.

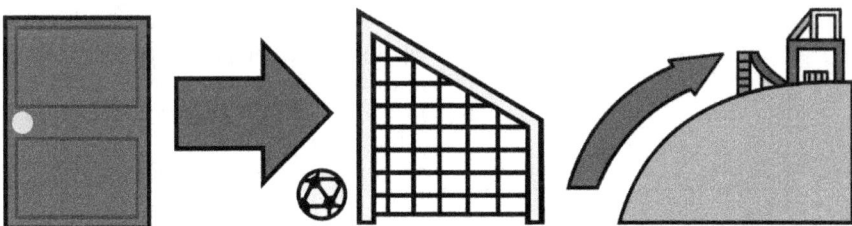

Figure 8.5 Symbol instructions

Map making years 4–6

Table 8.23 Scheme of work for using the testing theories framework for teaching map skills for years 4–6

Testing Theories Framework – Map Making		
Location	Learning objective	Activity
Outdoor	Identify features on a map. Measure in metres.	Show your students an aerial picture of your school grounds. Ask them to use tape measures to measure obvious features in your school grounds and label them on the picture. For example, measure the playground in metres.

(Continued)

Table 8.23 (Continued)

Testing Theories Framework – Map Making		
Location	Learning objective	Activity
Indoor	Understand scale. Use a ruler to measure. Look for patterns in data. Identify features on a map.	Ask your students to create a comparative table of 'on the ground' and 'on the map' measurements (see Table 8.24). Then ask them to measure the length of the same landforms on the photo in cm. Ask your students to look for patterns in the data. Using this pattern, they can calculate the scale of the map. Students then choose a new landform and measure it on the photo in cm. Using the scale they then calculate what the distance is on the ground.
Outdoor	Test the scale of a map.	Ask your students to measure the landform outside to see if the distance they predicted from the photo was accurate.
Indoor	Create a scale map from an aerial photo. Understand relative position on a map. Make a key.	Students can use the outline of the photo to create a scale map of the main landforms in your school grounds. Get them to cut around the school building and then draw around it on paper. Do the same for the playground, field, and any other landforms and habitats (see Figure 8.6). Ask your students to add a scale bar and a north arrow and create a key for the landforms on their map.
Indoor	Use a map to navigate. Use directional language accurately. Instructional writing.	Then your students can create a route around the map. They can use directional language and correct distances to write a route card with instructions, e.g. start by the school gate. Go north for 10 m until you get to the grass, turn east, and follow the playground for 25 m.
Outdoor	Follow a map. Follow directions. Assess the effectiveness of their own and others writing and suggest improvements.	Get your students to then test the directions and instructions for their route by giving the instructions to another group. Another group then follows their instructions and the map to see if they get to the correct location. Allow each group to provide feedback on their route, map, and directional language.
Indoor	Refine their map.	Students listen to the feedback on their map and instructions and adapt their map as necessary.
Outdoor	Complete their map of the school grounds.	Students then walk around your school grounds and add details from their map that are missing to improve its accuracy.
Indoor	Use the map.	You can then share the maps with another class. The class could set up an orienteering course, or treasure hunt for another class using the map.

Subject schemes of work

Table 8.24 Comparative table for map making

Length on the ground in metres	Length on the map in cm

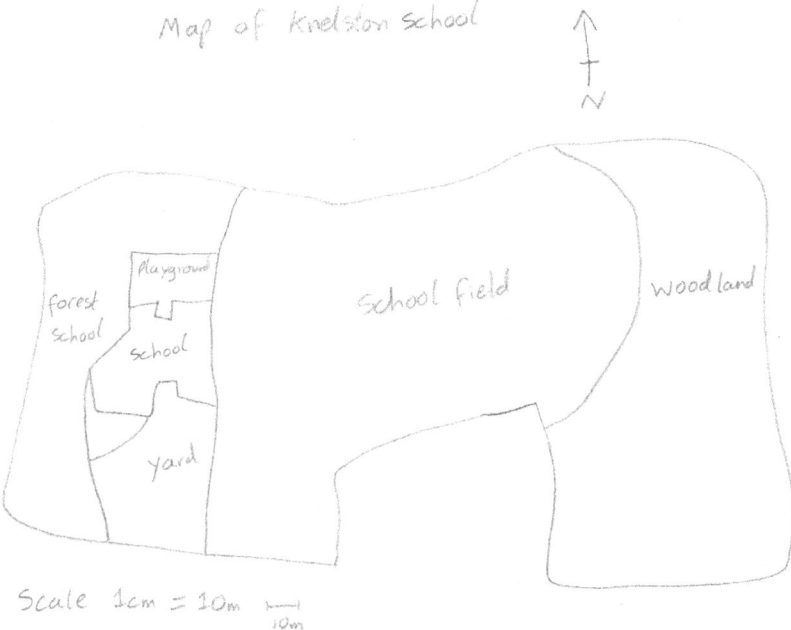

Figure 8.6 Scale map of school grounds. Photograph by the author.

A progression on from this map making is to use digital data collection such as Survey123 to create a digital map. See Information Technology Table 8.21.

You can continue to develop map use skills when undertaking field trips and residentials, see the field work and residential framework in Chapter 6.

Geographical enquiry years 5 and 6

Geographical enquiries are similar in structure to science investigations but not as rigid. The questions which can be asked can be broader than a scientific investigation and the data can be collected in qualitative forms, such as pictures or descriptions. The best geographical enquiries combine people and how they interact with the natural world. Data can be collected and presented through annotated photos, and does not have to involve measuring.

Table 8.25 uses the testing theories framework to teach the enquiry process.

Table 8.25 Scheme of work for using the testing theories framework for teaching geographical enquiry for years 5 and 6

Testing Theories Framework – Geographical Enquiry		
Location	Learning objective	Activity
Indoor	Understand the geographical enquiry process.	Outline the geographical enquiry process. • Enquiry question • Plan a method • Data collection • Present data • Analyse data • Come to conclusions • Evaluate process
Outdoor	Observe geographical features and processes.	Take your students outside and look for the geography there. They can observe and describe the features, e.g. hills, habitats, structures like buildings, roads. Or observe the geographical processes taking place, e.g. the water cycle, movement of people, erosion of the football pitch or footpath, pollution, seasonal changes. As a class come up with questions to investigate about these features or processes, e.g. What landforms are there near our school? Is there more air pollution closer to the road? Where does the water go after it rains? Is the footpath getting wider?
Indoor	Using experience and knowledge of geography to come up with an **enquiry question.**	In groups, get your students to discuss all the questions they could investigate looking at the geography of the school grounds and local area. They could use Google Earth to see what is outside the school grounds. Bring the ideas together and discuss one question which they could undertake an enquiry on.
Outdoor	**Trail a method** for the enquiry.	Allow your students to explore possible methods for undertaking the enquiry, e.g. Place masking tape at different distances from the road and see how much particulate matter falls on them. Use a map of the school grounds and colour or annotate different landforms. Use a map to colour in where the puddles are after it rains. Measure the size of the footpath at different distances from the school.
Indoor	Write a **method** for the enquiry. Plan how they will collect results.	Ask your students to use the outdoor experience to write a method to follow. Include instructions for how they plan to collect the results. Students need to create a results table or find a base map to collect the data on (see Table 8.26).

(Continued)

Table 8.25 (Continued)

Testing Theories Framework – Geographical Enquiry		
Location	Learning objective	Activity
Outdoor	Undertake the **data collection** for the enquiry.	Students can follow their method to collect the data in their results table or on a map, or take photos.
Outdoor	Present the **results**.	Students then use chalk or loose materials to present their data to show the results. They can be creative in the way they show what they have found out.
Indoor	**Present** the results.	Students then present their results in their books or on paper. The aim is to show the answer to the enquiry question using an image. It could be a graph in books or using a computer program, a map coloured in with a key or annotated pictures.
Indoor/Outdoor	Draw **conclusions**.	Students then present their conclusions to the enquiry either in books or as a presentation. They need to answer the enquiry question using proof from their results.
Outdoor	**Evaluate** the investigation.	Students can use the space outside to describe what they did and how it generated reliable data and how their method could be improved.
Outdoor	**Apply** the conclusions. Come up with more enquiry questions.	Take your students for a walk around your local learning area to find more evidence that their results are correct. They can predict what they will find in a different location. Visit a different environment and repeat the process of creating an enquiry question there, e.g. visit a beach, woodland, city centre, river, country park.

Table 8.26 Enquiry results table

Distance from school	Width of the footpath

How to teach history with the indoor-outdoor framework

Every school has some evidence of the history of the area around it. You may have an old school building or there may be old buildings in your local learning area such as churches, town halls or memorials. Table 8.27 uses the inspirational framework to teach about local history around your school site using first hand observational evidence and researching secondary sources of evidence.

Local history

Table 8.27 Scheme of work for using the inspirational framework for teaching local history

Inspirational Framework – Local History		
Location	Learning objective	Activity
Outdoor	Inspire students, using an outdoor experience, to be curious and **collect ideas.**	Take your students on a walk around your school grounds or local learning area and imagine what it would have been like in the past. For example, you could think back to before the school was built, during World War II, in the Stone Age, during the last ice age. Choose a time in history which you are studying.
Indoor	**Examine the ideas** collected. Research further.	Ask your students to explore the history of the local area through research and see if the ideas you discussed outdoors happened. For example, what was on the site of the school before it was built? Are there any ancient remains close by that give you clues about the past? Do local street names give you clues to what the area was used for? Are there any old photos of the area? Students can look at the site Geograph.org.uk for old photos of the UK.
Outdoor	**Find evidence** of the research they have undertaken indoors, outdoors.	Take your class to visit places they have researched in your local area and explore them. For example, you could walk around the streets looking at the street names to see what they tell you about the past. Visit local old buildings to explore their history, talk to local historians or residents about what the area used to be like.
Indoor	**Consolidate** the research and practical visits together. Make a historical guide.	Students then create a historic walking guide to their local learning area. For example, using old maps to find old landmarks or ruins locally, combine this with their research to produce an informative guide. They could use photos, maps, and descriptions.
Outdoor	**Share** with the wider community.	Students can then invite local residents or parents to go on a guided tour of the local history. With the students using their historical walking guide.

How to teach expressive art with the indoor-outdoor framework

Nature can provide inspiration for all the expressive arts. The aim of these frameworks is to use outdoor experiences to inspire creativity. It is important that you leave time to reflect on the experience of using nature as a source of inspiration and your students get to share their artwork with others to develop the skills of art appreciation and giving and receiving feedback.

Drawing

Table 8.28 uses the inspirational framework to teach about different aspects of drawing such as texture, shapes and patterns.

Table 8.28 Scheme of work for using the inspirational framework for teaching drawing

Inspirational Framework – Drawing		
Location	Learning objective	Activity
Outdoor	Inspire students, using an outdoor experience, to be curious and **collect ideas.**	Take your students on a walk around your school grounds and look for different lines and textures. Students can collect examples by sketching objects or drawing around objects, copying shapes, and using rubbings.
Indoor	**Examine the ideas** collected. Search for creative ideas.	Students then look at the shapes and textures they have collected outside. They can look for more examples of lines and texture inside using the same method.
Outdoor	Look at different forms of blending textures.	Ask students to look at how the different textures blend together. For example, use foil to rub on different textures and see how they can be blended together.
Indoor	**Consolidate** the research and practical visits together. **Create** their own drawing.	Ask your students to create their own drawing using the different lines and textures they have discovered outdoors.
Indoor/Outdoor	**Share** your art. Provide and take feedback. **Appreciate** artwork.	Students can then share their piece or art with the rest of the class and describe the inspiration for it. The rest of the class can provide feedback on the other's work.

Sculpture

Natural materials found outdoors are used as inspiration in Table 8.29 to teach sculpture using the inspirational framework.

Table 8.29 Scheme of work for using the inspirational framework for teaching sculpture

Inspirational Framework – Sculpture		
Location	Learning objective	Activity
Outdoor	Inspire students, using an outdoor experience, to be curious and **collect ideas.**	Take your students on a walk around your school grounds and look at the range of natural items you have for making a sculpture. Students then look at the objects collected.
Indoor	**Examine the ideas** collected. Search for creative ideas.	Ask students to research artists who use natural materials in their sculpture. For example, James Brunt, Andy Goldsworthy.

(Continued)

Table 8.29 (Continued)

Inspirational Framework – Sculpture		
Location	Learning objective	Activity
Outdoor	**Create** their own natural sculpture.	Ask your students to find the best place outdoors to build their sculpture. Then they collect the items they need to build and then build their sculpture.
Outdoor	**Share** their art. Provide and take feedback. **Appreciate** artwork.	Students then show other members of the class their sculpture and explain the inspiration for it. The rest of the class provides feedback on each other's work. Students then take photos of their sculpture.
Indoor	**Consolidate** the research and practical together.	Students can create a gallery guide to the artwork they made outside. They can include photos of their artwork and explain the inspiration behind it.
Indoor/Outdoor	**Share** your art.	Students can take another class for a guided tour around their outdoor sculpture park using the gallery guide they have created.

Drama and dance

In Table 8.30 the inspirational framework is used to teach students to create a piece of drama or dance.

Table 8.30 Scheme of work for using the inspirational framework for teaching drama

Inspirational Framework – Drama		
Location	Learning objective	Activity
Outdoor	Inspire students, using an outdoor experience, to be curious and **collect ideas.**	Take your students on a walk around the school grounds and look for movement and drama in nature. For example, the ways the leaves move in the breeze, birds flying or are arguing.
Indoor	**Examine the ideas** collected. Search for creative ideas.	Discuss what you saw outside, and ask your students to use their experience to inspire a piece of drama or dance. Students can undertake research into how dance and drama have been inspired by nature. For example, the play Toad of Toad Hall, the ballet Swan Lake. They can then use this research, and the experience observed outdoors to create their own piece of theatre or dance. For example, they could design a dance sequence based on birds murmurating, or a story of two animals going on an adventure around your school grounds.

(Continued)

Subject schemes of work 111

Table 8.30 (Continued)

Inspirational Framework – Drama		
Location	Learning objective	Activity
Outdoor	**Practice** their performance and rehearse. Consider the **audience** and setting of the piece.	Ask your students to find the right place to perform the piece outdoors. They can look at the space and the backdrop and think about where their audience will sit. If they are using dialogue, they could explore how the sound travels around the space, will everyone hear them? They then rehearse the piece in the space where it will be performed.
Indoor	**Consolidate** the research and practical visits together.	Students can create a program for their performance piece describing the inspiration behind it and what the performance is about.
Indoor/Outdoor	**Share** your performance. **Appreciate** performance. Give and receive feedback.	Groups then perform their piece to an audience. The rest of the class provide feedback on each other's work.

Music years 5 and 6

In Table 8.31 the inspirational framework is used to teach students to use found sounds from the environment to compose their own music.

Table 8.31 Scheme of work for using the inspirational framework for teaching music

Inspirational Framework – Music		
Location	Learning objective	Activity
Outdoor	Inspire students, using an outdoor experience, to be curious and **collect ideas.**	Take your class on a walk around the school grounds and listen to the different sounds. Get your students to try to mimic the different sounds they hear. They could record some of the sounds using a sound recorder.
Indoor	**Examine the ideas** collected. Search for creative ideas.	Ask your students to listen to the recording they have made of outdoor music. Can they remember what made each sound? Introduce the idea of found sounds – making music using sounds found outside. Get your students to research how found sounds are used to inspire and make music. For example, whale songs in meditative music, Money by Pink Floyd, Billie Eilish's Bad Guy.
Outdoor	Collect found sounds.	Students collect a range of found sounds for use in their composition.

(Continued)

Table 8.31 (Continued)

Inspirational Framework - Music		
Location	Learning objective	Activity
Indoor	Collect found sounds.	Students continue indoors to collect a range of found sounds for use in their composition.
Indoor	Create a piece of music using the found sounds.	Students then create their own piece of music using the different found sounds. For example, they could create a beat from a repeated sound they find or make one out of nature or other objects, e.g. Tapping stick together, tapping a fence. Then they can overlay with ambient sounds like bird song or the wind. They could add rhythm by making a tune with objects outdoor or indoors. Students then record the piece or write down how it will be performed.
Indoor/ Outdoor	**Share** their music. **Appreciate** music. Give and receive feedback.	Students can share their music by playing the recording in the place which best reflects their inspiration to the rest of the class. Or play a live version. Students can describe the inspiration for their musical composition. The rest of the class provides feedback on each other's work.

Ideas of how to apply chapter content

- Identify which subjects you want to start integrating the indoor-outdoor framework into.
- Start with one subject and identify some activities you could add to your planning for the subject. Use the indoor-outdoor framework to integrate them into your planning.
- Look at your planning for one of the topics described in this chapter. How can you use the fundamentals of the indoor-outdoor framework to apply to your teaching of the topic?
- Summarise the key features of the integrated indoor-outdoor frameworks that you could embed in your teaching. Review these with your staff and identify what would work for your school.
- Identify the features of the indoor-outdoor framework that you are not embedding. Why is this? What difference would it make if you integrated all features of the indoor-outdoor integrated framework?
- Come up with an action plan to embed the indoor-outdoor framework more.

References

1 Rundell, K. (2017). The explorer. Bloomsbury.
2 Morpuro, M. (1999). Kensuke's kingdom. Harper Collins.
3 Macfarlane, R. (2017). The lost words. Penguin Books.
4 Blake, W. (1794). Songs of experience collection. The Tyger.
5 Waters, F. (2018). I am the seed that grew the tree: A nature poem for every day of the year. Nosy Crow.

9 Cross curricular application

Aims of the chapter

- To demonstrate how using the indoor-outdoor integrated framework cross curricular application of knowledge and skills can be achieved.
- To provide a range of activities to use to integrate the indoor-outdoor frameworks into the teaching of various topics.
  - Scientific topics – plants and animals, transport, materials, light, and sound.
  - Geographical topics – navigation, water and rivers, weather and seasons, and global climate change.
  - Historical topics – my local area, the Romans, the Celts, castles, World War II.
  - Expressive art topics – colours.
  - Literacy-based topics – stories.
- To demonstrate how the different frameworks can be combined to teach cross curricular topics.

"I try to link my outdoor learning to our topics, but it isn't always possible". (If teachers are shoe-horning outdoor learning into their teaching of topics, it doesn't work.)

Introduction to cross curricular use of the indoor-outdoor integrated frameworks

In chapter 8 I outlined how the indoor-outdoor integrated frameworks can be used to teach concepts and skills required in specific subjects. However, the best use of outdoor learning is in its natural cross curricular application. The outdoors is not divided into subjects and naturally lends itself into exemplifying how different subjects interact and how all learning is interlinked.

This chapter provides examples of the way that topics can be taught using the frameworks. It interweaves many of the frameworks and includes field trips and visits as well as external visitors.

Science-based topics

Living things: Plants

The best time to study plants is when they are at the height of their growing season, either in spring and summer for flowers and bulbs, or autumn to look at seeds and seed dispersal. Some of the activities in Table 9.1 require prior planning and resourcing, such as collecting flowers for dissection and setting up rain gauges ahead of time.

Table 9.1 Scheme of work for the indoor-outdoor framework for the topic of living things: Plants

Location	Learning objective	Activity
Outdoor	Activate prior knowledge on plants.	Take your class on a walk outside to a place where there are plants. This could be a wood, planter, or border. Ask your students to identify the parts of the plant they recognise. Observe the variety of plants and how they differ from each other.
Indoor/ outdoor	Identify the parts of the plant.	Pull up a small plant to see the roots. Get your students to look at the colour of them. How are they different from the stem? Students can look for evidence of roots under trees. Then repeat the identification of plant parts with other types of plants like trees and bushes. Students can draw a picture of a plant and label the roots, stem, leaves, flower.
Outdoor	Sort and identify flowers. Collect data.	Get your students to undertake a survey of the flowers in your school grounds. They can complete a tally chart looking at colour, number of petals, or shape. See Table 9.2 for an example results table.
Indoor/ Outdoor	Present data in a graph. Analyse data	Students then use loose parts or chalk to make a pictogram of their results as a class. Then they draw a graph of the results on paper or digitally. See Figure 9.1. Discuss which type of flower there is the most of and which there is the least.
Indoor/ Outdoor	Label the parts of the flower. Understand what the different parts of the flower are for.	Discuss with your class why there are different colours and types of flowers. What are flowers for? Get each student to pick or give out a flower - use a simple flower such as a daffodil or tulip. Ask them to smell the flower. Why do they smell? Ask your students to pull off the petals and count them. Look carefully at them and how they are connected to the stem. Look for any sticky nectar close to the bottom of the petals. What are the petals for? Get your students to identify the anther where the pollen is - male part, sticky stigma - female part to catch the pollen, on the style - to hold the stigma up.

(Continued)

Table 9.1 (Continued)

Location	Learning objective	Activity
		Get your students to break open the bottom of the style – the ovary, to see if they can see a baby seed – ovum. Students can draw or take photos of the dissected flower and label the parts.
Indoor	Using experience and knowledge on flowers to come up with an investigation question.	Discuss what questions came up about flowers. How could they find the answer to these questions? For example, do bees prefer one colour? Why are there so many different coloured and shaped flowers? What are the different shapes for? As a class decide on a question to investigate. Then use the scientific method described in chapter 8 to design an investigation into their question.
Outdoor	Undertake a science investigation.	Get the class to collect data to find the answer to their question.
Indoor/ outdoor	Understand pollination.	Teach pollination either outside using a flower to demonstrate or inside.
Indoor	Understand what plants need to grow.	Teach that plants need water, light, and warmth to grow. You can show how water moves through a plant from the soil through the roots and out the leaves by placing a clear plastic bag around the leaves and looking for condensation forming inside the bag. You can also chop a celery stalk which has been sitting in food dye in half to see the tubes (xylem) the water travels up.
Outdoor	Collect data. Identify the best place for plants to grow.	Take your students on a walk around your school grounds to determine where would be the best place for plants to grow. They then undertake a survey to see which is the most suitable site. They can measure light levels with a light meter or app, temperature in the air or soil with a thermometer, and rain if you leave a rain gauges out for a few days in several places.
Indoor	Identify the best place for plants to grow.	Get your students to then repeat the survey inside for the most appropriate variables, for example, light levels, and temperature.
Indoor/ Outdoor	Make a prediction.	Students can then predict where the plants will grow the best and choose several locations for growing plants.
Indoor	Understand a fair test.	Discuss how to make the investigation fair, e.g. same plant, same amount of water inside. Ask your students to come up with a way of measuring the health of the plant. E.g. height over time – growth rate, colour, number of leaves, number of flowers. Choose a plant that grows quickly both inside and out, for example, lettuce, tomato plants, or cress.

(Continued)

Table 9.1 (Continued)

Location	Learning objective	Activity
Outdoor	Take measurements.	Students can take initial measurements of the health of the plants and then place the plants in the locations they have decided on. They then continue to take measurements daily or weekly depending on how fast the plants grow.
Indoor/ Outdoor	Calculate the range of the data. Calculate mean average of the data. Draw a bar or line graph. Come to a conclusion from analysing data. Evaluate a method.	If they have used numerical data to measure the health of the plant, then they can calculate the range in growth heights between the different locations. Each student then takes this value and the class lines up outside in number order of growth heights. Each student can then say what the conditions were in the location of their plant as you move down the line to see if there is a trend in the data. For example, have the plants outside or inside grown tallest? For each plant students can calculate the mean average growth rate by dividing the total height measurement minus the initial height measurement, divided by the number of days growing. Students can draw a bar graph of plant location against growth rate or create a correlation graph of other variables, for example, the amount of light against growth rate. Allow students to evaluate the method they used to see if it was fair test and the results are reliable. How could they improve their results?
Indoor/ Outdoor	Draw conclusions from evidence.	Looking at the graphs and results, students can decide where the best place to grow plants is. Students can take some measurements of the light levels and temperature at this location and use these to explain why their plant grew best there.
Outdoor	Find and identify seeds.	Ask your students what happens to the flowers once the bees have pollinated them? If you have an apple tree in blossom, then you can look at where the blossom has died and see the baby apple growing. Take your students on a seed hunt. See if any of the flowers you looked at in the beginning of the topic have now died and turned to seed. See if your students can identify the flower they came from. For example, dandelion clocks, tulips, daffodils. If you have no seeds in your school grounds, then bring in a range of seeds to look at. For example, peas or beans in their pods, pumpkin seeds, sunflower seeds, cress seeds, and mung beans.

(Continued)

Table 9.1 (Continued)

Location	Learning objective	Activity
Indoor	Identify and name the inside and outside parts of a seed. Make an accurate labelled drawing.	Show your class an apple and look at the stalk where the apple was hanging from the tree and the sepals where the flower was growing on the other side. The fruit has grown where the bottom of the style was, where they saw the ovary or baby seed. Cut an apple in half and show your class the seeds inside. Give out seeds for your class to look at. If they are in a pod, then let them open the pod to find the seeds inside. Get your students to look for the baby root and shoot growing on the outside of the bean. Which is which? If the seeds are large like a broad bean and are soft or have been soaked, then students can cut them open and see what is inside. Students can then draw a picture of the seed with the baby stem and baby root and label it.
Indoor/ Outdoor	Plan and undertake an experiment.	Recap what plants need to grow based on your student's last experiment and see if the class thinks seeds need anything else to sprout. Your students can plan an experiment like the one on plant growth to find out what seeds need to sprout. They can add a growing medium such as kitchen paper, soil, compost, or cotton wool as well as light, temperature, and water. Use the scientific framework as a guide. Create a question. Identify variables. Make a prediction. Make sure it is a fair test. Design a method. Set up experiment. Collect data. Present data. Analyse data. Draw conclusions. Evaluate method.
Outdoor	Investigate seed dispersal.	Use dandelion seeds to teach how plant's seeds disperse away from their parent plant. Students can search for other seeds that use different dispersal methods. For example, sticky weed, (cleavers) and burdock stick to fur or clothing, fruits are eaten and deposited, sycamore and ash keys have wings for helicopters, iris seeds explode.
Indoor	Seed dispersal investigation.	Students can undertake an investigation into seed dispersal. Which seeds travel the furthest? Ask your class to design a method for testing how far different seeds travel. They could use real seeds or make models.

(Continued)

Table 9.1 (Continued)

Location	Learning objective	Activity
Outdoor	Follow a method. Collect data. Take measurements.	Students can test the seeds to see which one goes the furthest. Then they can draw conclusions from the results. Which seeds went the furthest?
Indoor	Design the best seed. Present your design.	Students use the conclusion from their experiment to design a seed that will travel even further than the seeds they used. Then present their super seed to the class and explain why it will travel further.
Outdoor Field trip	Apply knowledge in a different environment.	Plan a visit to a habitat where plants grow which you have not got in your school grounds. Students can explore the plants growing there and measure the conditions. Are the plants like the plants growing in your school grounds? Look at the plants growing in this unfamiliar habitat. Do your students recognise them? Are any of them growing in your school grounds? If you visit a very different habitat such as sand dune, rocky shore, marsh, or heathland, look at the plants and see if your students can determine how they are different from the plants they have studied. Why are they different? How have they adapted to the conditions found in that environment? For example, you can look at seaweed on the rocky shore and see how the air bubbles help them float. Grasses on the sand dunes and see how the long roots suck up water and the rolled-up leaves stop water escaping. You can do a comparison between the different plants in the different environments.

Table 9.2 Flower investigation results table

Independent variable	Dependent variable
Flower colour	Tally
Flower shape	Tally
Number of petals	Tally

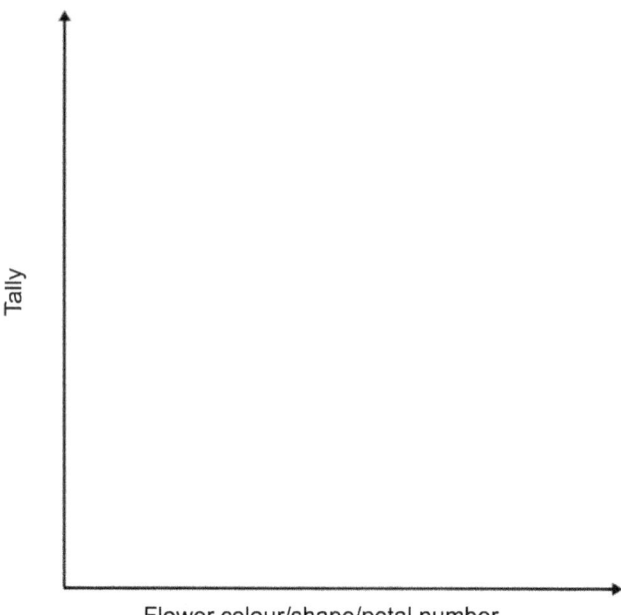

Figure 9.1 Graph axis for flower investigation

Living things: Animals

Animals are best studied in summer when they are the most active, especially if you want to see butterflies. Mini beasts in the soil can be found most time of the year but in the winter, you are unlikely to find as many. Teaching about animals using the framework in Table 9.3 is a good opportunity to teach caring for the environment so include how to keep the animals safe in any animal collecting you do.

Table 9.3 Scheme of work for the indoor-outdoor framework for the topic of living things: Animals

Location	Learning objective	Activity
Outdoor	Sort animals by characteristics.	Take your students on a mini beast hunt and collect the animals in a tray. Ask your students to prove they are animals and alive. Are they all the same? Students can sort them into groups. They can choose the groups and then justify the categories they have used. For example, number of legs, shape of body, the way they move, and their size.
Indoor	Observe the features of an animal. Use an identification key.	Ask your students to draw the mini beasts and label their characteristics. Identify the main body parts: head, thorax, abdomen, legs. Then list the ways in which they differ from each other. Students can use a key to identify the mini beasts.

(Continued)

Table 9.3 (Continued)

Location	Learning objective	Activity
		Get your students to look at the construction of the key. What kind of characteristics did it use? How many choices were there?
Outdoor	Observe the features of an animal.	Get your students to find a mini beast that they have not identified. Then create a name for it using this formula; the animal's colour, where it lives, distinguishing feature, how it moves, and the type of animal. For example, the red, log dwelling, long legged, scurrying beetle. Or come up with your own formula.
Indoor	Identify and name a variety of animals.	Teach your students about other animals which may live in your school grounds such as mammals, amphibians, fish, and birds. How do they differ from mini beasts? How are they similar?
Outdoor	Identify and name a variety of animals.	Take your students on an animal hunt. You can take binoculars and look for birds. Get students to observe how they move. Students could create a dance based on the bird's movement, see the dance framework in chapter 8. Look for evidence of any other animals. For example, stored and eaten nuts from squirrels, poo from badgers in square holes, or foxes on top of logs, footprints in wet mud.
Indoor	Survey mammals.	Discuss with your class how you can find out what animals are living in the school grounds when no one is there. Get your students to design a trap for surveying small and large mammals. For example, place double-sided sticky tape inside a toilet roll tube. Place an ink pad or flour inside the tube and some bird food. Place the tube outside overnight in a hedgerow or beside a wall. Or place flour around any holes in hedges. The next morning, check the traps for any eaten food, footprints in the flour or ink, fur stuck to the Sellotape, or droppings. Students can use these clues to guess what animals are living in your school grounds.
Indoor	Design an animal home.	Ask the students what animals are missing from your school grounds? How could you encourage them to move in? Students can then plan some habitat creation to encourage animals such as hedgehogs – piles of leaves, reptiles – corrugated sheets and piles of rock in sunny areas, amphibians – pond or marshy area. They can research what the animals need to survive.
Outdoor	Monitor the success of your design.	Using your student's research, they can create the animal home they have designed in the right location. Make sure students monitor if there are signs that it is being used. If you have a trail camera, monitor the place at night.

(Continued)

Table 9.3 (Continued)

Location	Learning objective	Activity
Indoor	Understand animal feeding relationships.	Look at the animals that live in your school grounds and ask your students to think about what they eat. Students can research to find out if they are herbivores, carnivores, or omnivores. In groups, students can create a food chain for the animals in your school grounds. For example, woodlice eat wood, robins eat woodlice, and owls eat robins. Then try to connect all the different groups' food chains into a food web.
Outdoor/ Indoor	Create a food web. Understand about interconnection in plants and animals.	Stand the pupils in a circle. Ask every child to choose an animal from the school grounds to represent. You or another adult stands in the middle of the circle as the plant holding onto the end of a long piece of string. Choose one of the pupils who is an herbivore to stand next to you also holding the string with you holding the end. Ask the students to choose an animal which eats the herbivore and the student who represents that animal takes hold of the string next to the herbivore. Carry on building one food chain. Then add more animals with new strings either from the plant or connected to animals already in the chain. Once all the animals are connected in the food web observe how complicated it is. Next say you are going to kill the plant. Let go of the string and say that if you ate a plant, then you have no food and will die. The dead animals drop the string. If the next animal along the string has no food they also die, and so on until all the animals are dead and the food web collapses. This should help show that all animals and plants are interconnected and if you destroy one, it impacts the others.
Indoor	Understand animal life cycles.	Teach your students about the life cycles of animals such as frogs, butterflies, beetles, dragonflies, water beetles. You can use the book *Monkey Puzzle* by Julia Donaldson [1].
Outdoor	Investigate life cycles.	Take your class out to look for animals with interesting life cycles you have heard about, for example, caterpillars in the trees and bushes, beetles in the soil or dead wood, frogs in wet woods, or tadpoles in ponds. If they find the larvae or young you can keep them in a safe place outside and revisit them to see how they develop. Take your students on a caterpillar, butterfly, or egg hunt by looking under leaves and shaking branches over sheets. They can use nets to carefully catch butterflies. Then create a life cycle diagram for all the animals they have found.
Indoor	Understand adaptation.	Teach your class about adaptation and how animals survive. For example, camouflage, movement, claws, teeth, venom, stings, breathing, flying.

(Continued)

Cross curricular application 123

Table 9.3 (Continued)

Location	Learning objective	Activity
Outdoor	Understand adaptation.	Take your class to look for an animal that is adapted to its environment. Students draw the animal and label all the ways it is adapted to survive.
Indoor	Design a new animal.	Ask your students to choose a different environment to your school grounds. Then they can design an animal that is adapted to the conditions in that environment. For example, the sea, a mountain, a swamp, a desert. Students then present their animal with its name and how it will survive.
Indoor	Plan a field trip.	Look at a Google Earth image of your school and pan out to see your local learning area. Ask your students to find a new habitat you do not have in your school grounds, for example, a river, a pond, the sea, a beach, a hill, or a forest. Take your class on a virtual field trip to the location on Google Street View. Help your class plan a field trip to the site using the fieldwork and visits framework in chapter 6.
Outdoor	Go on a field trip.	Take your class to visit a new habitat to investigate adaptation there. They can collect data on the number of different animals in the habitats.
Indoor	Present data in graphs. Draw conclusions.	Pupils can then create graphs of the different animals found on the field trip. Get then to compare the animals found on the field trip to those found in your school grounds.
Indoor	Plan an investigation.	Students can plan an investigation into the number of different mini beast in your school grounds. They can create a results table, see Table 9.4.
Outdoor	Collect data. Draw a graph.	Students collect data by counting how many different types of minibeasts are in each habitat and how many in total. Then they can create a graph of their data using loose parts.
Indoor	Draw a graph. Draw conclusions from data. Apply knowledge.	Students draw a graph of their results on paper or digitally. Ask the class what conclusions they can draw? Which habitat is the most diverse? Why? Which has the largest number of mini beasts? Why? Ask your class if they wanted to increase the number of mini beasts in your school grounds, which habitats should they develop?
Indoor	Write a guide. Create an identification key.	The students can draw all this knowledge together by creating fact files for all the animals they have found in your school grounds. Or they could create an identification guide or key for the animals in your school grounds.

Table 9.4 Minibeast survey results table

Name of Habitat	Number of different types of mini beasts	Tally	Total
Field	E.g. woodlice, worms, slugs = 3		
Woods			
Flower bed			

Materials

Materials are used to build everything and provides a practical topic to teach the understanding of equating properties to uses. This framework exemplified in Table 9.5, applies the theory of material properties to making a model boat, but any model can be used in its place that requires the right choice of material, e.g. waterproof umbrella, sunshade, or visor for an astronaut's helmet. The aim of the activity is to learn the importance of choosing the right material for the job based on its properties.

Table 9.5 Scheme of work for the indoor – outdoor framework for the topic of materials

Location	Learning objective	Activity
Outdoor	Identify human-made and natural materials. Undertake a survey.	Take your class on a walk around your school grounds and identify the different materials that are there. For example, natural materials like wood and human-made materials like plastic. They can undertake a materials survey around the school grounds. See Table 9.6.
Indoor	Sort materials by their properties. Understand properties of material and how they are used.	Your students can then continue the survey inside the school. Next, get your students to collate and analyse the data and calculate if there are more natural or human-made materials being used. Ask your students to consider why have these materials been chosen for their jobs? Teach your class about properties. Get students to apply this information by sorting a range of materials by their properties.
Indoor	Research properties of different materials. Create a design.	Set the task for your class to build a model boat. They can research and then choose the materials to make it out of. Next, they design their boat. You can use the design framework from chapter 8.

(Continued)

Table 9.5 (Continued)

Location	Learning objective	Activity
Outdoor	Test the design. Evaluate the effectiveness of the design. Adjust the design.	Provide a bowl of water for your students to test their designs. The students then adjust their designs to improve them and retest.
Outdoor	Present their model.	Once the model boats have been completed the students can show them to the rest of the class explaining how they work and how they chose the materials.
Indoor	Write instructions. Give clear instructions. Follow a set of instructions.	Students can then write a guide to their model. It could be an annotated picture showing how the materials connect together and work to produce a floating boat, linking to forces and material properties. Or they could write a set of instructions as a guide to make a model boat. Another group can then follow the instructions to build their own model.

Table 9.6 Materials survey results table

Object	Material	Natural	Human made
Bench	Wood	X	
Sign	Plastic		X

Sound

The topic of sound can be taught using the framework outlined in Table 9.7. Outdoors provides an opportunity to investigate the properties of different sounds as well as exploring how sound travels.

Table 9.7 Scheme of work for the indoor-outdoor framework for the topic of sound

Location	Learning objective	Activity
Indoor	Understand pitch and volume of sound.	Teach your class about sound including pitch and volume.
Outdoor	Understand how sound is made.	Take your class around the school grounds looking for different sounds. Students could use sticks on fences, sticks on sticks, empty buckets. Use cups of water to show sound is vibration. Let the students feel the vibration of the railings after the rungs make a noise. Ask your class what happens to the sound when you hit the object harder making it vibrate more strongly? You can talk about the volume of sound and how it is linked to the strength of vibrations that produce it.

(Continued)

Table 9.7 (Continued)

Location	Learning objective	Activity
Outdoor	Look for patterns in data. Recognise different pitches.	Students can investigate pitch using different objects to make different pitches. They can investigate if there is a pattern to the type of object that makes the higher or lower pitch.
Outdoor	Investigate how sound travels. Investigate sound barriers.	In pairs get your class to investigate how far away they can move away from a sound before they can't hear it. Get them to explore what happens to the sound as you move further away? Let the class try the same experiment but by moving behind an object and see what happens to the sound. They can experiment with different sound barriers such as a hedge, a building, a tree, or a fence. Ask them to test what makes the best sound barrier? Why do they think that is?
Indoor/ Outdoor	Follow the design process.	Set a challenge for your students to design a set of ear defenders to block out the sounds that are present in your school grounds. You can provide a design brief of which sound you want blocked, for example, the road, the nursery, and the playground. They can follow the design process in chapter 8 and make a prototype and test it outdoors.
Outdoor	Go on a sound survey. Collect data. Follow a map.	You can download a sound meter onto digital devices. Bring the sound meters outdoors and get the students to measure the sound level as they walk around your local learning area. Students can record the sound levels on a map.
Indoor	Analyse data. Draw conclusions.	Ask the students to look at the sound map and see if there are any patterns. Explore where the sound is the loudest and quietest and why? What is the source of the sound? Is there a sound barrier?
Indoor	Apply data. Create a trail.	Task your students to use the data they have collected from the investigation to design a sound walk in your local area. They could create an immersive soundscape experience, maximising the oratory experience, or they could design a mood-enhancing walk, for example, a calming walk.
Outdoor	Test their trail for impact. Analyse results. Explore their emotions and how they are impacted by experiences.	Take the class with their sound trails along the walks designed by the class and analyse the impact of the sounds on their moods. Ask the class to discuss how the sounds on the walk made them feel. Students can provide feedback on the trail to the groups.

(Continued)

Table 9.7 (Continued)

Location	Learning objective	Activity
Indoor	Create a still walk.	Your students can follow the framework on music in chapter 8 to create a still walk. This is a series of still photos with a soundtrack of found sounds so that a viewer can go on a virtual walk with all the visual and auditory experience.
Outdoor	Collect sounds.	Ask your students to record and collect found sounds from different locations for their still walk. Task them to take photos for each location which relates to the found sound or the location.
Indoor	Share their still walks.	Once your students have collated their sounds and images, they can share them with another class or even another school. You can share the still walk videos with a school from another area or location and get feedback on how they found the experience.

Light

The theory and properties of light can be investigate using the framework in Table 9.8. These activities may require certain amounts of light outdoors so check the weather forecast before planning the session.

Table 9.8 Scheme of work for the indoor-outdoor framework for the topic of light

Location	Learning objective	Activity
Outdoor	Explore shadows.	On a sunny day, take your class outside and get them to draw around shadows from buildings, benches, or other static objects with chalk. Note the time the shadows were drawn.
Indoor	Understand how shadows are formed.	Teach the concept of light and shadows. Allow students to experiment with making shadows bigger and smaller using torches and objects.
Outdoor	Draw conclusions from evidence. Ask questions about data.	Take your class outdoors to check the outlines of the shadows they drew earlier. Ask your class to draw around the new shadow in a different colour. Compare the two shadows. Ask your students to think about the theory and experimenting they did on shadows inside. Ask them to try to come up with a reason why the size of the shadows has changed. For example, has the sun moved further away from the Earth? Has the sun moved down or up?
Indoor	Investigate how shadows change.	Get students to experiment with shadows again to test the questions they posed outside. If the sun has not moved further or closer away, how else can the shadows change?

(Continued)

Table 9.8 (Continued)

Location	Learning objective	Activity
Outdoor	Make a prediction. Draw conclusions from data.	Take your class to check the shadows again and draw a third outline in a different colour. Ask your class to look at the location of the sun in the sky and using what was learnt from the experiment inside, predict where the shadow will be later in the day. Ask the class to draw a fourth line in a different colour on the ground of their prediction.
Indoor	Communicate the conclusions from the experiments.	Your students can make a poster or presentation explaining all they have learnt about shadows and their size.
Outdoor	Collect data.	Take your class outside to check on their predicted shadow outline and see if you were right. Students can then collect data on size of the shadows over time, see Table 9.9.
Indoor	Present data in a graph. Draw conclusions.	Students can present the data on shadow length in a line graph. They can then use the data to draw conclusions about what happens to the length of shadows.
Indoor	Design a shadow puppet theatre. Apply knowledge in a different context. Write a story.	Task students to create a shadow puppet show using their knowledge on how shadows are formed. They can design the puppet theatre so that the shadow puppets work for the audience. Next, they can write a short story that involves one character changing size.
Indoor	Perform a story to an audience. Apply knowledge of shadows to tell the story.	Groups can then perform their shadow puppet show to the rest of the class or another class, making the same shadow puppet grow and shrink.
Outdoor	Investigate reflection.	Take your students on a walk around your school grounds with mirrors. Get students to experiment with using the mirrors to reflect light to one another and over long distances. Challenge the class to send the light around a corner.
Indoor	Design a periscope. Build a periscope.	Use the experience from outdoors to get your class to design a periscope to see over a wall. They could research reflection first and the use of periscopes to help them see what they are aiming for. You can provide a range of boxes and mirrors.
Outdoor	Test their design.	Students can take their periscope outside and test if they work seeing around corners. Then they can redesign if necessary and test again. You can use the design framework in chapter 8.
Indoor	Evaluate your design. Instructional writing.	Once completed, students can write instructions for building a periscope.

(Continued)

Table 9.8 (Continued)

Location	Learning objective	Activity
Outdoor	Investigate light.	Give UV-reactive beads to your class but don't tell them what activates them. Ask them to work out what they are sensitive to. Discuss possibilities.
Indoor	Investigate light.	Try exposing the beads to LED light and see if they change colour.
Indoor	Understand that light comes from the sun and can be dangerous. Understand that light is made up of many colours.	Teach about the concept of visible light being part of a spectrum of light from the sun. Show rainbows by shining light through a prism or on a CD. The light we don't see can damage our skin and eyes; ultraviolet light causes sun burn.
Indoors	Design a pair of sunglasses.	Set the class the challenge to design a pair of UV filtering sunglasses.
Outdoor	Test their design. Make modifications. Collect data.	They can test the effectiveness of the sunglasses using the UV-sensitive bead. Provide a scale for the beads that shows how much UV they have been exposed to. They can modify the sunglasses and retest until they stop the UV.
Indoor	Test their design. Make modifications. Collect data.	Once all students have created a UV filter the class have to test if the sunglasses are fit for purpose. For example, can they see through them? If not, they will have to redesign the sunglasses so that they can.
Outdoor	Present their model. Take and give feedback.	Students then take turns to present their sunglasses showing how they work. They need to describe what problems they found and how they overcome them. They then receive feedback from other groups.

Table 9.9 Results table for shadow size

Time of day	Shadow's length

Transport

Teaching forces through outdoor learning, as shown in Table 9.10, can reinforce the applicational understanding of balanced and unbalanced forces. The important part is not the design itself but the pupil's explanation of how the design works with the forces to meet the design brief. You can video these explanations to share with other stakeholders, or to show a younger class before they attempt the challenge.

Table 9.10 Scheme of work for the indoor-outdoor framework for the topic of transport

Location	Learning objective	Activity
Indoor	Understand what forces are.	Teach forces such as gravity and air resistance.
Outdoor	Understand forces and the theory of their use to explain what happens.	Ask your students to explain forces using examples found outdoors. For example, why a feather falls slower than a stick, why a ball falls faster than a Frisbee. Look out for the understanding using the correct terminology.
Indoor	Understand balanced forces.	Clarify or revisit any misconceptions identified in the practical task. Introduce the idea of balanced forces.
Indoor/Outdoor	Use problem-solving skills to apply the concept of forces.	Present a problem to the class which requires the application of the understanding of forces to answer. E.g. How can we make a ball fall slower? Ask your class to research ways to reduce the rate of fall and use these ideas to come up with a model to test. E.g. parachutes, balloons, umbrellas.
Outdoor	Create a design. Test their design. Use measuring skills.	Ask your students to build the model to apply to the ball. Then they can test the effectiveness of the model.
Indoor	Evaluate the effectiveness of their design. Adjust their design.	Ask students to discuss if the model is working and if it can be improved. Get them to adjust their design to improve its effectiveness.
Outdoor	Test their design. Use measuring skills.	Students can then test the effectiveness of their model again and see if it is better.
Indoor/Outdoor	Present their model.	Once their models have been completed, they can show them to the rest of the class explaining how it works to change the balance of forces applied to the ball.
Outdoor	Identify the value of the concept through real-life application.	Take the students to look around your school ground to observe where nature has increased air resistance to slow the rate of fall. Did nature use any of the same ideas they did in their designs? You can go on to undertake a seed dispersal experiment from the plant's framework in this chapter, Table 9.1.
Indoor	Understand forces.	Introduce the concept of lift and upthrust forces in aeroplanes and boats.

(Continued)

Table 9.10 (Continued)

Location	Learning objective	Activity
Indoor	Research to build a design.	Students use their understanding of forces to design a plane. They can research a design to start with.
Outdoor	Create a design. Test their design. Use measuring skills.	Students then build the model plane and test how far the plane goes.
Indoor	Evaluate the effectiveness of their design. Adjust their design.	Students discuss if their model plane is working and how it be improved. Allow them to adjust the design to improve its effectiveness.
Outdoor	Test their design. Use measuring skills.	Students can test the effectiveness of their model again and see if it is better.
Outdoor	Present their model.	Once the model plane has been completed students can show it to the rest of the class explaining how it works using the different forces and terminology, and how they reviewed and adjusted the design. (The same design process can also be used for a boat to see how much weight it can hold before sinking.)
Indoor	Research to build a design.	Task students with investigating wind-powered vehicles, for example, land yachts, sea yachts, kite buggies. Task them with planning their own wind-powered vehicle. For example, they could use Knex or Lego and add a sail.
Outdoor	Test their design. Use measuring skills.	They can test their design and work out a way of measuring how fast it goes.
Outdoor	Present their model.	Once the models have been completed they can show them to the rest of the class explaining how they work using different forces, and how they reviewed and adjusted the design.

Geography-based topics

Navigation

The framework in Table 9.11 builds on the map-making skills framework outlined in chapter 8. If you have not made a scale map of your school grounds, you can use a printout from Google Maps, but you may have to add a few features if your grounds look featureless on the map. This framework develops navigation skills then moves onto a walk around the local learning area and then using map skills in an unknown area. This is a great opportunity to test map skills and can be integrated into a field trip or residential.

Table 9.11 Scheme of work for the indoor – outdoor framework for the topic of navigation

Location	Learning objective	Activity
Outdoor	Learn to orientate a map.	Take your class on a walk around your school grounds and identify key landscape features which would be on a map. For example, the field, playground, boundary fence, or path. Discuss what shape they would be from above. Give out a copy of a map of the school grounds to your class. Ask them to identify the landforms you have seen on the ground, on the map. Show how to orientate the map so the landforms are facing the same way as the map. Walk around the grounds again with the students keeping their finger on the spot where they are on the map. Stop and ask them to show their location periodically.
Indoor	Learn the parts of a compass. Understand the names of the cardinal points and the degrees they represent.	Teach the class the parts of the compass, the dial, base plate, compass needle, compass housing, direction of travel arrow, orientating arrow, compass direction values, or declination marks. Identify the cardinal points on the compass and what degrees or bearings are represented by each. For example, North is 0° or 360° South is 180° East is 90° West is 270°.
Outdoor	Learn to walk on a compass bearing.	Go through the process of walking on a compass bearing. For example, hold the compass flat with the direction of travel arrow pointing in front of you. Turn the dial until north (0°) is in line with the direction of travel arrow. Turn your body and the compass until the red compass needle is inside the red stripy orientating arrow. Walk the way the direction of travel arrow is pointing, and you are walking north. In the playground or field get pairs of students to place a cone where they are standing. In pairs they take turns to walk five paces north, then swap compasses over. Starting from the same spot, then set the compass to east and walk five paces. Swap over the compass and then set the compass to south and walk five paces south. Swap compasses then set the compass to west and walk five paces west and they should end up at the starting point. If they don't, then try again.
Indoor	Understand the position and significance of key geographical features on the globe.	Teach about the wider scale of position and the significance of compass points and features on the globe such as longitude and latitude, the equator, the northern hemisphere, the Arctic, etc.

(Continued)

Table 9.11 (Continued)

Location	Learning objective	Activity
Outdoor	Apply skills in compass work.	Create a star orienteering course for your school grounds with compass bearings. For example, work out the bearing from a significant starting point to a landmark such as the corner of a building. Place a number or picture or a stamp at the location as a control. Repeat from the start point to other locations. See Figure 9.2. Once all the locations are set up give your students a list of the bearings and a sheet to collect all the stamps or pictures, see Table 9.12, orienteering control marker card. Get the students to follow the bearings and find the controls; they write the number, picture, or stamp in the right box.
Indoor	Use the scale of a map. Understand and read 2-, 4-, or 6-figure grid references.	Students can create grid lines on your school grounds map. Get students to take the map of the school and draw equal distance lines across and up to form a grid. Using the scale, they should make the grid lines about 10m apart. Next, they can number the lines from left to right and bottom to top. For example, depending on the ability of the class they could use 1-10 along the bottom and 11-20 along the side or letters, or use the same numbers. See Figure 9.3. Teach your class how to use 2-, 4-, and 6-figure grid references. Students can then find the grid reference of objects in the school grounds.
Outdoor	Read grid references. Read a map.	In pairs, one student picks a location on the map and then tells their partner the grid reference for the location. Their partner then has to find the right location in the school grounds and stand at it. Their partner watches and tells them if they are correct. Swap over. You can observe any misconceptions to grid referencing and map reading.
Indoor	Understand how to read an OS map. Read 6-figure grid references.	Show your class an OS map of the area around your school. Teach about the symbols on an OS map. Identify the grid references and use them to find local landmarks. Choose some key landmarks and ask students to identify their 6-figure grid references.

(Continued)

Table 9.11 (Continued)

Location	Learning objective	Activity
Indoor	Use directional language accurately. Design a route on a map. Read grid references. Measure scale on a map.	Together use the OS map to design a route to all the landmarks. Students then create a route card for the walk, see Table 9.13. Or use directional language to write a set of instruction to get to each landmark.
Outdoor	Follow a route on a map.	Take your class outside and using the route card, directions, compass, and map, follow the route to all the landmarks. Ask your students to take photos of the landmarks.
Indoor/Outdoor	Share their local landmark route with others.	Your students can share their route map to the local landmarks with another class or stakeholder. (This can be linked with the local history trail in the history My Place framework in this chapter, Table 9.22.)
Outdoor	Complete an orienteering course.	Take your class to an unknown location which has an orienteering course and get the students to use their compass and navigation skills to complete the course. This could be undertaken on a residential or on a field trip to a site with a permanent orienteering course.
Indoor	Design an orienteering course.	Students can then create their own orienteering course in the school grounds. This could be a permanent course of posts with numbers or letters on, or a temporary course for a treasure hunt for another class. They can use directional language or compass skills, or the map and grid references.

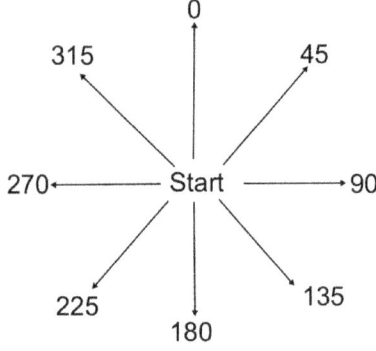

Figure 9.2 Star orienteering course

Cross curricular application 135

Table 9.12 Orienteering control marker sheet

1.	2.	3.	4.	5.	6.
7.	8.	9.	10.	11.	12.

Table 9.13 Route card

Leg	Start grid reference	Direction	Distance	Time to walk	Time of arrival	End point
1.	School gates 513, 814	150°	1000m	20mins	9:50 am	Church
2.	Church 513, 824	0°	200m	4mins	9:54 am	Townhall

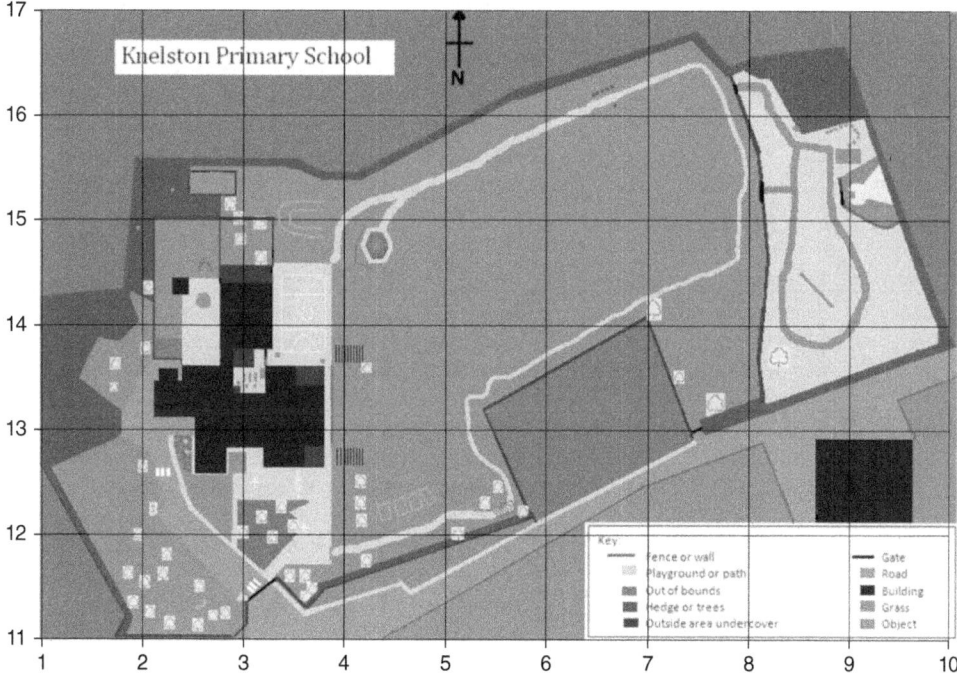

Figure 9.3 School grounds map with grid lines

Water and rivers

Table 9.14 uses the framework for undertaking a river study, which is a practical way of teaching about the water cycles and river landforms. It also provides opportunities for applying map work skills and measuring skills. Giving ownership of a field trip to a river to the class means they fully understand why they are there and what they are trying to achieve. Try to find a river locally which you can visit close to its source, at the middle and mouth of the river. Ensure it is not too long a distance, if you are walking, or too deep, so you can enter the river safely. When you return, build on the experience of visiting the river by drawing together what you saw and discovered.

Table 9.14 Scheme of work for the indoor – outdoor framework for the topic of water and rivers

Location	Learning objective	Activity
Outdoor	Understand the school's role in the water cycle.	Take your students around the school grounds identifying where the rain goes. Ask your students to look for where water enters the school grounds, for example, through rain. Places where water flows, for example, drainpipes. Where water is stored, for example, puddles, and where it leaves the school grounds, for example, drains.
Indoor	Understand the parts of the water cycle.	Teach the water cycle, sources, stores, and flows.
Outdoor	Survey and map water.	Task your students to map the water in the school grounds. Students can draw on a map of the school grounds showing where the water travels with arrows. Or create a film of a raindrop's journey through their school grounds.
Indoor	Read a map.	With your class, look at maps of your local learning area and identify local rivers, lakes, ponds, or the sea. Get students to trace a river from the source to the sea. Then using the map's scale measure its length from where it starts to where it ends. Teach the parts of a river including source, mouth, meanders, flood plain, bank, and riverbed.
Indoor	Plan a river study. Read a map. Understand how to be safe beside a river.	Plan a trip to your local river. Discuss with your class how to be safe beside rivers and research the size and depth of the river you are going to visit. Then look on Google Street View and go on a virtual visit to see what access to the river is like. Together find three locations along the river where you may be able to take some measurements. Discuss with your class what you could measure about the river and create a results table. See Table 9.15. Ask your class to come up with a prediction as to what they think will happen to the river as they move from the source to the mouth. For example, will it get deeper, wider, and faster? Discuss with your class what equipment they will need to bring on the field trip.
Outdoor Field trip	Conduct a river study. Collect data by taking measurements.	Travel to the first site on the river. Discuss with your class how they are going to measure the depth, width, and speed of the river safely. For example, if you can enter the river, you can use a meter ruler, and measure the time it takes for a stick to float a set distance. If you can't enter the river, they could use a bridge and a piece of string with a weight. Students then collect data for the first site.

(Continued)

Cross curricular application 137

Table 9.14 (Continued)

Location	Learning objective	Activity
		They can draw a sketch or take photos of the river features at the site. Repeat for all the other sites.
Indoor	Analyse data. Calculate mean averages. Draw graphs. Draw conclusions.	Collate the class data from the river study. Give the collated data to the class and get them to calculate mean averages for each site and make a class set of average results. With the collated data ask the class to draw graphs to look for trends to check their predictions. For example, a line graph of distance from source against average depth of river or a bar graph of river width for the three sites. Students can calculate the speed of the river by dividing the distance the stick travelled in meters by the time in seconds. They can then graph the speed readings. Students then use the graphs to draw conclusions about the river. Ask them if their predictions were right.
Outdoor	Create a model of a river. Identify river features.	Task your students to use the map, photos, or sketches taken on the field trip and the river measurements, to create an accurate model of the river. They could build it in a tray and use soil or sand. Make sure they include river landforms they have seen in the correct locations along the river. See Figure 9.4. They can add labels of the features.
Indoor/ Outdoor	Share their model.	Groups can share their river models with the rest of the class explaining what each landform is.
Indoor	Research the world's rivers.	Students use their knowledge of a local river to research other rivers around the world and see if they have similar features to your local river.

Table 9.15 River results table

		River depth			
River site	River width	Left bank	Centre	Right bank	Speed of river
1. Source					
2. Middle					
3. Mouth					

Figure 9.4 Model river
Source: Photograph by the author.

This water and rivers framework can be adapted and used for visiting any local landforms, for example, a beach, hill, forest, or city centre.

Weather and climate

Weather and climate are great topics to teach in the autumn and winter months when it is harder to get outdoors. The framework in Table 9.16 can be used to teach about the weather and climate and develop data collection and measuring skills. If you are collecting data on the weather, then use this to develop data analysis and data presentation skills such as drawing and interpreting graphs and calculating mean averages. If you have created a map of your school grounds using the mapping framework in chapter 8, then this can be used to collect the data on the weather.

Table 9.16 Scheme of work for the indoor-outdoor framework for the topic of weather and climate

Location	Learning objective	Activity
Indoor	Understand the weather.	Teach about the weather in your local area. Do your students think the school has any impact on the weather?
Outdoor	Explore and experience the local weather.	Take your class on a walk around your school grounds and identify all aspects of the weather. For example, the wind, temperature, sun, and rain. Get students to notice as they walk around if any of these factors change.
Indoor	Create an enquiry question.	As a class come up with an enquiry question which investigates how the weather is different around the school grounds. For example, Where is the windiest place? Where is the hottest place? Where is the wettest place?
Indoor	Research data collection methods.	Discuss with your class how you can measure the factors you need to measure. Students can research how they measure them in a weather station. Then they can choose the correct equipment for the data collection.
Indoor	Make a weather station.	Get your class to make a range of weather instruments. For example, a weather vane, a windsock, a pinwheel, or a rain gauge.
Outdoor	Trail the use of weather equipment.	Let your students experiment with their equipment and explore how they can collect data with the equipment. For example, can they count how many times the pinwheel rotates? Can they measure how strong the wind is with the windsock? Does the thermometer work outdoors? Do buildings change the wind?
Indoor	Undertake research. Adapt design.	As a class, research and adapt the equipment to make them functional, for example, place some tape on the stick of the pinwheel so it makes a noise when the sails rotate. Use the Beaufort scale to measure wind speed with the windsock. Use a compass with the weather vane.
Indoor	Write a method for the enquiry. Plan how they will collect their results.	Ask your students to write a method to follow. This should include instructions on how they plan to collect their results. For example, where are they going to do their measuring? For how long are they going to measure? Students need to draw a results table or find a base map to collect their data on. See Table 9.17.
Outdoor	Undertake data collection for their enquiry.	Pupils follow their method to collect the data in a results table or on a map. For example, write the temperature on the map where the reading was taken, or create a colour code for temperatures and colour in the location the correct colour.

(Continued)

Table 9.16 (Continued)

Location	Learning objective	Activity
Outdoor	Present their results.	If they have used a results table, students can use chalk or loose materials to present the data to show the results outdoors.
Indoor	Present the results.	Students can then present their results in their books or on paper. The aim is to show the answer to the enquiry question using an image. It could be a graph in their books or using a computer program, or the map they coloured in with a key.
Indoor/outdoor	Draw conclusions.	Students then present their conclusions to the enquiry either in their books or as a presentation. They need to answer their enquiry question using proof from their results.
Outdoor	Evaluate the investigation.	Students can use the space outside to describe what they did and how it generated reliable data and how their method could be improved. For example, demonstrate how they collected the data and any problems they found.
Outdoor	Apply the conclusions. Come up with more enquiry questions.	Ask your students to identify the best place in the school grounds for certain activities with reference to their data. For example, where is the best place to have a picnic? Where is the best place to fly a kite? Where is the best place to go sunbathing?
Outdoor	Repeat the enquiry in another location.	Take your class for a walk around your local learning area to find if the weather changes there too. Students can predict what you would expect to find in different locations. For example, beside tall buildings, in a woodland, on the beach, up a hill. Visit different environments and repeat the weather enquiry there, e.g. visit a beach, sand dune system, woodland, city centre, country park.
Indoor/Outdoor	Collect data. Use a spreadsheet.	Get your class to create a long-term data set by continuing to collect weather data for your school grounds every day. Pupils can input this data into a spreadsheet for use in the future for data analysis of the school's climate.
Indoor	Understand climate data. Draw climate graphs. Analyse climate graphs.	Students can use the spreadsheet data on weather for the year to compare with climate data in other countries. They can draw graphs of rainfall, temperature, and wind speed. Then compare the graphs to climate graphs in other countries.

Table 9.17 Weather results table

Distance from school	Wind speed

Seasons

Depending on the time of year the topic of seasons can be used to teach about the weather, life cycles of animals and plants, or colours as shown in Table 9.18. If you can repeat some of these activities in different seasons, then the pupils will get a better understanding of the differences between them. For example, completing the season picture and colours survey can provide a visual representation of each season for a seasonal display.

Table 9.18 Scheme of work for the indoor-outdoor framework for the topic of seasons

Location	Learning objective	Activity
Outdoor	Name the four seasons. Describe the weather associated with the season.	Take your pupils for a walk around your school grounds or local learning area and look at what is happening in nature. Ask your students to look for signs of the season. For example, bulbs emerging in spring, flowers in summer, nuts in autumn, leaves turning in autumn. Discuss with your class why these things are happening now. Link to the weather of the season. Students can collect or take photos of items that link to the season.
Indoor/Outdoor	Create a seasonal picture.	Ask your students to build a seasonal picture out of their items. This could be on a nature table or paper. Take photos to compare to other seasonal pictures they make.
Outdoor	Observe seasonal change.	Get your students to go on a seasonal hunt. Give out a spotter sheet for the season. Students then go around the school grounds and try to find the signs of the season.
Indoor	Design an investigation.	Discuss with your class what colour the season is. How can we find out? Introduce a method for collecting data on the colour of the season. The class could choose colours to survey in nature and create a results table for them to tally on. See Table 9.19.
Outdoor	Collect data. Create graphs. Interpret data.	Get students to walk around your school grounds and tally the number of different colours they find in nature. They can create a graph using their data out of loose parts. For example, each stick represents a tally, and they are laid out in a line next to the colour cone. Discuss with your class which colour there was the most of. What colour is the season?

(Continued)

Table 9.18 (Continued)

Location	Learning objective	Activity
Outdoor	Experience and observe the changing seasons.	Lay a tarpaulin beneath a tree. Get your class to lie down on the tarp facing up. What can they see? Depending on the season, they will see less or more of the sky. Repeat this activity over the seasons to see how the tree changes in its life cycle. For example, watch as the leaves fall, as the tree skeleton of branches appears, as the buds burst, as the leaves grow, as the birds build nests, as the canopy closes out the sky. Students can sketch or take a photo from where they are lying. Relate these changes to the weather and the amount of sun reaching the ground. Then relate the amount of sun reaching the ground to the spring flowers growing and then dying again as the canopy closes.
Indoor	Create a seasons display.	As a class you can create a photo collage of the tree. Over the year you can repeat this activity and make three more collages for the other seasons.

Table 9.19 Colour of the season results table

Colour	Tally	Total
Yellow		
Red		
Green		

Other activities depend on the season. Life cycles can be investigated in spring and summer; see the animal's framework, Table 9.3, for ideas. Flowers can be investigated in summer; see the plant's framework, Table 9.1, for ideas. Seeds can be investigated in autumn; see the plant's framework for ideas, Table 9.1.

Going out regularly to see how the seasons change can be a continual aim for your outdoor learning session. Link the seasons with the weather by collecting data on the weather; see the weather and climate framework, Table 9.16.

Global climate change

Global climate change is such an important topic to teach pupils; however, it can seem so far removed from their lives. This framework, outlined in Table 9.20, is based on looking at how each student contributes to global climate change and what they can do to reduce their impact. There are also several science investigations you can undertake that show the implications of global climate change and how contributing to citizen science projects can provide ongoing monitoring data. It is important to empower the students to take action and not just outline the negatives of global climate change.

Table 9.20 Scheme of work for the indoor-outdoor framework for the topic of global climate change

Location	Learning objective	Activity
Indoor	Understand what global climate change is.	Teach the theory of global climate change.
Outdoor	Survey their school's impact on global climate change.	Take your class outside and undertake a survey of carbon sinks and sources. For example, trees, plants, and the soil are a sink for carbon. Cars, animals, buildings are a source of carbon. Discuss with your class if they think the school is absorbing more carbon or releasing more? Or is your school carbon neutral, when the two balance?
Indoor	Calculate their carbon footprint.	Teach the concept of a carbon footprint. Support your students to use online resources to calculate each of their carbon footprints for one year. Ask the class if they think the school grounds sinks (absorbs) all the carbon they emit in their daily lives? Get your students to calculate the size of tree it would take to store the amount of carbon in their carbon footprint using Table 9.21 on the carbon storage in trees.
Outdoor	Measure the carbon content of a tree.	Discuss with your class how they could measure the circumference of a tree and where to measure it. For example, measure at 1.3 meters off the ground or chest height. Ask your students to find a tree similar to the circumference they have read from the table that would store their emitted carbon. Students can calculate the age of the tree they have found to see how long it has taken for their tree to absorb all their carbon. For example, divide the circumference of the tree in cm by 2.5 to calculate the tree's age in years.
Indoor	Discuss data and impact of knowledge on their emotions. Research ways of reducing carbon use. Generate an enquiry question.	Discuss with your class how it felt to find out how long it took for a tree to absorb all the carbon released by their activities in one year? Each student can come up with a strategy to reduce their carbon footprint. Discuss if the school could reduce its carbon footprint. Students can research ways to reduce carbon use at the school. They can then use this research to come up with an enquiry question. For example, how much energy could the school generate from renewable sources? How can we reduce the use of carbon in the school?

(Continued)

Table 9.20 (Continued)

Location	Learning objective	Activity
Outdoor	Trail a method for their enquiry.	Support your students to explore possible methods for undertaking their enquiry into reducing carbon use by the school. E.g. Measure the size of the roof of the school and the size of solar panels and see how many will fit on your school. Measure the wind speed around the school grounds and look for a location for a wind turbine. Look at ways of switching off lights or reducing electricity usage. Look at ways of sharing cars to school. Plan to plant more trees in your school grounds.
Indoor	Write a method for their enquiry. Plan how they will collect their results. Create a results table.	Students can design a method to follow to answer their enquiry question; they could write instructions in a written method or a video instruction piece describing how they will collect their results. Students need to make a results table or find a base map to collect their data on.
Outdoor	Collect data for their enquiry.	Students then follow their method to collect the data in a results table or on a map, or take photos.
Indoor	Present their results.	Students present their results in their books or on paper. The aim is to show the answer to the enquiry question using an image. It could be a graph in books or using a computer program, a map coloured in with a key, or an annotated picture.
Indoor/ outdoor	Draw conclusions.	Students present their conclusions to the enquiry either in books or as a presentation. They need to answer their enquiry question using proof from their results.
Outdoor	Evaluate the investigation.	Students then use the space outside to describe what they did and how it generated reliable data and how their method could be improved.
Outdoor	Apply their conclusions. Write a persuasive letter.	Students can then use their enquiry data to write a letter to the head teacher or governing body with suggestions for reducing the carbon footprint of the school.
Indoor	Take part in a discussion.	Discuss with your class if they think global climate change is happening in their area. How do they know?
Outdoor	Use equipment to measure temperature.	Start to undertake a long-term study of the temperature in your school grounds. Every day, get students to measure the temperature outdoors. They can input the data into a spreadsheet. (You may have this from work in the weather and climate framework, Table 9.16.) Over time you will be able to use this data to see if global climate change is having an impact on your school grounds.

(Continued)

Table 9.20 (Continued)

Location	Learning objective	Activity
Outdoor	Take part in citizen science.	Get your class to undertake a citizen science project like The Woodland Trust's Nature's Calendar to monitor when key seasonal events happen in your school grounds. For example, bud burst and blackberry ripening.
Indoor	Research the impact of global climate change.	Get your students to look at the phenology calendar on Nature's Calendar website. See if there is another citizen science survey you could undertake in your school grounds. Look at the results on the website to see how the seasons have shifted forward over the last 100 years. Get your students to predict what the seasons will look like in the future.
Indoor	Research the impacts of global climate change.	Get your students to research about the consequences of global climate change on the poles. Once the ice melts, there will be less reflective surfaces on the Earth and more darker surfaces. Discuss what impact that will have on the world's climate.
Indoor	Create an investigation question.	Support your class to use the testing theories framework in chapter 6, to undertake an investigation into the impact of less ice on air temperature. For example, use an investigation question like, How does the colour of a surface affect the amount of solar energy it absorbs? Do dark surfaces absorb more heat? Do reflective surfaces keep the ground cold?
Outdoor	Undertake a preliminary experiment to test ideas for a method and skills in data collection.	Allow your students to experiment with methods for collecting the data to answer the question. For example, they could place a thermometer beneath different coloured paper, white versus black, place out in the sun, and see which one gets hotter. They could place an ice cube on different coloured paper outside and see which melts first. They could measure the temperature of different coloured surfaces outside.
Indoor	Write a method for the investigation.	Students could use their outdoor experience to write a method to follow. They need to include instructions for the location to use and how to use the equipment.
Outdoor	Undertake the data collection for their investigation.	Students follow their method to collect the data in a results table.
Indoor	Present their results.	Students need to use the most appropriate method to present their results. It could be a graph in books or using a computer program or as a presentation.

(Continued)

Table 9.20 (Continued)

Location	Learning objective	Activity
Indoor/ outdoor	Draw conclusions.	Students present their conclusions to the experiment either in books or as a presentation. Which colour surface absorbs the most heat? What does this mean if the ice is melting?
Outdoor	Present their finding.	Task your students to use their results from the enquiry and their research to make a presentation to the rest of their class on global climate change. What it is, how it is formed, how everyone is contributing, what will happen in the future, and how can we make it better.

Table 9.21 Carbon storage in trees table

Circumference of tree at chest height (cm)	Carbon stored in tree (Kg)
1.5	0.0045
2.5	0.02
5	0.115
10	0.7
20	4.5
30	13.5
40	41
50	53
75	155
100	334
125	604
150	982
175	1626.5
200	2110.5

Source: NRW.

Historical-based topics

You can visit the area within walking distance around your school to inspire understanding of the history and culture of your local area using the framework in Table 9.22. The old buildings and ruins located close to your school are a way to connect to the past of the area and vary from school to school. Use the Local history framework in chapter 8 to investigate any interesting building or sites. Table 9.22 is a more specific framework for using graveyards as a teaching tool.

My place – graveyard study

Table 9.22 Scheme of work for the indoor-outdoor framework for the topic of my place

Location	Learning objective	Activity
Indoor	Identify Interesting places in their local area. Read a map. Undertake research. Map a route.	With your class look on Google Earth and local maps to identify the location of your school and the boundaries of your local learning area, where you can walk in 20 minutes. Look in the area for any places of interest. For example, churches, old building, ruins, green spaces, or landforms like hills or rivers. Choose one of those places to investigate. Ask your class to undertake research into the place. How old is it? What is it used for? Who owns it? Identify a local church with a graveyard within walking distance from your school. Your pupils can use their mapping skills to plan a route to walk to it. Using the scale of the map the pupils can measure the distance to the churchyard.
Outdoor	Calculate their walking pace.	Measure a 100 m stretch and get your students to count the number of steps it takes each of them to walk the 100 m. Then time how long it takes them to walk 100 m. This is their walking pace. They can convert the pace for 100 m to a pace for a km. For example, if it took 2.5 minutes to walk 100 m it will take 25 minutes to walk a km.
Indoor	Calculate the time it will take to walk.	Use Google Earth to take a virtual journey from your school to the church following the route the class planned. Ask the class to estimate how long it will take them to get to the churchyard.
Outdoor	Follow a route on a map.	With your students leading the way, follow the planned route to the church using a map, measuring the time it takes. When you get there compare the time taken to the predicted time.
Outdoor	Collect data. Make observations.	Lead your class to investigate the graveyard by undertaking a graveyard study. For example, find the oldest grave. Find the oldest person to be buried there. Find any war graves or memorials. Look for local family names by collecting data, see results in Table 9.23. Undertake data collection of the number of deaths between certain dates.
Outdoor	Sketch images.	Get your class to draw pictures or take photos, or rubbings of interesting gravestones. Walk back to school.
Indoor	Analyse data. Create graphs of data. Look for trends in data. Undertake research.	Get your class to complete the results table by totalling the tallies. Ask your class to analyse the data looking for the most common name, most unusual name, any names of people in the school. They can draw graphs to represent their data.

(Continued)

Table 9.22 (Continued)

Location	Learning objective	Activity
		Ask them to look at their graphs of dates of death. Are there any trends? What is the reason behind any trends? Get your students to undertake research on those dates to see what happened. For example, after World War II there was a flu epidemic.
Indoor	Ask questions about an experience. Interview or listen to an expert.	Discuss with your class what questions they have about the visit to the graveyard. Invite a local historian into your school to ask them the questions your students have identified.
Indoor	Identify other places of interest.	After listening to the historian, look back at the other places of interest your class identified in your local area. Choose another location that interests your class to research and plan a visit to it.

Table 9.23 Graveyard study results table

Surname	Tally	Total

Date	Tally	Total
Before 1750		
1750-1799		
1800-1849		
1850-1899		
1900-1949		
1950-1999		
After 2000		

Back in time

When starting a topic based on a specific time in history you can use the inspirational framework to launch the topic, shown in Tables 9.24 and 9.25. Visit a location associated with that time or a museum with artefacts from that time. I have included potential visits for the topics which can be used for inspiration or for testing theories and concepts taught in the school and the school grounds. If possible, you could undertake two visits, one more abstract one at the beginning of the topic to inspire interest and questions and one at the end to build on your student's prior knowledge and put the learning into context.

The Romans

Table 9.24 Scheme of work for the indoor-outdoor framework for the topic of the Romans

Location	Learning objective	Activity
Outdoor Field trip	Inspire students, using an outdoor experience, to be curious and collect ideas.	Visit a site associated with the Romans. It may be a ruin of an amphitheatre, a Roman road, a Roman fort. Look at Historic UK website to see sites near your school in the UK. Take your class for a walk around the site and ask questions about the location. For example, how old is it? Who built it? What is it for? Take lots of photos.
Indoor	Undertake research.	Get your class to sort the questions generated by the visit. Then ask your class to research the site they visited and see if they can answer any of the questions they identified.
Indoor	Place the time of the Romans in relation to other times.	Teach about the time of the Romans and explore what it was like to be a Roman. Look at Roman villas and the mosaics within them.
Outdoor	Using knowledge of the past, design and create a model Roman villa.	Get your students to use loose parts such as sticks and leaves to design and build a model Roman villa. Ask them to include as many of the features as they can from that time, for example, porticos, pools, gardens, porches, pillars, and underfloor heating.
Outdoor	Design and create a mosaic.	Students can collect leaves of different colours or petals of different colours. Then use the different colours to design and create a mosaic for the floor of their Roman villa.
Outdoor	Present your design.	Allow students to present their model Roman villa to the rest of the class explaining the features.
Indoor/ Outdoor	Research Roman pottery. Create a Roman pot.	Get your students to research the pottery of the Roman times, such as the amphora used for storing wine and olive oil. Ask your students to make some model Roman pottery. They can decorate it with textures or stories from the Roman times. They can collect items from outside to make imprints in the clay.
Indoor	Understand what life was like as a Roman soldier.	Introduce life as a Roman soldier and what Roman soldiers wore. Get your students to design and make a full-size Roman shield.
Outdoor	Practice being a Roman legion.	Get the class to use their shields to practice marching in formation as a legion of Roman soldiers. Try battle manoeuvres like testudo (tortoise), with all the shields protecting the legion.

(Continued)

Table 9.24 (Continued)

Location	Learning objective	Activity
Indoor	Research Roman life. Plan a Roman feast. Take part in a Roman feast.	Get your class to research the food that the Romans ate and the clothes that they wore. They can then use this information to plan a Roman feast. What would they eat and wear? Students can then invite others to their Roman feast. Celebrate all that is Roman with a feast with everyone dressed in Roman clothes, eating Roman food, and having Roman entertainment.
Outdoor Field trip	Visit a Roman villa	Locate a Roman site, for example, a Roman villa, an amphitheatre, a Roman mosaic, a Roman fort, or a Roman display in a museum to visit. Allow your students to look at the actual Roman artefacts or structures and see how they differ from their models and imaginings of Roman life.
Indoor/ Outdoor	Display all their work and share with others. Write a museum guide.	Get the class to create their own Roman museum with all the work they have done and models they have made. Write a guide to the objects and displays for another class or their parents to visit. They could display their marching skills outside.

The Celts

Table 9.25 Scheme of work for the indoor-outdoor framework for the topic of the Celts

Location	Learning objective	Activity
Outdoor	Inspire students, using an outdoor experience, to be curious and collect ideas.	Visit a Celtic site. It could be a stone circle, a burial site, a Celtic cross, or a barrow. Take your pupils for a walk around the site and ask questions about the location. For example, how old is it? Who built it? What is it for? Take lots of photos.
Indoor	Undertake research.	Get your class to sort the questions generated by the visit. Then ask the class to research the site they visited and see if they can answer any of the questions they identified.
Indoor	Place the time of the Celts in relation to other times.	Teach about the time of the Celts and explore what it was like to be a Celt. Look at Celtic roundhouses and how they were constructed using wattle and daub.
Outdoor	Create a wattle and daub fence.	Ask your class to collect sticks and use them to weave a wattle fence; it can be a small section. Then they can mix up mud with water and daub it on the wattle fence to complete the wall. (Willow is bendy and good for the weaving.) Look at the student's fences and discuss if they would protect them from the weather.

(Continued)

Table 9.25 (Continued)

Location	Learning objective	Activity
Outdoor	Using knowledge of the past design and create a model Celtic roundhouse.	Remind your class of how the Celts lived. Show them pictures of Celtic roundhouses. Students can then use loose parts such as sticks and leaves to design and build a model Celtic roundhouse. They need to include as many of the features as they can from that time, for example, wattle and daub walls, and a thatched roof. See Figures 9.5 and 9.6.
Outdoor	Design the inside of the Celtic roundhouse.	Discuss what it would have been like inside the roundhouse and what the Celts would have had inside, for example, a fireplace, a weaving loom, beds.
Indoor	Research Celtic art designs.	Get your class to research the designs the Celts painted on the inside and outside of their roundhouses.
Outdoor	Paint the outside of the Celtic roundhouse.	Ask your students to paint the outside of their roundhouses and decorate them.
Outdoor	Present your design.	Students can then present their model Celtic roundhouse to the rest of the class explaining the features.
Indoor/Outdoor	Experience weaving.	Introduce weaving and how the Celts used looms to make material. Let the class use paper to try the process of weaving. Then get the class to collect forked sticks from outside. Support them to have a go at weaving wool on a stick. See Figure 9.7. Discuss how easy it was to weave.
Indoor	Understand the use of plants for dying.	Ask your students to research how the Celts made coloured cloth by dying with plants. They could look at the use of plants like woad to make blue dye.
Indoor/Outdoor	Try dying material with plants.	Students can experiment with making their own dyes using plants. For example, boiled beetroot, red cabbage, turmeric, stinging nettles, or spinach. While the dyes are warm add material to the dyes and wait for them to dye. Leave them out to dry. You can try buddle dying to make tie dye.
Outdoor	Experience fire lighting.	Introduce fire lighting using a flint and steel. Let your students have a go at lighting cotton wool with a striker, a modern-day flint and steel. **Make sure you are confident to light fires and have close supervision at all times.**

(Continued)

152 *Learning Indoors and Out in the Primary School*

Table 9.25 (Continued)

Location	Learning objective	Activity
Indoor	Consolidate learning. Write a first-person account of a day in the life of a Celt.	As a class reflect on what life would have been like in Celtic times. Discuss all the skills that they would need and all the jobs they would have to do. Ask your students to write a diary for a day as a Celtic child. What chores would they have had to do? What would they have eaten? Where would they have slept? How did they feel about their life?
Outdoor	Visit a Celtic living museum or a roundhouse.	Locate a well-preserved Celtic site, for example, a reconstructed Celtic roundhouse, Celtic display in a museum. Let your students explore the actual Celtic roundhouses and artefacts and see how they differ from their models and imaginings of Celtic life.

Figure 9.5 Photo of Celtic roundhouse model
Source: Photograph by the author.

Figure 9.6 Photo of wattle and daub fence
Source: Photograph by the author.

Figure 9.7 Photo of stick weaving
Source: Photograph by the author.

Castles

Table 9.26 uses the inspirational framework to introduce and teach the topic of castles. Look for examples of castles to visit close to your school so that your students have the whole immersive experience.

Table 9.26 Scheme of work for the indoor-outdoor framework for the topic of the castles

Location	Learning objective	Activity
Outdoor Field trip	Inspire students, using an outdoor experience, to be curious and collect ideas.	Take your class to visit a ruin of a castle. Let them walk around the site and ask questions about the location. For example, how old is it? Who built it? What is it for? Take lots of photos.
Indoor	Undertake research.	Get your class to sort the questions generated by the visit. Then ask the class to research the site they visited and see if they can answer any of the questions they identified.
Indoor	Place the medieval time in relation to other times.	Teach about the time the castle was built and the features and functions of the castle. Give your class pictures of castles and their defensive features to look at and examine.
Outdoor	Using knowledge of the past to design and create a model castle.	Get your students to use loose parts such as sticks, sand or mud, and leaves to design and build a model castle. Ask them to include as many of the features as they can from that time, for example, portcullis, moat, crenulations, drawbridge, castle walls.
Outdoor	Present their design.	Pupils can then present their model castle to the rest of the class explaining the features.
Indoor/ Outdoor	Research medieval weapons. Create a model siege weapon.	Get your class to research the weapons of the medieval times such as the trebuchet, ballista, and catapult. Task them to make some model siege weapons out of sticks, string, and elastic. They can use the design framework in chapter 6 to build a prototype for a larger model.
Indoor	Build a working siege machine.	Introduce the use of knots for tying sticks together using lashing. Students can then use larger sticks, such as bamboo to build a working model of their siege machine.
Outdoor	Investigate siege machines. Take measurements.	Let your students try out their siege machines by firing marshmallows. They can undertake an investigation into which type of siege machine fires the furthest.
Indoor	Instructional writing.	Get your students to use this experience to write instructions for building a siege machine and firing it.

(Continued)

Table 9.26 (Continued)

Location	Learning objective	Activity
Outdoor Field trip	Visit a castle.	Locate a castle to visit. Take your class around and look at the building and see how it differs from their models and imaginings of castle life.
Indoor	Research Medieval life. Plan a Medieval feast. Take part in a Medieval feast.	Get your students to research the food that they ate in Medieval times and the clothes they wore. Students can then plan a Medieval feast. What would they eat and wear? They can research the entertainment they had in the castle. For example, jousting, plays, and medieval games. They can invite others to their feast.

World War II

Table 9.27 uses the inspirational framework to teach about World War II. Most villages or towns have war memorials which can be used to inspire a more focused investigation into the war for your students.

Table 9.27 Scheme of work for the indoor-outdoor framework for the topic of World War II

Location	Learning objective	Activity
Outdoor Field visit	Inspire students, using an outdoor experience, to be curious and collect ideas. Collect data.	Visit a war memorial. Get your students to look at the ages of the people who died in the war. They could undertake some data collection on the men and women who died in the war and where they were from. Ask your students to come up with questions about the memorial to research back at school.
Indoor	Undertake research.	Get your class to sort the questions generated by the visit. Then ask the class to research to find the answers to the questions they had about the war. Discover the number of men who gave their lives in your area in the two World Wars.
Indoor	Place the World Wars in relation to other times.	Teach about the time of the World Wars and what life was like for those at home. Show your class pictures or air raid shelters.
Indoor/ Outdoor	Using knowledge of the past to design and create a model of an air raid shelter.	Students can use loose parts such as sticks, sand or mud, and cardboard to design and build a model air raid shelter. They need to include as many of the features as they can from that time, for example, dug into the ground, sandbags, vegetable patch. They can use the design framework in chapter 6 to build a prototype for a larger model.

(Continued)

Table 9.27 (Continued)

Location	Learning objective	Activity
Outdoor	Present their design.	Students then present their model air raid shelter to the rest of the class explaining the features.
Indoor	Research dig for victory. Create a vegetable patch. Plan to grow your own vegetables.	Ask students to research dig for victory and what the women and children had to do to get food such as rationing. Then ask them to design a vegetable patch for their class to grow their own food.
Outdoor	Grow your own vegetables.	If you have a vegetable patch, get your class to try to grow as many vegetables as you can in the area. You can use the opportunity to build maths skills when following the instructions on the back of the seed packet to plant them out at the right depth and distance apart.
Indoor	Investigate wartime recipes.	Task students with researching recipes from wartime. They can identify ingredients that you can forage from your school grounds such as acorns, stinging nettles, rosehips, blackberries, and apples.
Outdoor	Discover foraged food.	Take your class on a foraging walk around your school grounds to see what they could eat that is growing there. **Do not eat it, just observe.**
Indoor	Write a foraging guide to your school grounds.	Using the observations on their foraging walk your class can undertake research to make a foraging guide to your school grounds. For example, make fact files on plants you can use to eat like acorns for making acorn flour, dandelion roots for making coffee, stinging nettles for making cordage, conifer sap for making glue, rosehips for making cough medicine.
Indoor	Research VE Day. Plan a VE Day street party. Take part in a VE Day street party.	Teach about the end of the war and the VE Day street parties. Get your class to plan their own VE Day street party. They could use the recipes they discovered from that time to create food for a VE Day street party, for example, wild garlic scones, oat biscuits, blackberry shortbread, vinegar cake, and carrot cakes. If the vegetables from your veg patch are ready, harvest them and use them in your cooking. You could invite others to your party especially older relatives who remember the VE Day celebrations.

Table 9.28 Scheme of work for the indoor-outdoor framework for the topic of stories for early years – Year 2

Location	Learning objective	Activity
Outdoor	Listen to a story.	Find a location outside which is the backdrop to the story. For example, read *The Gruffalo* [2] in a woodland.
Indoor	Create a story map.	Create a story map of the story with your class. Then look at all the parts of the story.
Outdoor	Retell a story.	Take your class for a walk in your school grounds and find the locations mentioned in the story. For example, where would the foxes' log pile house be? Where would the owl's tree-top house be? Where would the Gruffalo live? When you get to each location, ask the class to retell that part of the story and lead the class to the next location.
Indoor	Make characters from the story.	Get your class to create characters from the story out of clay.
Outdoor	Use details from the story to build a home for the characters.	Take the classes characters outdoors and find the best location for their home. Ask your students to build a home for each of the characters.
Outdoor	Retell a story.	The class then takes their characters to the different homes and uses them to retell the story. Take photos of the characters in their homes.
Indoor	Collect ideas into chronological order.	Use the pictures of the homes to make a book of the Gruffalo using your school grounds and characters. Students can write sentences to describe the story.
Outdoor	Retell a story.	Get your class to share the new book with another class, reading each page in the right location.

Literacy-based topics

Stories – early years – Year 2

There are so many books for this age group which are set outdoors. Anyone can be used to build a scheme of work around the inspirational framework using Table 9.28. Weaving a scheme of work around a story set outdoors is a great way to embed outdoor learning into your teaching.

Stories – Year 3–6

Key stage 2 reading can also provide a vehicle for embedding outdoor learning as shown in Table 9.29. Books which are set outside or use the outdoors in interactive and engaging ways are the best ones to choose. The activities in Table 9.29 can be undertaken in the school grounds or on visits to the most appropriate location.

Table 9.29 Scheme of work for the indoor-outdoor framework for the topic of stories for Key stage 2 - Year 3-6

Location	Learning objective	Activity
Indoor	Read fluently and comprehend.	In class read *Kensuke's Kingdom* [3] up until Michael is shipwrecked and lands on the island.
Outdoor	Experience being alone and stranded.	Spread your class around the school grounds so they are not near each other. They can then read the section when Michael arrives alone on the island. Ask your students to write down what they see, hear, smell, and feel, both externally and internally. (This activity works even better on a beach.) Gather back together and ask your class to describe how it felt to be alone. Relate the experience to Michael's situation in the book.
Indoor	Read fluently and comprehend.	Read the next part of the story when Micheal walks up to survey the land.
Indoor	Draw a map.	Take your class for a walk up to a vantage point, such as the top of a hill. Ask them to imagine this is the island that Michael sees. Get them to draw a map of the island taking inspiration from what they can see. They can label anything that would be helpful for Michael to survive. For example, shelter, food, and water.
Indoor	Discuss priorities of survival.	Discuss what Michael's priorities should be to survive. Get your pupil in groups to discuss and complete the rules of survival, see Table 9.30. Ask them to decide what Michael must do first. You can use the design framework from chapter 6 to build a shelter.
Outdoor	Work as a group to design and build a shelter.	Provide resources for the class to build a shelter for Michael, in groups. For example, sticks, tarpaulins, and string,
Outdoor	Present your shelter. Evaluate your group work and shelter design.	Students then show the other groups their shelters. Explaining what they did. What problems they had and how they overcome them.
Indoor	Research survival. Design a water collecting device.	Get your class to research how much water a person needs to survive. Discuss how Michael is going to get drinking water? Task the class with designing a water collecting device.
Outdoor	Build a water collecting device.	Provide your class with the resources to build their water collecting devices. For example, plastic bottles, string. Groups then create their water collecting device and set them up to collect water overnight.

(Continued)

Table 9.29 (Continued)

Location	Learning objective	Activity
Outdoor	Take measurements. Improve designs.	After it has rained get your students to measure the amount of water the devices have collected. Have they collected enough water to survive? Get the groups to evaluate the designs and make any improvements.
Indoor	Investigate water collecting devices. Build a solar still.	Ask your students to research how to collect water. They could look at solar stills or getting water from plants. Using the research, ask your students to create a solar still outside. Set up a plastic bag over a plant and tie it closed. Leave the water collecting devices.
Outdoor	Take measurements.	After the solar stills have been in the sun for a few hours, get the students to measure the volume of water collected by this method. Is it enough water to survive? Show the class the water or condensation inside the plastic bag and explain how water evaporates out of leaves.
Indoor	Experiment with methods of cleaning water.	Discuss how clean water is and if it is safe to drink. Students can undertake a science investigation into different methods of filtering water and how effective they are. Allow your students to experiment with cleaning water using filters, sieves, and funnels.
Outdoor	Create a water filter. Test the water filter.	Introduce your class to natural filters such as moss and clay. Give out empty water filters. Ask pupils to create a natural water filter using materials they find outside. They can test their filter to see how clean it gets the water.
Indoor	Research wild food.	Get your class to research wild food and what food they could eat that is growing in your school grounds.
Outdoor	Use a guide or key to identify plants.	Take your class on a foraging walk and identify all the plants you could eat growing in your school grounds. Use an identification guide or key. **Do not eat anything.**
Indoor	Create a foraging guide to your school grounds.	Get your class to research the plants growing in your school grounds and write a foraging guide, for example, stinging nettles for soup, cleavers for salad, dandelion roots for a drink, honeysuckle flowers.
Outdoor	Recount part of the story. Persevere and be resilient.	Get your class to recount how Michael tries to make fire with some glass he found. On a sunny day, see if your class can set paper on fire using magnifying glasses. **Be aware of any fires through strict supervision.** Evaluate how they got on.

(Continued)

Table 9.29 (Continued)

Location	Learning objective	Activity
Indoors	Design a raft.	Discuss if they think Michael will be rescued from the island and if so, how? Get your class to design a raft to escape the island. You can use the design framework in chapter 6. They can make a model of their raft out of kebab sticks and elastic bands.
Outdoor	Build a raft. Test their raft.	Get your class to build a larger version of the raft to test. Place it in a bucket of water and investigate how stable it is. Let the class investigate how much weight it can carry. Discuss how Michael could steer it. Ask your students to add a sail.
Outdoor	Reflect on their achievements. Write an informative letter.	Finish reading the story outside and give your class a moment to reflect on the journey Michael had, and they have had, and the skills they have learnt along the way. What advice would they give Michael at the start of the story? Get your students to write a letter to Michael for him to receive when he has just arrived on the island. Give him some advice and courage.

Table 9.30 Rules of survival

You can survive only 3 seconds without **Thinking**
You can survive for only 3 minutes without **Air**
You can survive for only 3 hours without **Shelter (including clothes and warmth)**
You can survive for only 3 days without **Water**
You can survive for only 3 weeks without **Food**
You can survive for only 3 months without **Company**

Expressive art-based topics

Colours

Depending on the time of year the number of colours available outside varies. Aim to do this topic described using the inspirational framework in Table 9.31 when the summer flowers or spring greens are growing. You can bring in some flowers or plants if you don't have many growing in your school grounds, or if you don't want them all picked. Dandelions and buttercups make great yellow paint. Grass makes a powerful green. Leaves in autumn unfortunately do not produce the colours you see on them so avoid those. In autumn, you can use different coloured leaves to make an artist's palette or leaf rainbow.

Table 9.31 Scheme of work for the indoor-outdoor framework for the topic of colour

Location	Learning objective	Activity
Outdoor	Sort objects.	Take your class on a walk around your school grounds and look for different leaves. Get your students to collect them and sort them into piles. The class can choose the categories, or you can, for example, by shape, colour, or texture.
Indoor	Create a collage. Use rubbings to make different textures.	Get your class to look at the leaves they have collected outside. Ask them to make a pattern out of the leaves on paper. It could be a picture or a pattern. Next get them to make rubbings of the leaves using crayons. What do they notice about the patterns the leaves make?
Outdoor	Explore and look for different textures.	Take the paper outside and let the pupils find other textures using rubbings. For example, drain covers, tree bark, grooves in wood.
Indoor	Create artwork incorporating all the different textures.	Ask your class to look at the different textures they have made. Ask them to cut them into shapes of things the texture remind them of. For example, a scaly texture maybe a dinosaur, or a lined texture might be a zebra. As a class create a picture using all the cut outs of different textures. They could add outlines or colouring to complete the piece.
Outdoor	Collect colours.	Take your class on a colour hunt. They could collect flowers and plants of different colours.
Indoor	Discover natural paints. Use natural paint to create a picture.	Get your students to rub the coloured plants and flowers on paper to find out what coloured paint they make. Is it the colour they expected? They can use the natural paints to create a picture. They could create a seasonal picture. There is the possibility of undertaking the "what colour is the season?" investigation described in the season's framework Table 9.18 in this chapter.
Outdoor	Create a natural paintbrush.	Ask each student to find a stick for their paint brush handle which is the right size for their hand. Then they can collect items to make the bristles. They could use grass, or ferns, or moss. Attach them to the handle using elastic band or string. See Figure 9.8.
Indoor/ Outdoor	Experiment with natural paint brushes.	Get your students to experiment with the paint brush using paint to see what designs they make. They can experiment with different natural materials to compare the patterns and shapes they make.
Indoor	Research and explore dyed fabric.	Get your students to explore coloured fabrics and research dying.

(Continued)

162 Learning Indoors and Out in the Primary School

Table 9.31 (Continued)

Location	Learning objective	Activity
Outdoor	Dye fabric with plants.	Outside get your class to collect green plants and colourful flowers. Then place a piece of fabric, such as an old pillowcase, on a hard surface. Get the students to arrange the leaves and flowers on half of the fabric. Fold the other half of fabric on top. Next using a rubber mallet, the students can hit the material until the colours come through. **Make sure your pupils use two hands on the mallet and don't hold the fabric.** Let your students experiment with different plants and arrangements. They could make bunting or flags, or t-shirt designs.
Indoor/ Outdoor	Try dying material with plants.	Help your students make some dyes using plants. For example, boiled beetroot, red cabbage, turmeric, stinging nettles, or spinach. While the dyes are warm add material to the dyes and wait for them to change colour. They could add vinegar to the red cabbage dye to change its colour. Leave them out to dry. They could try buddle dying to make tie dye or experiment with different plants found outside.
Indoor	Create artwork using all your skills.	Get your class to combine all the creative skills they have acquired over the topic to create a piece of art.

Figure 9.8 Picture of natural paint brushes

Source: Photograph by the author.

Ideas of how to apply chapter content

- Identify a topic you teach in school which is covered in this chapter.
- Compare your planning for a topic to the indoor-outdoor integrated framework plan for the same topic. What are the main differences?
- How can you adjust your planning to make better use of the outdoor experiences?
- Add a preparatory and follow-up lesson to all your planned outdoor learning sessions.
- Review the impact of the outdoor learning experience when you have added the preparation and follow-up sessions.
- Integrate some of the topics and activities described in this chapter into your planning and experiment with integrating the indoor and outdoor learning.

References

1 Donaldson. J. (2016). Monkey puzzle. Published by Pan Macmillan.
2 Donaldson. J. (2017). The Gruffalo. Published by Pan Macmillan.
3 Morpurgo. M. (1999). Kensuke's kingdom. Published by Harper Collins.

10 Maintaining momentum

> **Aims of the chapter**
> - How to use the indoor-outdoor integrated framework for teaching new activities and topics.
>   - How to plan with the outdoors in mind
>   - How to find inspiration for future outdoor learning
>   - Trails
>   - Your school's stories
> - How to build on the indoor-outdoor integrated framework
>   - Field trips
>   - Developing long-term outdoor projects
>   - Monitoring sustainability projects
>   - Community involvement
>   - Developing progressive adventurous outdoor learning
> - How to build on the strategic aspect of the indoor-outdoor integrated framework
> - Provide case studies of best practice of outdoor learning in schools

"I've taught everything I can outside, what do I do now?" (Teachers who have been following ideas from an INSET on outdoor learning or have found activities in books or the internet, don't know where to go next to improve outdoor learning in their school.)

How to use the indoor-outdoor framework for teaching new topics

Once you have worked your way through the examples in Chapters 8 and 9 you may feel you have no more outdoor learning to draw on. However, in following any of the suggested ideas you have hopefully seen the adaptability of the indoor-outdoor integrated framework and how it works in practice. Maybe you couldn't follow it rigidly and went a bit rogue and found you could see potential for different outdoor opportunities or follow-up indoor activities. This is the next step.

There are a lot of outdoor learning activity ideas available online or in books if you do need inspiration. But hopefully, what I have left you with is a way to look at those outdoor activities and the indoor lessons you creatively plan and with support from the framework, the skills to weave the two into a meaningful system that makes the best use of the outdoor experience.

If you take one of the examples in Chapters 8 and 9 and relate it to the learning outcomes for your next topic, then you can develop a planning indoor-outdoor process that adapts to any topic you are teaching. There are very few topics you can't teach part of outside, and if you are struggling then focus on skills in specific subjects such as numeracy or science which lend themselves to practical application outside. If the topics are of no relevance outdoors, I can't think of an example, then maybe the topic is not very meaningful to your students. If you can't apply the learning to real life, then why are you teaching it?

How to plan with the outdoors in mind

Planning with the outdoors in mind is the best way to ensure outdoor learning is meaningful and embedded.

There are two ways to do this:

1 Have a map of your school grounds alongside you as you are planning.
   This will help you identify the best place to teach each objective. Also, look at the school's wider area to include visits to the local learning area and further afield in your planning.
2 Plan outside.
   Take your laptop or planning sheet outside. Then, when you are struggling for inspiration, the outdoors will deliver. I walk around the outdoor space where I teach with the learning objectives in mind and look for ways the outdoors links or can be used to teach content or skills.

Change the view

I also recommend walking around the area where you are going to teach, your school grounds or another site, and put on your maths eyes, or science eyes, and just identify as many curriculum opportunities as you can see within that space. This will provide you with outdoor links to the curriculum for later in your planning.

In your school there will always be an expert in being outdoors or outdoor learning. Share ideas with them and see if you can adapt their ideas to your year group and build a bank of adaptable ideas. A lot of outdoor activities can be adapted to many different topics.

For example, I have made model round houses for the Celts, Roman temples, Tudor houses, castles, and earthquake-proof houses. These are all in essence the same activity, but the learning objective is to use knowledge of the building from that time in history to build a model, so the outcomes are very different structures. When undertaking outdoor learning sessions which work well, consider how they could be adapted for a different topic or cohort in the future.

How to find inspiration for future outdoor learning

Trails

There is one activity which provides an endless potential for outdoor learning across the subjects, and that is the use of trails.

Trails can be a good extension activity and assessment activity. Trails should not require you to undertake a lot of setting up, although this is one possibility. I like to use whatever is permanently outside. Trails are not something you can download or borrow from someone else's setting; they need to be adapted or made for your school grounds.

A good place to start is developing a maths trail. Survey what you see outside and identify all the potential maths you can. For example, 2D shapes of the windows and bricks, 3D shapes of the outdoor classroom or planters, angles of the branches to the tree trunk, symmetry of the doors, measuring lengths of the playground lines, volume of the sheds, time to walk the path, etc.

Then start to look deeper at potential applied maths concepts you could test. For example, what is the area of the playground, how high is the tree, estimate the number of bricks in the wall, and calculate the number of tyres in the car park.

Progressing on from there you can introduce complex problem-solving questions which require several mathematical skills. For example, if the tree in the field fell, would it hit the school building? How much energy can we generate from the school roof? Where is the best place to erect a wind turbine? How much paint do we need to repaint the school? How much would it cost to fence in the playground?

Depending on the age group, maths trails can be used to test one concept, e.g. measuring skills or geometry, or can be used to show the interconnectedness of different maths skills in a practical way. If you want to combine maths and map-reading skills, then you can create a map with grid references and then use the answers to the questions to locate the next coordinate. But always be mindful that you are testing the application of skills, and the accuracy of the answer is not the important thing. So, when the pupils all come back with different answers to the height of the tree, you don't take out the right answer and mark them; you ask them **how** they got to that answer and assess the methods they used to get to their answer. This also means that you do not need to have the answers to the maths questions for them to undertake a meaningful trail.

Trails can also be used in other subjects too. Looking for adjectives or metaphors, or characters for a story. Going on a simile hunt or alliteration hunt can all be ways to collect inspiration from the outdoors.

Your school's stories

Build on the Stories framework in Chapter 9 by creating a whole library of your school's version of traditional tales or popular stories. Some great books to use are *Stick Man* by Julia Donaldson [1], *We're Going on a Bear Hunt* by Micheal Rosen [2], *The Explorer* by Katherine

Rundell [3], and *Kensuke's Kingdom* by Michael Morpurgo [4]. Also, traditional tales like the Gingerbread Man, Little Red Hen, and the Enormous Turnip.

Weaving outdoor learning around stories can ensure the continued use of indoor-outdoor teaching if the books are set outside.

In early years, Stick Man is a great way to introduce the school grounds to the pupils and imagine what would happen to Stick Man in your school grounds. Retelling classic stories in your school grounds can be a useful way of making them more meaningful and relatable to your students as well as gaining skills in retelling and creativity.

How to build on the indoor-outdoor integrated framework

Once your school has developed the ethos of the strategic indoor-outdoor integrated framework, then consider introducing some more adventurous and longer-term projects. This can increase the use of outdoor learning across the school and broaden its scope.

Field trips

When planning your topics and curriculum content, one aspect of outdoor learning that tends to be an afterthought is field trips. Most schools outsource these to outdoor learning providers which works if the provider is aware of your classes' requirements.

The next step is to develop these opportunities, so they weave better into the indoor teaching and outdoor learning undertaken in the school grounds.

Feeling confident to run your own field trip may take some training in aspects of outdoor learning such as risk assessing and risk management. If this is a possibility for your school, then developing bespoke field trips that meet your classes' needs will improve your pupil's field work experiences. If this is something you do not feel confident to do yet, then create a good relationship with any providers you use. Communicate the requirements of the school and each class, and ask for specific outcomes to be covered.

Where possible meet the provider face to face in the field so they can show you the planned activities, and you can identify any additional needs of your pupils or differentiation that may be required with the activities. Then prior to the field trip such issues can be prepared for so that all pupils can access the activity and get the most out of the experience. Also look for the Learning Outside the Classroom Quality Badge with any provider as this will ensure quality of risk management and educational provision.

Look for ways to work with any outdoor learning providers to improve the service they offer to meet your pupils' needs.

Case study of integrated field trips at Dan Y Coed autistic school

Dan Y Coed school, a specialist school and home for children with autism and learning disabilities based in Swansea, South Wales, undertook a field trip to St Fagan's National Museum of History. When the students arrived at the site, many pupils were overwhelmed by how different the place was from their school and could not engage or, in some cases, even enter the museum. The museum seeing the issues the school was having in accessing their site approached the teacher and ascertained what the barriers were for the pupils.

Based on that conversation, the museum worked with Dan Y Coed staff to develop a welcome video story for schools visiting the museum to watch to prepare them for their visit. They also created visual resources with symbols to facilitate the student's needs from the school. Now the museum has become much more accessible for students with special needs and a productive relationship has developed between the school and the museum.

There is research by Ballantyne and Packer [5] that has found that novel experiences, such as a first trip to a location, can actually make pupils fearful and this can be a barrier to students having a positive experience on their first visit to a place. However, the research also found that pupils who had done pre-visit activities at school were looking forward to their visit more than those who had not. [5] Also, on the second visit pupils were much less fearful so could access much more learning from a repeat visit. If you do not have access to a lot of different locations for field trips, then consider repeat visits and creating a progression framework for skills or curriculum content for that location.

If you are not lucky enough to have transport to go on regular field trips, then you can still go on a walking field trip to places in your local learning area. Take time to explore the area you can walk to safely from your school and use Google Earth to see what habitats and spaces are local to your school. You could create a progression map for activities or skills developed through visiting the same location regularly and look for ways to embed regular use of the local learning area across the school.

Case study of repeat site visits at Casllwchwr primary school, Estuary education

Casllwchwr school is a primary school in Swansea, South Wales,

After lockdown, Casllwchwr wanted to improve their outdoor learning provision to increase wellbeing in their students. The school grounds were used but also the Loughor estuary which was within walking distance, flanked with a beautiful woodland Machynys beach and Parc Williams. The school's "Estuary Education" outdoor learning days were planned for years 2-6.

"We want to foster a love of the outdoors; developing pupils' stamina, resilience, collaboration, practical skills, risk management, natural knowledge and life skills, and are lucky enough to have the most wonderful resource on our doorstep."

Now Estuary Education is integrated and planned into the school day and repeat visits to the area are used to develop a range of skills across all subject areas.

Developing long-term outdoor projects

Outdoor learning projects can quite easily expand beyond the term a topic is being taught in. School grounds development is one way to engage your pupils in outdoor learning which will have a lasting impact on the school. This is a great legacy project for year 6 that they can revisit once they have left the school.

You could design a peace mala or reflection garden, an allotment area, plant a new woodland, a wildflower meadow, or dig a pond.

The design process provides opportunities for the pupils to survey the opinions of other students, make measurements, research costings, and budget. Then the actual building requires technical skills such as tool use, planting, and consideration of the microclimate and trampling.

Once the area has been developed there will be upkeep, so consider this in any development. I have visited so many schools who have large overgrown pond which they cannot access or use for outdoor learning because they could not maintain it.

Alongside the creation of the project consider what ongoing curriculum teaching the area will provide in the future.

Long-term projects like school grounds development need a longer-term planning view and integration into grounds maintenance plans.

Case study of integrated school grounds development, Knelston Primary school

Knelston Primary School is a small rural school in Gower in Swansea, South Wales.

In Knelston Primary, the year 6s used the design process to develop their outdoor area as an outdoor maths area. The teacher set a design brief.

The product must:

- Be located in the class outdoor area and not impede movement around the area.
- Have several different uses so that it can be used to experiment with several STEM activities.
- Be accessible and suitable for all members of the class to learn through.
- Last a long time.
- Be functional – can be used repeatedly.
- Fun and interesting to learn through.
- Value for money.

In groups the students designed different games and activities to improve the outdoor area. They presented their ideas, and the rest of the class ranked them using the design brief as an assessment tool. The winning designs were then built by the whole class and used for future outdoor learning sessions.

The project took a term with one session a week. The main issue they met was the pupil's lack of woodworking skills to be able to build something that would last. But they still managed to build a large marble run out of guttering, a bird watching station and a treasure box game. If they had used a longer-term approach maybe over the years, they could have integrated the practical skills required in the previous years so that once students got to year 6, they had the skills to deliver their designs.

Growing projects

The use of allotments, vegetable patches, and polytunnels has the potential for meeting many outdoor learning objectives. However, when growing areas are established, just remember that the ongoing upkeep needs to be done by someone. Gardening clubs are very useful in lunchtime or after school. Or inviting in a keen gardener, such as parent, governor, or grandparent, to take responsibility in the holidays.

Growing areas provide an opportunity for enterprise in schools. If you give each student a 1 m² patch to develop and give them a small budget, say £1, to cultivate it, then they can be responsible over the year to buy seeds, plant the seeds, weed and harvest, and then sell their produce, or make something to sell out of the produce. They can see how much money can be made and use the profits to improve their harvest the next year. Maintaining a small patch is much more sustainable than having a whole raised bed to deal with.

Case study of school grounds development at Penyrheol primary tree planting and growing project

Penyrheol Primary is an urban school in Swansea, South Wales.

Penyrheol Primary has provided first-hand experiences of nurturing nature alongside developing biodiversity in their school grounds. The pupils have planted over 600 trees including a locally sourced heritage orchard. This hands-on experience was part of the Queen's Green Canopy stewardship project. The Queen actually sent a personal message of recognition to the children.

The school grounds have been developed to promote learning about biology, ecology, and the importance of sustainability and putting the Sustainable Development Goals into practice.

The impact of these outdoor learning activities and tree planting initiatives has been profound. Children use numeracy skills such as estimating, quantity, spatial awareness, and measurements whilst being involved within an extensive range of garden activities.

Children use literacy skills to talk about their gardening journey and develop narratives to generate new ideas for growing projects.

Children are curious and captivated after gaining authentic knowledge and real science of soil, botany, and cultivation for life-long learning for a changing climate.

> Children are developing the knowledge of growing food using permaculture science and recognise the need to protect food and nature for a wide variety of climate conditions. Children thrive in open-air spaces, freedom of movement enriches conversations, enhances wellbeing, and enables pupils to increase their attentiveness in class.
>
> Food grown organically with the care of pupils is distributed and shared with the whole school; pupils are proud of their produce and delight in sharing.

Monitoring sustainability projects

Other ongoing projects linked to weather monitoring outlined in Chapter 4 on incidental outdoor learning, include surveying the sustainability of your school.

This can include monitoring:

- Pollinators,
- Decomposers such as worms,
- The number of species of flowering plants,
- Carbon content and sequestration by trees,
- The amount of soil erosion on a path or in the playing field's goals.

This could be a job for an eco-club or integrated into a sustainability topic.

There are lots of science investigations that could be undertaken to inform any development aimed at improving the sustainability of your school grounds.

- Which colour flowers do pollinators prefer?
- How much carbon is your school grounds absorbing?
- Can you make your school carbon zero?
- Do mini beast hotels increase the number of mini beasts?
- How much water could you collect from the rain in a water butt?

Long-term data sets on when trees or hedges were planted are useful for data analysis and presentation over time. There are also lots of citizen science projects available that your students can contribute to, looking at how the seasons and quality of the environment are changing. The Woodland Trust's Nature's Calendar is a great resource for collecting meaningful data that contributes to a national database of evidence.

Local community opportunities

There may be organisations, businesses, or universities who have projects they can share with your school. This will depend on where your school is and how you connect with your stakeholders. A good place to start is to send out questionnaires to all your stakeholders to find out who they have links with and how you can develop those links.

Survey your pupil's parents, grandparents, staff, including kitchen and caretaking, and governors. If you find an expertise or interest, then approach them and see if they could provide an opportunity to link with the school. It could be that they take part in a topic launch day or run a workshop or after-school club. You may be able to visit their organisation or get people power for school grounds development. Look at each potential link and see how it can broaden the opportunities for your pupils.

Case study of local community opportunities at Knelston Primary for launch days

Knelston primary is a small rural school in Gower in Swansea, South Wales.

Through a questionnaire to pupil's parents and talking to staff and governors, Knelston Primary School have developed a database of local businesses who are eager to engage with the school.

At the start of each topic, they deliver a launch day. This provides an opportunity for the pupils to meet and listen to experts from outside the school to find inspiration for the future planning of the topic.

For example, for the topic of "Travel" they invited a local tour provider, a safari boat operator, an overseas expedition leader, a tropical butterfly collector, and the coast-guard to their launch day at the start of the topic. Each of these businesspeople provided a hands-on experience for the pupils, to inspire them to ask questions on the topic of travel. Through the rest of the term the planning incorporated opportunities for pupils to answer these questions through the topic's content.

Case study of schools visiting other schools with Knelston Primary and Dan Y Graig Primary School

Knelston Primary is a small rural school in Gower in Swansea, South Wales.

Dan Y Graig is a multicultural inner- city urban school in East Swansea, South Wales

Knelston Primary's year 4s were studying the topic of senses and undertook a series of outdoor learning sessions in their school grounds linked to the indoor work on the five senses. They undertook a blind fold walk, played bat and moth, a listening game, went on a texture hunt with foil, created a sound map, went on a smell hunt, and met a tree.

At the end of the topic as their celebration of all they had learnt they invited an inner-city school to visit their school grounds. The year 4s planned, resourced, and then led their favourite outdoor learning sessions on the senses for the year 4 class from Dan Y Graig Primary School. The experiences were talked about by pupils and staff for years and the opportunities for cultural exchange and leadership by the year 4s could not have been achieved within the school environment without this link.

Developing links with the community surrounding your school or linking up with another school or community further afield is the next step to developing your school's outdoor learning experiences. It is useful to find a school with differing environments than your own so you can share your school's uniqueness and discuss different challenges and how you have overcome them. The cultural exchange of ideas is also valuable if the two schools differ significantly.

Overseas case study of Penyrheol Primary and The Inglés Center (The English Centre), Cádiz, Spain.

The Inglés Center is a privately owned mixed family school which teaches the National Curriculum and International Curriculum to Spanish children from 2-year-olds to 18-year-olds in Cadiz, Southern Spain.

The head teacher at Penyrheol Primary School discovered a local link to a school in Cadiz, Spain. This school has a residential centre in Caswell, Swansea where they were planning to regularly bring year 6 students for a cultural exchange to Wales. For the last three years two classes from The Inglés Center have shared a week of experiences with the students of Penyrheol Primary School. This has included going on joint field trips to the beach, forest school session in the school grounds, surfing lessons together and social events. The Inglés Center now visits Caswell on two occasions and links with another school to undertake further field trips visiting a river.

This year the pupils of Penyrheol Primary fund raised and acquired funding for 12 of the year 6s and four teachers to travel to Spain and visit The Inglés Centre.

Developing progressive adventurous outdoor learning

Another aspect of outdoor learning which can be better developed in schools is the adventurous activity offer. Most schools provide one opportunity in year 6 for pupils to undertake adventurous activities such as water sports, climbing, and caving, while on residentials. Just like residential progression, providing more opportunities for adventurous activities throughout the school will improve skills and ensure progression in those skills.

Adventurous activity case study secondary school – Olchfa School and The Inglés Center Cádiz, Spain

Olchfa school is a large secondary comprehensive school in West Swansea.

The Inglés Center is a privately owned mixed family school in Cadiz, Spain.

Building on the links made through Penyrheol Primary, the head of activities at The English Centre contacted me to see if I could create an activity week for their year 8s integrating adventurous activities such as climbing, hiking, and coasteering with curriculum-based outdoor learning. They also linked up with a secondary school in

Swansea, Olchfa school, to share the experience with them and use the subject leads from the school to plan and run the field work.

Together we designed a series of sessions which combined a long shore drift study with climbing, coasteering with flora and fauna study, and hiking with self-development. The whole week was based around a group project on their perception of Wales, which the students then presented to me. The focus was on personal development and connecting with the landscape.

I was really impressed with the standard of the presentations and the different topics the groups chose to concentrate on. It was clear that they had developed a deeper understanding of the places they had visited then they would have done through a wholly activity-based week.

The Inglés Center has now developed multiple opportunities for their students to visit Wales.

Year 6 pupils undertake the Pioneers programme described above including field trips and visiting two primary schools.
Year 7 pupils return to Wales on a choir tour and have cultural activities and perform together with pupils from Penyrheol Primary.
Year 8 pupils go on the Adventurer programme with Olchfa school.

Other physical skills development required by pupils can also be included in outdoor learning, for example, cycling. Most schools undertake cycling proficiency training but that is all with limited progression towards that end. Some early years are now introducing balance bikes, but this does not progress to cycling skills on two-wheel bikes in older years groups.

Case study of Penyrheol primary active transport – bikes

Penyrheol primary is located in a residential area of Gorseinon town in Swansea with limited parking. The school undertook a survey of their pupil's journeys to school and found the majority were not using active transport, even though many were living locally. To promote a healthier lifestyle, reduce congestion outside the school and instill a culture of active travel to school, they collaborated with Sustrans and Safer Streets Wales. The aim was to make active transport an attractive, safe, and viable option for pupils and their families.

Their approach included providing access to balance bikes during curriculum time, ensuring that upon leaving reception class, all pupils possessed the skills to ride a two-wheel bike. The program also included infrastructure support such as secure bike storage, promoting road safety awareness, and Cycling Proficiency training. The school also planned engaging activities that integrate active travel into the daily routine of physical activity of the children.

> The impact on the pupils has been improved mood, concentration, and overall well-being as well as increased physical activity at break and lunch times when classes have access to the school bikes and a dedicated part of the playground, allowing them to develop their cycling skills safely.
>
> The initiative also links to the school's Sustainable Development Goals contributing to environmental sustainability by reducing vehicular congestion and emissions around school premises.
>
> The staff have observed enhanced pupil behaviour, engagement, and readiness for learning. There is a noticeable decrease in local traffic congestion during drop-off and pick-up times, leading to safer and more pleasant school surroundings
>
> In the future, the school plans to undertake trips from the school site using the bikes and the local cycle trail network.

How to build on the strategic indoor-outdoor integrated framework

In the UK the Council for Learning Outside the Classroom (CLOtC) provides a Quality Mark for schools.

"The LOtC Mark is a quality assurance scheme that supports and celebrates schools who provide meaningful experiences beyond the classroom across the whole curriculum, indoors and out, on and off-site" [6].

Learning Beyond is their "programme of support for teachers to develop a culture of learning beyond the classroom to ensure students thrive and succeed." This award is for schools who are undertaking an integrated use of learning beyond the classroom to apply for. It is not restricted to being outdoors but includes visits to anywhere that isn't your school and visitors coming to your school. Broadening the scope of the outdoor learning in your school to include all learning beyond the classroom is an effective way to build on the progress you have made.

The Learning Beyond tracker that is used in assessing the Quality Mark is a perfect next step to assess the progress you have made and to have that achievement recognised. It can also be used by schools who are not yet undertaking an integrated approach to outdoor learning but want to, as it provides a supportive framework for looking at all the school's systems and identifies what to include when embedding learning beyond the classroom. You can also get mentoring through the CLOtC to help you complete this award or once you have received the gold Mark become a mentor yourself.

Monitoring progress and impact

It is also important to maintain a strategic overview of outdoor learning across the school by continuing to monitor the progression and impact of the outdoor learning. Make sure that outdoor learning continues to be embedded in whole school evaluation and keep it at the forefront of any future developments. Through this monitoring you can collect data on what strategies or activities are having the greatest impact on pupils. You then may

176 *Learning Indoors and Out in the Primary School*

wish to focus on a specific aspect of outdoor learning which would be of advantage to your pupils.

If you ask of any new initiative,

"How can outdoor learning be used to facilitate this?"

Then you may find some excellent ways to further develop your use of the outdoors.

It is also important from the strategic side to monitor the trips your school is engaging in and keep track of how well they meet your pupil's needs. Involve all staff in the evaluation of all trips and visits, and look for ways of making better use of available trips and visits in the future.

Case study of monitoring King's Edward VI Norton School for Boys

King Edward VI Norton School for Boys in Birmingham, England.

King's Norton Boys' School has created an outdoor learning folder for each subject on their school's online filing system. All staff can access and upload their own lesson plans to share ideas. Alongside the lesson plans there is a system for adding comments on how it worked for the age group and how they might improve it so other teachers could build a better resource. The same was undertaken for school visits, speakers, and residentials. A spreadsheet of outdoor learning opportunities is shared with staff containing information on what topics were taught, how it met the learning objectives, and how pupils had engaged with the experience. This was updated after every trip and so was a dynamic resource for all staff to use. The spreadsheet was monitored by the outdoor learning coordinator to review the outdoor learning taking place across the school.

To embed the indoor-outdoor integrated framework, a spreadsheet of outdoor learning opportunities like this case study could be expanded to explain how the outdoor learning built on the indoor learning and what future indoor and outdoor learning was undertaken as a result of the experience to consolidate it or assess its impact.

Resources for addressing training needs

An assessment of outdoor learning activity and practice in schools undertaken by O'Donnell et al. in 2006 [7] identified that "teacher confidence was one of the key factors underpinning the extent of provision." As well as the "belief in senior leadership support" as having a positive influence on the extent of outdoor learning taking place in schools. Therefore, creating and fostering a supportive culture for outdoor learning in your school is key. Other research from NAEE [8] identified "prioritising of teacher training and professional development so all educators have knowledge, skills and confidence to deliver high-quality experiences" was recommended. So, implementing an ongoing program of professional training and support is important to maintain confidence in staff and progress in the outdoor learning being undertaken by staff across the school.

As confidence in staff increases then you can reduce the amount of guidance you are providing the teaching staff to undertake outdoor learning using fading. As the staff get more confident in their abilities to teach outside your role will move to facilitating their further development by helping them identify any training needs or resource requirements to help them develop. This could be by a shift from creating outdoor ideas and activities for teachers, to asking them to implement interventions for certain students or classes. This could provide a research project for staff to run into what outdoor learning has the greatest impact on your pupils. Continue to challenge your staff to come up with more exciting and adventurous outdoor activity ideas by celebrating the outdoor learning that is taking place in staff performance management.

Going forward buddy up new staff with confident outdoor learning teachers and support them to monitor and share best practice with others. As an outdoor learning coordinator your aim should be for every member of staff to have distributed leadership and responsibility in providing integrated outdoor learning, so it is fully embedded. Make sure you monitor this progress and celebrate it with all stakeholders. Continuous vigilance and congruence with the aims of your outdoor learning policy with keep you on the path to continued improvement in your outdoor learning provision.

Case study of a journey to indoor-outdoor teaching at Knelston Primary School

I have been working with Knelston Primary School for over 18 years. Before I started teaching in the school the Early Years leader had undertaken some forest school training and was the only member of staff undertaking any outdoor learning. In fact, the reason I chose the school for my son was because I felt I could improve his opportunities to undertake outdoor learning by being involved in the school.

When I first started teaching there, I was teaching weekly forest school sessions for my son's class in Nursery. Over time, as my son moved up the school, I taught every year group for one session a week. Though it was called forest school it was all curriculum-based and linked to their topic but not necessarily their in-class work, as there was no collaboration with the class teacher; the teachers would leave me with the class and a teaching assistant and get on with some other work inside.

Over 18 years and four head teachers the situation in the school in terms of outdoor learning has totally changed. The biggest shift has been in mindset. When I started all the teachers would consider what I was doing was enough outdoor learning to "tick that box" and were grateful because then they didn't have to do it.

Over the last few years, I have pushed the school to embrace the indoor-outdoor integrated framework for teaching, which has worked excellently in parallel with the roll out of the Curriculum for Wales. My role has been to provide training to all the staff, increase their confidence by team teaching and demonstrating best practice with all the teachers, helping with launch days and providing a sounding board for outdoor learning ideas. The team teaching was a perfect way for the class teachers

> to link the indoor work to the outdoor session I was leading, and the teachers would always say that they could see how to follow the session up in class and progress the learning.
>
> Now I am very pleased to say that the school does not need me to teach anymore and that was my aim, to remove their dependence on me as an external outdoor learning practitioner. As a governor, I speak to the pupils and hear about the outdoor learning the teachers are providing, and I love talking to the staff who enthusiastically share what they have done with their topics to integrate the indoor and outdoor teaching and learning. My proudest moment was being on the appointment panel for the latest headteacher whose vision for the school was to make it a centre for excellence for outdoor learning.
>
> The whole school undertakes more outdoor learning than they have ever done and not only are the sessions regular and frequent providing a broad and deep outdoor learning experience, but they link into all the indoor teaching and learning that takes place. I just need to convince the early years staff to run a residential!

In summary, progression in the use of outdoor learning in your school can be undertaken through.

- An increase in the time pupils spend outside.
- Development of more adventurous use of the outdoors.
- Inclusion of more complex outdoor learning challenges.
- Building in progression from the school grounds to further outdoor learning opportunities.
- Use of outdoors in more aspects of the school such as whole school celebrations, health and wellbeing, or other targeted interventions.
- Integrating longer-term projects such as school grounds development.
- Linking up with other members of the community.
- Sharing your school grounds and outdoor learning with other schools.
- Mentoring your staff to continue to grow their outdoor learning offer through training.

Ideas of how to apply chapter content

- Evaluate your school's use of the indoor-outdoor integrated framework.
    - What is working and what is not?
    - How could you build on your successes and improve the areas that need it?
- Experiment with the suggested planning methods such as planning outside.
- Try to develop a number of different trails so that you can add them to your outdoor learning experiences.
- Identify any training needs you have to progress your skills in outdoor learning.
- Identify some longer-term projects for your school.

References

1. Donaldson, J. (2008). Stick man. Scholastic.
2. Rosen, M. (1989). We're going on a bear hunt. Walker Books.
3. Rundell, K. (2017). The explorer. Bloomsbury.
4. Morpurgo, M. (1999). Kensuke's kingdom. Harper Collins.
5. Ballantyne, R., & Packer, J. (2002). Nature-based excursions: school students' perceptions of learning in natural environments. *Journal of International Research in Geographical and Environmental Education, 11*, 218–236.
6. Council for Learning Outside the Classroom (CLOtC). Helping you take your teaching beyond the classroom. Council for Learning Outside the Classroom (CLOtC). https://www.lotc.org.uk
7. O'Donnell, L., Morris M., and Wilson R. (2006). Education outside the classroom: An assessment of activity and practice in schools and local authorities. National Foundation for Educational Research and Department for Education and Skills. https://dera.ioe.ac.uk/id/eprint/6550/1/RR803.pdf
8. NAEE. (2024). Engaging the Next Generation. The state of environmental, sustainability and climate education in UK schools and effective practice in the classroom. National Association for Environmental Education. https://naee.org.uk/wp-content/uploads/2024/11/NAEE-Report-Engaging-the-Next-Generation.pdf

Final thoughts

Impacting education

I hope that this book has taken you on an inspirational journey and opened your eyes to the endless possibilities of strategically integrating indoor and outdoor learning.

Strategically embedding a whole school approach to outdoor learning takes time and is professional development for your school. So don't give up and bring as many staff members as you can along with you. The impact on the school, its staff, and pupils, I hope, will far exceed any expectations you have. The possibility is there, you just have to grab it. But if we don't embrace the full potential the outdoors provides, then we are letting the students down, especially the ones who are struggling indoors.

In this age with so many mental health problems, nature disconnection, and global emergencies, we need a future workforce that values the outdoors and sees its role in their own personal development. Schools can make that difference, not in the content of the curriculum but in the experiences they create, the memorable moments in their children's lives.

If you think back to your best school memory, I wonder, do you remember the classroom or the experience? Was it indoors or outdoors? Let's make some impactful memories for our children!

Appendix

Whole school outdoor learning audit

Outdoor learning provision:

1. How much outdoor learning does each class do?
2. What outdoor learning does each class do?
3. Where does the outdoor learning take place?
4. In terms of staff confidence what level are the staff at in each class? See spectrum of outdoor learning.
5. What barriers do staff have to progressing to undertake further outdoor learning?
6. What support do the staff need to progress outdoor learning?
7. Is the outdoor learning linked to in-school teaching for each class?
8. Are outdoor sessions built upon in follow-up class sessions?
9. When is outdoor learning considered in the planning process?
10. Do you think the school and senior leaders value outdoor learning?

Strategic outdoor learning:

1. Is there an outdoor learning coordinator?
2. Have you surveyed the school staff to audit the outdoor learning provision?
3. What barriers to outdoor learning are procedural or policy led? Lack of staff, evidence gathering, expectation by senior leaders.
4. What barriers to outdoor learning are confidence based?
5. What support do staff need to progress outdoor learning? Who is the best person to provide this support? Is it training, resources, or mentoring?
6. What structures are missing in the school to support outdoor learning? Storage for waterproofs, local learning area permission forms, list of volunteer helpers, knowledge of local learning area, and trips.
7. What physical resources are missing? Waterproofs, outdoor storage, seating, covered areas, lesson ideas, risk assessments.
8. What is the staff's attitude to outdoor learning? How can this be improved?
9. Are there local schools or organisations you could link up with?
10. Is there progression in your outdoor learning across the school?

11. Which class is outdoor learning the most established? How can you share this practice? Which class needs more support?
12. Is outdoor learning integrated into policies and procedures such as outdoor learning policy, teaching and learning policy, health and safety policy, uniform policy, school ethos, and values?
13. Is outdoor learning imbedded into school evaluation? Is each outdoor learning and visit evaluated and improved on? Is outdoor learning in performance management, pupil progress, staff meeting, governor's meetings, reporting?
14. Are the school grounds being used to their best for outdoor learning? If not, why not, and what needs doing to improve that?
15. Is there a central bank for resources, and do staff know where to go?
16. What is the next step to progressing outdoor learning? See the strategic outdoor learning model.
17. What does strategically integrated indoor-outdoor learning look like at your school? What are the next steps to get there?

Outdoor learning policy outline

1. Rationale: Outdoor learning at　　　　　　　　(name of setting) is
Links to development plan and other policies:
Vision:
Aims:
Objectives:
Action plan: When and where does outdoor learning take place?
Strategies for successful outdoor learning:
Management:
Review, monitoring, and evaluation:
Specific staff responsibility:
Approval procedure:
Risk management:
Statement of support from senior management:

Planning ideas

Cycle A: Year Group									
Topic:									
Trip/Visitor:									
English		**Numeracy**		**Science & Technology**		**Expressive Arts**		**Humanities**	
	Location		Location		Location		Location		Location

Appendix 185

Transition exercises

Descriptions of the following transition exercises can be found on the online resources supporting learning indoors and out on the Nature Days YouTube channel, https://youtu.be/TD9ku81Uknw.

- Immersive introductory ideas:
    - Connecting activity
    - Magic spot
    - Knowledge line
    - Pair share
    - Snow balling
    - Visualisation
- Activity starters:
    - Walk around school grounds
    - Trails
    - Storytelling
    - Group challenges
    - Shelter building
    - Maze building

Extract from Estyn school inspector report for Blaen Y Maes primary school

Teachers consider the interests of pupils when planning activities and use this to engage and motivate them. The school's curriculum makes good use of the locality and community resources and this helps broaden learning opportunities for pupils. For example, leaders at the school liaise with the Gower Tae Can project and local community farm to provide opportunities for pupils to plant vegetables that they harvest and use to make soup. Parents are invited into school to taste the soup and learn about how they can make healthy, affordable meals at home. These activities help create a purposeful curriculum and valuable connections between family and school life.

Leaders are beginning to develop a bespoke curriculum that aligns with the ethos and expectations set out in Curriculum for Wales and recognises the diverse nature of the local community. The curriculum is based on the 50 experiences Blaenymaes Primary pupils should access and this helps ensure that there is a breadth of knowledge and learning experiences for all. Leaders make effective use of the Pupil Development Grant to ensure that there is equity of provision and opportunities for all pupils.

Extract from Estyn school inspector report for Dan Y Coed specialist school

Strengthen the opportunities for pupils to develop work-related opportunities

The school has made strong progress against this recommendation. The school has appointed a senior leader with responsibility for overseeing the provision and evaluation of work-related opportunities for all pupils across the curriculum.

Leaders at the school have developed valuable opportunities for pupils to learn in a range of exciting activities outside the classroom. As a result, pupils develop a range of important skills such as independence, confidence, and resilience. These skills prepare pupils well for experiences beyond school.

Nearly all pupils are involved in appropriate work-related activities both within the school and the community. These activities relate well to pupils' additional learning needs and interests. Pupils develop worthwhile skills which support their understanding of the world of work.

Staff have identified and made beneficial links with a range of local providers to offer work experience opportunities for pupils. For example, many pupils benefit from valuable regular work experience programmes at a local organic company, at the school bank and at a local enterprise, which includes opportunities to work at a shop, café, laundry, office, and kitchen. In addition, pupils gain worthwhile accreditation for this work.

As a result of pupils' engagement in work-related opportunities, many pupils' attendance has improved, and a very few pupils have transferred to a local mainstream college because of skills acquired on work experience placement. In addition, the school has recently been presented with a recognised quality award for its outdoor and work-related curriculum offer.

Glossary

Word	Meaning
Blooms Taxonomy	A hierarchical ordering of cognitive skills that can be used for teaching.
Council for Learning Outside the Classroom (CLOtC)	CLOtC is a registered charity existing to champion learning outside the classroom (LOtC).
Field trip	Usually, a bus ride away to a location different from your school grounds where you can explore. E.g. a beach, river, woodland, city centre.
Forest School	A child-centred inspirational learning process.
Integrated Outdoor Learning	Outdoor learning used to teach curriculum content and inextricably linked to the indoor teaching and learning.
Local Learning Area	The area you can walk to outside your school gates in about half an hour. E.g. local park, shops, church, post office.
Outdoor Learning	For the purposes of this book, curriculum-based teaching and learning undertaken outside the school building.
Outdoor Learning Coordinator	Member of staff with management responsibility on the use of the outdoors. Sometimes called an educational visits coordinator (EVC) but covers in-school outdoor learning as well as visits and residentials.
Pedagogy	The method and practice of teaching.
Progression	Pupils gaining more knowledge and skills.
Composite Rectilinear Shapes	A 2D shape created by combining two or more rectangles.
Residential	An overnight experience.
School Grounds	The outdoor space enclosed by your school boundary, e.g. playground, field, car park, school woodland.
Senior Leadership Team (SLT)	School staff with management responsibilities.

Further reading

Outdoor learning training:

Agored Cymru Award in Outdoor Learning Practice. www.agored.cymru

Cambium sustainable Curriculum-Based Outdoor Learning Practitioner award. www.cambiumsustainable.co.uk

ITC Level 3 Award in Learning Beyond the Classroom aimed at teachers designed to show participants how to maximise curriculum linked outdoor learning opportunities. www.itcfirst.org.uk

Learning Beyond programme on the LOtC Quality Mark, more information can be found at the Council for Learning outside the classroom website. www.lotc.org.uk

Nature Days provides recorded training on integrated outdoor learning as well as face to face training on strategically embedding outdoor learning into your school. www.naturedays.co.uk

Outdoor learning organisations:

Council for Learning Outside the Classroom membership provides access to resources and recorded online training. www.lotc.org.uk

Curriculum-Based Outdoor Learning and Field Studies Professional Practice Group part of the Institute for Outdoor Learning (IOL). Provides support for members of the IOL as well as links to other providers' resources on the teaching hub. www.outdoor-learning.org

Outdoor learning activity ideas:

Creative Star Learning Ltd provides hundreds of ideas for outdoor learning focused on outdoor maths and literacy outdoors. www.creativestarlearning.co.uk

Learning through Landscapes provides many free resources on their website on outdoor learning ideas. www.ltl.org.uk

Natural Resources Wales (NRW) has created a range of curriculum-linked outdoor learning resources. www.naturalresources.wales

Nature Days has created outdoor challenge cards which cover all subjects in the curriculum and are designed for upper primary to undertake independent outdoor learning. www.naturedays.co.uk/shop

Nature Days YouTube channel @Nature_days has outdoor learning support videos for teachers and outdoor learning challenges for children to undertake.

The Woodland Trust has written a free Outdoor Learning Pack with many outdoor activity ideas. www.woodlandtrust.org.uk

Tirlun is a portal for outdoor learning activities based on the designated landscapes of Wales. www.tirlun.wales

Pupil awards:

ASDAN is an education charity and awarding organisation providing courses, accredited curriculum programmes and regulated qualification on life skills for students with SEND. www.asdan.org.uk

John Muir Award is a nationally recognised, individual award scheme for engaging with wild spaces. www.johnmuirtrust.org

National Outdoor Learning Awards. More information can be found on the Institute for Outdoor Learning (IOL) website. https://www.outdoor-learning.org

The National Education Nature Park programme, which aims to embed nature-based learning in the curriculum. www.educationnaturepark.org.uk

Index

Note: Page references in *italics* denote figures, in **bold** tables.

2D shapes **79**, 102, 166
3D shapes **79**, 166

academic attainment 61
access to outdoors 11
added value 16
ad hoc level 27
adventurous outdoor learning 173-174
angles 79, **80-81**; *see also* geometry
animals **54**, 120, **120-123**, 143; adaptation 97, **122-123**; bar chart of speed of 31; characteristics **120-121**; feeding relationships **122**; home **98-99**, 121; hunt 121; life cycles of **122**; night sky and nocturnal 56; variety of **121**
area calculation **77-78**
ASDAN 14
assessment 33-34, 60, 74, 166, 176; baseline 60; of outdoor learning 31-33, *32*; peer 32; of pupils 52; reflective cycle for 34; risk 24, 25, 41, *42*; time for 34; tool *33*, 169
attendance 14, 61, 187

Bad Guy (Eilish) **111**
Ballantyne, R. 168
baseline assessment 60; *see also* assessment
beach field trip 62-63
behavioural improvements 15
Blaenymaes Primary School 66, 186
block graph *83*
Bloom's taxonomy 68
Brunt, James **109**

carbon storage **143-144**, 146, 171; *see also* global climate change
case study: assessment of outdoor learning session 31-32, *32*; beach field trip 62-63; Blaenymaes Primary School 66; Casllwchwr primary school, repeat site visits 168; Dan Y Coed specialist school 14, 167-168; The Inglés Center 173-174; of integrated field trips 167-168; King Edward VI King's Norton School for Boys 25, 176; Knelston Primary School 169-170, 177-178; of local community opportunities 172; Olchfa school 173-174; of Penyrheol Primary school 173, 174-175; of school grounds development 170-171; of schools visiting other schools 172
Casllwchwr primary school 168
castles 5, 154, **154-155**, 165
Celtic roundhouse model **151**, *152*
Celts **150-152**, 165
changing view 165-166
Christmas 63
citizen science project 142, **145**, 171
classroom 29-35; access to outdoors from 11; control 43; external providers in 41-42; getting outside 42; management 9, 10; measuring and calculating area **77-78**; return to 45-46; safety 42; *see also* cross curricular application; education; school; students; subject schemes of work; teacher/teaching
climate 138, **139-140**; *see also* global climate change; weather
colours 142, 160, **161-162**

Index

community opportunities 171-173
compass 56, **132-134, 139**; *see also* navigation
composite rectilinear shapes **77**
Continual professional development (CPD) 34
continuous data **84, 85**, 97
Council for Learning Outside the Classroom (CLOtC) 175
cross curricular application 114-163; expressive art-based topics 160-162; geography-based topics 131-146; historical-based topics 147-157; introduction to 114; literacy-based topics 157-160; science-based topics 115-131
curriculum 14, 49, 73, 165, 175, 186; access 15; added value 16; application of 15, 23; content 3, 5, 8, 14, 167, 168, 180; indoor-outdoor integrated 19, 39, 40; mapping 6; planning of 71
Curriculum for Wales 6, 186
cycling skills 174

Dan Y Coed school 14, 167-168, 187
Dan Y Graig Primary School 172
data 28, 50, 138, 171; analysis **79-80**, 138, 171; bar graph of **80, 82, 84**, 97, **117, 137**; continuous **84, 85, 97**; discrete **83, 84**; empirical 33, 60; quantitative and qualitative 61, 100; sources of 30, **100**; spreadsheet **140**; *see also* research
data collection 81-85; digital 100, **100-101**; for investigation **145**; methods 62, **85, 101, 139**; and presentation 81, **81-83**; and statistics 84, **84-85**
den-building activity 69
design technology 98, **98-99**, 126, 169; *see also* technology
differentiation outdoors 69-70
digital data collection 100, **100-101**
discrete data **83, 84**
Donaldson, J. 30, **122**, 166
drama and dance 110, **110-111**
drawing 45, 50, 108, **109, 118**, 135, 138

Early Years leader 177
education 3, 8, 15, 25, 40, 168; *see also* classroom; school; students; teacher/teaching
effective outdoor learning 19, 24, 27, 29-31
Eilish, Billie **111**

English 86-95; explanatory/informational texts 92, **92-93**; instructional/procedural text writing **91-92**; narrative writing 86, **86-88**; persuasive text writing 94, **94-95**; poetry 89-91
enquiry question **106-107, 139-140, 143-144**
Estuary Education 168
Estyn 14, 186, 187
explanatory/informational texts 92, **92-93**
The Explorer (Rundell) 30, 166
expressive art 108-112, 160-162; colours 160, **161-162**; drama and dance 110, **110-111**; drawing 45, 50, 108, **109, 118**, 135, 138; music 111, **111-112**; sculpture 109, **109-110**
extension tasks 68-69
external providers 41-42

fair test **96, 116-118**
field trips 4, 67, 105, 167-168, 174
field work and visits framework 53, *53*, **54**
fire lighting 65, **151**
flexible 31, 46
flower: collecting for dissection 91; coloured 160, **161-162**; investigation **119**, *120*, 142; parts of **115**; pollination **116-117**, 171; *see also* plants
focused level 27
forest school 3-5, 173, 177

geography 101-107; based topics 131-146; enquiry 84, 105, **106-107**; global climate change 142, **143-146**; map making **102-105**; navigation 131, **132-134**; seasons 141-142, **141-142**; skills 101-105; water and rivers 135, **136-137**; weather and climate 138, **139-140**
geometry 79-81; *see also* angles; shapes
global climate change 57, **94**, 142, **143-146**; *see also* carbon storage
Global Positioning System (GPS) 100
Goldsworthy, Andy **109**
Google Earth 100, **106**, 123, 147
Google Maps **100**, 131
Google Street View **123, 136**
Gower Tae Can project 186
graveyard study **147-148**
grid references **133**
growing projects 170-171
The Gruffalo (Donaldson) **157**

health and wellbeing 61
history 107-108; based topics 147-157; castles 154, **154-155**; Celts **150-152**; local 107, **108**, 146; my place **147-148**; Romans 148, **149-150**; World War II 155, **155-156**
hurricane 29, 30

I Am the Seed That Grew the Tree (Waters) **90**
incidental outdoor learning 57
independent outdoor challenges 68, 69
indoor-outdoor integrated framework 5-6, 48-58; aim of 5-6; build on 167-168; combining different 56; cross curricular use of 114; defined 6, 48-49; embedded 6, 10-13; field work and visits 53, *53*, **54**; framework 10-12; inspirational *49*, 49-50, **50**; knowledge and skills 52, 52-53, **52-53**; literacy lesson **32**; maths with 74-86; overcoming barriers 10-13; residential 54-56, **55**, *55*; scientific experimental process 50; strategic 175-178; teacher practically undertake 56-57; for teaching new topics 164-165; using different locations 57, *58*; *see also* outdoor learning; subject schemes of work
information technology 76, 100-101, 105; *see also* technology
The Inglés Center 173-174
inspirational framework *49*, 49-50, **50**, **75-78**, **85-95**, **98-99**, **108-112**, 160
instructional/procedural text writing **91-92**
integrated outdoor learning 4
International Curriculum 173
intervention impact 61
investigation question **51**, **84**, **96**, **97**, **116**, **145**

Kensuke's Kingdom (Morpurgo) 30, **87**, **158**, 167
King Edward VI King's Norton School for Boys 25, 176
Knelston Primary School 169-170, 172, 177-178
knowledge and skills framework 52, 52-53, **52-53**, **74-75**

leader/leadership *see* senior leaders; strategic leadership
The Learning Beyond tracker 175
learning outdoors *see* outdoor learning
Learning Outside the Classroom (LOtC) 5, 42, 167

length measurement **75-76**
light 24, 127, **127-129**; *see also* shadows
line graph **84**, **85**, *85*, **137**
literacy-based topics 157-160; *see also* stories
living things 115, **115-119**, 120, **120-123**; *see also* animals; plants
local history 107, **108**, 146; *see also* history
location 4, 42, 57, *58*, 71, 157; outdoor learning 4-5; progression 62-63, *63*; in school grounds *58*, 63; for teaching 49
long-term planning 29, 30, 56
Lost Words (Macfarlane) **89**, **90**

maintaining momentum 164-178
map/mapping **102-105**, **147**; curriculum 6; making skills **102-105**; progression 168; of school grounds *105*, *135*; water **136**; *see also* navigation
materials 67, 124, **124-125**; chalk/loose **82**, **85**, **97**, **107**; natural 67, 109, **124**, **161**; properties of 124, **124**; survey **125**
maths 74-86; area calculation **77-78**; geometry 79-81; measuring length **75-76**; number **74-75**; perimeter 76, **76-77**; skills in 102, 166
measurement 61-62; and calculating area **77-78**; impact of outdoor learning 60-61; length **75-76**; perimeter 76, **76-77**
medium-term planning 30
mentoring 25, 27, 175, 178
mini beasts 29, 31, 60, **96**, **99-100**, 120, **120**, 171
model of progression *63*, *64*, **64**, 64-68; *see also* progression
moment of learning 34
monitoring 15, 26, 34, 64, 142; continuous 57; progress and impact 175-176; pupils progress 34; sustainability projects 171; teachers 26
Monkey Puzzle (Donaldson) **122**
Morpurgo, M. 30, 167
motivation 8, 15, 49
music 111, **111-112**, **127**; *see also* sound

NAEE 176
narrative writing 86, **86-88**
National Curriculum 173
National Outdoor Learning Award (NOLA) 66
natural paint **161**, *162*

navigation 66, 131, **132-134**; *see also* compass; map/mapping
non-fiction writing 86, 91, 92, 94
numeracy 74, **74-75**

O'Donnell, L. 10, 13, 176
Olchfa school 173-174
orienteering **133**, *135*
OS map **133-134**
Outdoor Education Advisers Panel (OEAP) 40
outdoor learning 3-7, 39-47, 181; assessment of 31-32, *32*; barriers to 9; benefits of 8-9; boxes contents **40**; classroom return 45-46; coordinator 14, 28, 60, 66, 176, 177; culture 21-23, *22*; defined 3-4; delivery 44-45; effective 19, 24, 27, 29-31; embedded *12*, 12-15, 26-28, 43; evidence of 31, 33; extension challenges **69**; external provider for 41-42; flexible 46; forest school and 5; future 166-167; impact of 61; levels of 44; location 4-5, 42-44; objectives 39-42, 60; permissions 41; planning in mind 165-166; policy 14, 28, 177, 183; progression in (*see* progression); projects 169-175; ratios and staffing 40-41; reflection 45-46; resources 39-40; routine 30, 57; routines 46; safety 42; session 6, 9, 13, 30, 45, 172; skills 34-35, 61, *65*; starting 39; strategic leadership in 23-24; structuring 45-46; symbol 30; trend in amount of *60*; *see also* pupils; senior leaders; students; teacher/teaching
over time progression 63; *see also* progression

Packer, J. 168
pedagogy 4-6, 13, 15, 23, 27, 59
peer assessment 32; *see also* assessment
Penyrheol Primary school 170-171, 173, 174-175
perimeter measurement 76, **76-77**
permaculture science 171
permissions 40, 41, 181
persuade teachers 15-16; *see also* teacher/teaching
persuasive text writing 94, **94-95**
pervasive level 27-28
pictograms **81-82**, 115
Pink Floyd **111**

planning 4, 29-30, 71, 186; of curriculum 71; ideas 184; long-term 29, 30, 56, 169; medium-term 30; methods and tools for 30; with outdoors in mind 165-166; short-term 31, 34
plants 28, 57, **96**, 115, **115-119**; dying **151**, **162**; experiment **118**; growth **96**, **116-117**; parts of **115**; picking 43; in a sand dune **97**; seeds **117-119**, 170; water 40, 53, **116**, 135, **136-137**, **158-160**; *see also* flower; seasons; trees
poetry 89, **89-91**
policies 15, 23, 24, 41, 177, 183
pollination **116-117**, 171; *see also* flower
procedures 23-24, 41, 42
professional development 176, 180
progression 59-70; across school 66-67; extension tasks 68-69, **69**; in field trips 67; location 57, 62-63, *63*; map 168; model of 64, 64-68, *65*; in outdoor learning *12*, 12-15, 59-60, 62-63, 64-66, 178; over time 63; questioning and 68; in residential **67**, 67-68; senior leaders of 6
Pupil Development Grant 186
pupils 14, 49, 69, 141, 180; assessment tools *33*, 33-34; attainment 5, 61; attitude 31; curriculum access for 15; cycling skills 175; data collection (*see* data collection); engagement 187; extension tasks for 68-69; field trips 167-168; health and wellbeing 61; opportunities for 186, 187; outdoor learning culture for 21-23, *22*; performance 23; progress monitoring 34; questioning 68; training 31, 63; voice 61-62

quantitative and qualitative data 61, 100
Queen's Green Canopy stewardship project 170
questioning 43, 63, 68

ratios and staffing 40-41
reflection 45-46, 56, 169
research 8-9, **50**, **99**, **108-111**, **139**, **154-156**, 176, 177; *see also* data
residential framework 54-56, **55**, *55*
residential progression **67**, 67-68; *see also* progression
resources 12, 25, 39-40, 69, 176-178
Rickinson, M. 9, 13

risk assessment 24, 25, 41, 42; *see also* assessment
river **136-137**, *138*; *see also* water
Romans 148, **149-150**
Rosen, Micheal 166
route card **104**, *135*
routines 10, 30, 31, 42, 46, 57, 174
rules of survival **158, 160**
Rundell, Katherine 30, 166-167

safety 23, 41, 42, 53, 56, 174
school: aerial photo of **77**; awareness 24; bikes 175; buildings 4, 11, 44, 63, 107; curriculum 186; evaluation 62, 175; impact on global climate change **143**; policies 23; primary 174, 186; procedures 23-24; progression 66-67; risk management 24; stories 166-167; visits 41; *see also* classroom; education; students; teacher/teaching; specific school
School Development Plan 21
school grounds 10, 40, 69, 138, 167, 178, 182; development 170-171; field work and visits framework 53, *53*, **54**; integrated 169-170; locations in *58*, 63; map of *105*, 131, *135*; sustainability of 171; temperature in **51, 144**; walk around **94, 98, 100, 108-111, 132, 141**
science 95-98; based topics 115-131; experimental process 50; investigation 60; light 127, **127-129**; living things 115, **115-119**, 120, **120-123**; materials 124, **124-125**; method 95, **95-97**; results graph axis 98; sound 125, **125-127**; transport 129, **130-131**
sculpture 109, **109-110**
seasons 30, 44, 57, 115, 141-142, **141-142**; *see also* plants
senior leaders 21-28; creating outdoor learning culture 21-23, *22*; progression 6, 26-28; resources 25; risk assessments 24, 42; role of 25, 60; supporting class teachers 24-26; support provided by 27; whole school awareness 24
Senior Leadership Team (SLT) 10, 15-16, 19, 21, 39
shadows **127-129**; *see also* light
shapes 79, **79-80**; *see also* geometry
short-term planning 31, 34
siege weapons **154**

skills: cycling 174; development planning 56; knowledge and *52*, 52-53, **52-53**; outdoor learning 34-35; technology 169
small start 44
sound 125, **125-127**; *see also* music
staff: attitude 9, 11; confidence 10, 63, 176-177; knowledge 9, 10; lack of support 11; meetings 24; mentoring system 25; ratios and 40-41; training 15
star orienteering course 102, 104, **133, 134**, *134*
STEM activities 169
St Fagan's National Museum of History 167
Stick Man (Donaldson) 30, 166, 167
stick weaving *153*
stories: for 3-6 years 157, **158-160**; characters from **157**; for early years to 2 years 157, **157**; retelling of **87**, 167
strategic leadership 23-24
strategic level 27
strategic outdoor learning 4, *12*, 12-15, *24, 26*, 26-28, 181-182
students 5, 43, 68, 108, 142, 180; data collection 81-85; opportunities for 28, 174; progress 57, 63, 68; routines 46; with special needs 168; training 42; *see also* classroom; education; outdoor learning; school; teacher/teaching
subject schemes of work 73-112; for assessment of application of knowledge and skills **74-75**; design technology 98-99; English 86-95; expressive art 108-112; geography 101-107; history 107-108; information technology 100-101; for inspirational framework **75-78, 85-95, 98-99, 108-112**; introduction to 73-74; maths 74-86; science 95-98; for testing theories framework **79-85, 95-97, 100-104, 106-107**
Survey123 100, **100-101**, *101*, 105
Sustainable Development Goals 175
Swan Lake **110**
symbol instructions *103*

tactical level 27
tally charts **81-82**
teacher/teaching 29-35, 43; added value 16; assessment 32; confidence 10; curriculum content (*see* curriculum); indoor-outdoor integrated framework 56-57; location for 49;

maths 74–86; mentoring 25; monitoring 26; persuade 15–16; prior knowledge 34; professional development 176, 180; resources 25; staff (see staff); styles of 46; supporting 24–26; training 24, 176; see also classroom; cross curricular application; education; subject schemes of work

technology: design 98–99; information 76, 100–101, 105; skills 169

tell, show do model 68

testing theories framework 49–50, *51*, **51-52**, **79-85**, **95-97**, **100-104**, **106-107**, 148

Tiger Tiger Burning Bright **90**

time within week 10–11

Toad of Toad Hall **110**

trails **96**, **106**, 166, 175, 185

training 15, 24, 34, 42, 63, 176–178

transition exercises 43, 185

transport 129, **130-131**, 168, 174

trees: apple **117-118**; carbon storage in **143**, **146**; and growing project 170–171; identification skills 34; see also plants

Tudor houses 165

UV filtering sunglasses **129**

VE Day street party **156**

water 40, 53, **116**, 135, **136-137**, **158-160**; see also river

wattle and daub fence **150**, *153*

weather 9, 25, 40, 62, 141, 142; change 42, 46; and climate 30, 138, **139-140**; forecast 127; monitoring 171; results table **140**; working with **47**

We're Going on a Bear Hunt (Rosen) 166

what a good one looks like (WAGOLL) 68

whole school: approach 6, 10–14, 19, 21, 26, 180; awareness 24; outdoor learning audit 181–182

The Woodland Trust's Nature's Calendar 171

World War II **108**, 155, **155-156**

writing see specific writing

For Product Safety Concerns and Information please contact our EU representative GPSR@taylorandfrancis.com
Taylor & Francis Verlag GmbH, Kaufingerstraße 24, 80331 München, Germany

www.ingramcontent.com/pod-product-compliance
Lightning Source LLC
Chambersburg PA
CBHW082100230426
43670CB00017B/2901